Whose Hunger?

BORDERLINES

For more books in the series, see p. vi.

Whose Hunger?

Concepts of Famine, Practices of Aid

JENNY EDKINS

BORDERLINES, VOLUME 17

 University of Minnesota Press

Minneapolis

London

HC
79
.F3
E35
2000

The University of Minnesota Press gratefully acknowledges permission to reprint the following. Portions of chapters 3 and 6 originally appeared as "Legality with a Vengeance: Famines and Humanitarian Relief in 'Complex Emergencies,'" by Jenny Edkins, in *Millennium: Journal of International Studies* 23, no. 3 (1996); copyright *Millennium: Journal of International Studies* and reproduced with permission of the publisher.

Published by the University of Minnesota Press
111 Third Avenue South, Suite 290
Minneapolis, MN 55401-2520
http://www.upress.umn.edu

Printed in the United States of America on acid-free paper

Library of Congress Cataloging-in-Publication Data

Edkins, Jenny.
    Whose hunger? : concepts of famine, practices of aid / Jenny Edkins.
      p.   cm.—(Borderlines ; v. 17)
    Includes bibliographical references and index.
    ISBN 0-8166-3506-4 (hard : alk. paper)—ISBN 0-8166-3507-2 (pbk. : alk. paper)
    1. Famines.   2. Food relief.   I. Title.   II. Borderlines (Minneapolis, Minn.) ; v. 17.
    HC79.F3 E35 2000
    363.8--dc21
                                                    00-009377

12 11 10 09 08 07 06 05 04 03 02 01 00   10 9 8 7 6 5 4 3 2 1

For Tim

BORDERLINES

Contents

Abbreviations

CERA	Commission for Eritrean Refugee Affairs
EAA	Euro-Action Accord
EC	European Community
EEC	European Economic Community
EIAC	Eritrean Inter-agency Agricultural Consortium
EPLF	Eritrean People's Liberation Front
ERA	Eritrean Relief Association
ERRA	Eritrean Relief and Rehabilitation Association
EU	European Union
FAO	Food and Agriculture Organisation
FFW	Food For Work
IAG	Inter Africa Group
IDS	Institute of Development Studies
IES	Institute for Ethiopian Studies
LDCs	less-developed countries
MT	metric tons
NCA	Norwegian Church Aid
NGOs	nongovernmental organizations
ODA	Overseas Development Administration
REST	Relief Society of Tigray

TPLF	Tigray People's Liberation Front
UNDP	United Nations Development Programme
UNHCR	United Nations High Commissioner for Refugees
USAID	United States Agency for International Development
WFP	World Food Programme
WWI	Worldwatch Institute

Acknowledgments

The preparation of this book was undertaken with financial support from the Economic and Social Research Council of the UK, and the final revisions took place while I was Leverhulme Special Research Fellow at the Department of International Politics at the University of Wales Aberystwyth; I am grateful to both organizations.

For help in planning my visit to Eritrea and Ethiopia in March and April 1995, I would like to thank Ken Booth; Ian Robinson of the Centre for Arid Zone Studies in Bangor; Lionel Cliffe, June Rock, and others at the School of Development Studies in Leeds, particularly Teklemikiel Woldegiorgis; Trish Silkin; and, for help during the course of the visit, Simon Bush of the British Council in Asmara, Dr. Negusse who personally arranged many of the interviews, Guy Watson, Liz and Sam who gave me hospitality, and all those who agreed to be interviewed, including Dr. Assefaw Tekeste, Dr. Azbaha Haile, Martine Billanou, Laraine Black, Douglas Broderick, Ghirmai Mebrahtu, Tony Hall, Mike Harvey, Arild Jacobsen, Lalit Godamunne, Musa Hussein Naib, Dr. Nerayo Teklemichael, Lois Purdham, Emma Roberts, Saba Essayes, Ibrahim Said, Vanessa Sayers, Jacky Sutton, Teklewoini Assefa, and Bram Voets. I am greatly indebted to the kindness shown by Manuel Montecinos in agreeing to let me travel with him in Eritrea and to Ibrahim Said in suggesting it in the first place. I am very grateful to everyone else who was so helpful during the course of the fieldwork, including the many people in Afabet, Agordat,

Halhal, Keren, Nacfa, and Tessanie who let me take part in meetings and discussions.

Conversations with colleagues in development studies, politics, international relations, policy research, and government have been crucial at many stages. During the year I spent at the University of Manchester, I was able to convene a Politics of Emergency workshop, and I owe colleagues in the Departments of Government and Sociology and in the Institute of Development Policy and Management thanks for their support in this project, particularly Paul Cammack, the late Elizabeth Carlo, Pandeli Glavanis, Philip Gummett, David Hulme, Peter Lawler, David Pool, and Ralph Young. This workshop led to the setting up of an ESRC-funded research seminar series and the Emerging Political Complexes discussion group. The latter group, convened by Mark Duffield in Birmingham, including David Campbell, Mick Dillon, David Keen, Joanna Macrae, John Ryle, and Nick Stockton, provided both encouragement and constructive feedback on my work. Discussion at all these various meetings has been stimulating and helpful in the final stages of preparation of the manuscript. Students in my masters courses on the international politics of famine at Manchester and Aberystwyth, my course on famine and conflict in Africa, and my extramural classes in Aberystwyth have all contributed in significant ways to the development of the arguments in this book. John Gurr, Mair Jones, and Jen Stuttle are owed particular thanks.

Without the comments of two anonymous readers and the editors of the Borderlines series, David Campbell and Mike Shapiro, the book would have been very much the poorer. I would also like to thank Sarah Owen Vandersluis and Paris Yeros for their invaluable comments on an earlier version of parts of chapters 3 and 6, which was published as "Legality with a Vengeance: Famines and Humanitarian Relief in 'Complex Emergencies,'" *Millennium: Journal of International Studies* 25, no. 3 (1996): 547–75. This later appeared under the same title in *Poverty in World Politics: Whose Global Era?*, edited by Sarah Owen Vandersluis and Paris Yeros (Basingstoke: Macmillan, 2000), 59–90. Finally, among many others, I would like to thank Christopher Clapham for invaluable comments on a draft of the whole book; Alex de Waal, Nalini Persram, Colin Wight, and Marysia Zalewski for generously commenting on various parts of the emerging text; and Cynthia Enloe, Pete Moorehead Wright, Babu

Rahman, Rob Walker, Cynthia Weber, and Nicholas Wheeler, for many helpful conversations. Véronique Pin-Fat has been an invaluable friend and ally throughout. Other intellectual debts remain, of course, and the usual disclaimers apply; none of the above is responsible for the arguments advanced in what follows.

There is one other person I must mention. I owe a particular debt to Steve Smith, who prompted me to examine famine in the first place and whose support has sustained the project since.

Finally, no one will be more pleased that this book is finally complete than my family: I have drawn heavily on their support and encouragement throughout.

Introduction

A biblical famine—now, in the twentieth century.[1]

Famines seem anachronistic. They appear to belong to an era more primitive and less technologically advanced than our own. During the Ethiopian famine of the 1980s there was surprise that a crisis of this sort could take place at all in the twentieth century. It seemed biblical in its scale and imagery. Famines are seen as failures of development and modernization and, what is more, failures that can be overcome by progress and more advanced technology. There are disagreements as to where the difficulty lies, whether in the agricultural system, in economic distribution, or in population growth. There is even recognition that political breakdown can cause famines, too, and that what we find these days are not famines as much as "complex political emergencies." But whatever the nuances of emphasis, there is widespread agreement that what is at stake is how we are to refine and improve our techniques for the analysis and management of famines in the light of these difficulties. Famines are seen as technical problems that modern social and natural science will eventually resolve.

In this book I take issue with this position. Famines in the contemporary world are not the antithesis of modernity but its symptom. What this means is that rather than being something that modernization will solve, famines are produced by and symptomatic of modernity.[2] Modernity is a distinctive form of life and a particular way of resolving the questions that being human entails. It is a way of life that involves historically contingent political formations and a specific regime of truth.

The political systems of modernity revolve around the legal authority of the sovereign state, with its corresponding view of the individual as citizen. This configuration of politics has been called "biopolitics," and the form of life to which the citizen is reduced has been called "bare life."[3] In the modern era, bare life becomes central to the calculations of state power. Sovereign power is concerned with the governance of populations and biological life. No longer is a politically qualified life the subject of politics, but life itself, as opposed to death. In this sense, politics is depoliticized: we are concerned with the preservation of life as such, rather than the continuance of a specific political way of life. Aid processes treat lives to be saved as bare life, not as lives with a political voice.

Modernity's regime of truth is based on scientific method. What makes knowledge legitimate (and powerful) in the modern world is not tradition or divine authority but a particular scientific mode of validation.[4] In a Westernized modernity, truth no longer derives from religious faith. What counts as true is what scientific research can demonstrate. This is a particular mode of knowing: calculable, generalizable, and objective. Not only are contemporary understandings of famine produced in this way, attempts at ending hunger are also framed within the same discourse. Both the problem of famine and its solutions are constituted within the horizons of modernity.

The framing of famine in discourses of modernity has two very important corollaries. First, it means that hunger and how it should be combated are depoliticized. Technical solutions are sought, solutions that draw on modernity's professed ability to both identify and resolve problems through abstract analysis and the formulation of general principles. Calculability and measurability are emphasized.[5] This is the case whether what is being measured are crop yields, nutritional status, population movements, entitlement bundles, or food stocks. Such solutions are inevitably inadequate to the problem, which is not a technical one but one that accompanies specific forms of social and political organization or the emergence of new arrangements. Technical solutions merely reinstate and reproduce one of the precise forms of politics—modern politics—that produce famine in the first place.

For some time, writers have acknowledged that famine involves politics. But what is still lacking is any appreciation of what this implies, which would require a closer analysis of politics and the political.[6] If famine is seen as an unfortunate by-product of combat, proposed solutions often take the form of conflict resolution techniques. These can leave unresolved the issues that led to the dispute in the first place. They depoliticize by treating both sides in a conflict as equally culpable and by regarding the absence of hostility as unproblematically desirable. It is argued that relief agencies should be wary of inadvertent involvement in conflict, and techniques of aid that "do no harm" are elaborated.[7] This approach can still end up with a technical solution, one that involves a depoliticization of politics itself. The repoliticization required has to go much further than this. It has to involve a reassessment of the whole question of what qualifies as political.

The second corollary of the way famine is framed within discourses of modernity is that the humanitarian relief industry is largely impervious to challenge or critique. However much censure is aimed at "the humanitarian international," it still has "an extraordinary capacity to absorb criticism, not reform itself and yet emerge strengthened. . . . The legitimacy of Western relief agencies, donor institutions and even military forces seems to be enhanced by those who dispute their effectiveness."[8] Debate about humanitarianism, whether critical or supportive of current practices, is self-reinforcing. Talk of humanitarianism, famine, and famine relief produces these "objects"—humanitarians, famines, relief agencies—in specific and particular ways: "the humanitarian discourse itself, whatever its content, reinforces the humanitarians' moral ownership of famine and similar crises."[9] Humanitarianism's ability to resist criticism (and to reincorporate it) arises from its central location within discourses of modernity.

To examine how effective humanitarian interventions might be or to ask who are the final recipients of food aid and who benefits from the relief is thus to a great extent to participate in this discourse. Such questions have to take place within the framework that sets interventions in train in the first place. It is very difficult to engage with these issues without accepting the premise that humanitarianism is meant to be beneficial and without buying in to particular views of what humanity is, the views prevalent in modernity. The power of discursive practices is such that the entities they bring into being seem to be products of nature rather than discourse—and hence beyond question.

One particular strand is how modernity as a discourse relies on notions of scarcity. It is seen as axiomatic that we exist under conditions of insufficiency, where the maintenance of life depends on a battle with nature for limited resources. But scarcity itself is a central feature of modernity's way of constituting the world, not something natural.[10] Through the production of separations between man and nature, the growth of human populations can be contrasted with the increase in their "natural" means of subsistence. This means that the notion of famine, shortage, or scarcity is particularly embedded in the way modernity is constituted.

Although there is now much greater and more sustained involvement by the humanitarian organizations than there was in the past, famine crises appear to be less possible to solve, "more intractable" than before.[11] De Waal asks whether it may be the very intrusion of humanitarian organizations that causes this problem, arguing that it removes the capacity of the people involved to find their own solution. For de Waal, local political action is the answer. However, if we recall Foucault's analysis of the prison, we are led to a different conclusion. Foucault argues that contrary to a commonsense view, the failure of prisons to rehabilitate offenders (their stated purpose) is to be regarded functionally as a success. It reproduces "delinquents" as a particular category of subject: differentiated, subject to surveillance, and produced as objects of knowledge. By being labeled "criminal," their actions are depoliticized. A form of power relation—disciplinary power—is institutionalized. In the continuing involvement of humanitarian aid organizations in crises we have something similar. A situation of "permanent emergency" arises.[12] It is a situation where those apparently engaged in trying to bring about change are benefiting from the continuing crisis.[13]

An irony of the relationship between famines and modernity is the way in which modernity's own hunger for certainty impedes its ability to do anything about hunger in the physical sense. At the root of much modern thought and social scientific investigation is a drive for epistemological certainty, for a secure route to knowledge.[14] Without knowledge, we seem unable to act. This desire for certainty is found, for example, in the search for a new moral framework for humanitarianism. We feel a need for a set of principles against which we can measure our decisions before we act. But this search for a moral framework is futile: "whatever the attractions of such a construct, there is no escaping the fact that this process of decisioning about responsibility is irretrievably political and immune to epistemological equations. . . . Little can be achieved by searching for abstracted theoretical formulas."[15] In the same way, we look for general answers to questions about the causes of famine before we feel empowered to act. Moreover, the solutions put in place have to provide the feedback to satisfy assessment requirements. Aid projects have to be capable of providing measurable data. These results verify and legitimize the actions taken and the discursive practices in which they are framed.

There is a continual tension between modernity's hunger for truth and the struggle to end famine. There is a similar dialectical process in the response to calls for repoliticization. These calls take place both in contestations over famine "theory" and in debates about what should happen in "practice." The two sides of the coin are not separable. In Foucault's words: "Theory does not express, translate or serve to apply practice: it is practice."[16] In both cases, the call for a return to the political seems to be invariably followed by another depoliticization. The critique is reincorporated into the mainstream and another movement of challenge or contestation becomes necessary.

This book examines instances of the technologization of famine, a series of moves of repoliticization, and their reincorporation and institutionalization. These moves are traced both in theory—in the work of Thomas Malthus, Amartya Sen, and David Keen, for example—and in practice—in food for work programs in Eritrea and in the Band Aid movement of the 1980s. Although other writers have pointed to the need for politicization, my aim here is to begin to elucidate why such attempts are continually co-opted, through an examination of famine's close relationship to modernity. I shall also ask what the implications of these conclusions are for responsibility and political action.

The first chapter starts by raising the issue of the representation of famines in modernity. Commemorations of the tenth anniversary of the famine in Ethiopia in the 1980s and the 150th anniversary of the Irish Famine of the 1840s are examined. These accounts demonstrate the strength of the modern view of famine as a crisis of food supply and a natural disaster involving mass starvation.

The second chapter examines how this modernization came about and shows how distinctive it is. I locate the disjuncture that produces "modernity" as a framework for knowledge about and solutions to famine, and sketch an archaeo-genealogy of famine. Foucault identifies a number of changes at the turn of the eighteenth century as crucial in the rise of the human sciences. A whole series of epistemic shifts took place at a range of disciplinary sites. The result of these was what Foucault calls the modern *episteme,* or way of knowing. The production of "famine" and the starving subject was part of this modern episteme.

Three moves are examined in chapter 2. Together these are constitutive of famine in the modern episteme. First, famine is understood in scientific terms: Famine is defined and its underlying essence identified. The emphasis on price movements in premodern discussions of famines becomes an analysis of food production or food shortage. There is a change in the way that food appears: it becomes biologically rather than socially constituted and is combined with a medicalization of hunger. The result is that famine is constituted as a natural disaster with a scientific cause.

Second, famines are framed in terms of scarcity. Thomas Malthus's work is important here, and it has been and remains basic to many contemporary representations of famines. Strangely enough, it was a first attempt to argue against the rising social sciences of the day, which believed in the perfectability of social institutions through scientific knowledge. The Malthusian account has produced its own prehistory.

The third move is the way politics becomes biopolitics. The final section of chapter 2 traces the political implications of the modern episteme. It examines how the modern picture of famine is framed within a sovereign politics that sees life as bare life, not politically qualified life. The feminization of famine is part of this confinement of starvation to the *oikos* or domestic sphere.[17] By means of these three moves, modernity depoliticizes famine.

In the third chapter I turn to Amartya Sen's attempt to repoliticize the Malthusian view of famine. Sen's claim was that famine was not a question of food supply—a purely technical concept—but of food ownership—a question that is socially constituted. A person's entitlement to food depends on the series of social relationships within which that person's life is embedded. It is not an abstract, ahistorical fact. Each famine is the product of particular, historical social relations set within a framework of a particular political and economic structure. These relations establish what can be owned and how food is regarded; they settle what obligations exist between people within that social group. This approach to famine produces a much more particularistic analysis, where it is not whole populations who starve but particular employment groups who suffer.

However, I argue that, despite the considerable achievements of the entitlement approach, Sen's attempt at repoliticization fails because he does not take it far enough. In the end he does not take sufficient account of exactly how the social relations in which entitlement are embedded come into being in the first place or how they are maintained by the force of law, even in times of starvation. In other words, he assumes as given precisely that which is constituted in times of social upheaval that famines often accompany: a particular legal and social system. This assumption depoliticizes. It allows his work to provide techniques for dealing with famine as an economic breakdown within a system but does not permit him to question the system itself.

The fourth chapter moves from depoliticization in theoretical accounts to the way technologization operates in practices of famine relief. Sen's analysis of famine as related to entitlement breakdown leads to programs designed to replace lost entitlements by the provision of welfare or employment schemes. Chapter 4 examines food aid as a discursive practice and then looks at a particular instance of its institutionalization: food for work programs in Eritrea in 1995. I argue that these programs exemplify the technologization of aid and that they produce depoliticized subjects.

The next chapter is also focused on practices: it turns to the question of how we might begin to account for personal responses to famines and other crises. I argue that the responses to the Ethiopian famine in 1984/85 were, initially at least, a repoliticization of the question of famine. Professionals in the development and aid industry denounced the popular famine movement that gained expression through the Band Aid and Live Aid events. The outpouring of aid was a response to the gaze of the victim. Famine can be seen as a symptom of modernity and the success of the Band Aid movement comes in part from an exploitation of that relationship. I explore how questions of desire and the need to reconstitute an international community are implicated in our responses to other people's hunger.

In chapter 6, I return to academic and policy discourse, this time to that centered on the notion of complex emergencies. Much of the work of writers such as David Keen, Mark Duffield, and Alex de Waal arose from their reaction to Sen's entitlement approach. They were all involved in various ways in the famines in the Horn of Africa in the 1980s. The chapter shows how their attempts to repoliticize famine and famine relief have been incorporated into new technologies of humanitarianism and complex emergency. I conclude this chapter by discussing how we might retain a hold, however precarious, on the political and what this means for relief and aid processes and practitioners. I explore how my argument makes a difference to what we might do.

Finally, in the conclusion of the book, I explore how modernity's hunger for closure and completion is the driving force in its economy of desire and how this produces the impetus to technologization that has been so damaging in modernity's treatment of famines.

1

Pictures of Hunger

Famine is embedded in the discursive practices of modernity. Hunger has only recently been brought within the province of the human sciences, and these disciplines themselves, with "man" as their object, only came into being at the end of the eighteenth and beginning of the nineteenth centuries.[1] The incorporation of hunger into the episteme, or way of thinking, of the modern human sciences has refashioned it according to different, specifically modern, rationalities. It has been removed from the realm of the ethical and the political and brought under the sway of experts and technologists of nutrition, food distribution, and development. Its position there, as an appropriate subject for expert knowledge, remains a political position, but one that can lay claim to a political neutrality because of the specific way that science is construed as "truth" in modernity.

Famine's incorporation into the human sciences defines famine and food in scientific ways and leads us inexorably to particular technical forms of solution. Famine is seen as a disaster with a scientific cause. Ending famine is reduced to the question of acquiring the appropriate knowledge of the causes of famine and developing the techniques needed to apply that knowledge to produce a cure. Other views see food as more than fuel for the human machine and hunger as a recurring social tragedy, not a problem that can be solved by technology.

Famine, as a scarcity of food, is part of the struggle of modernity with the question of scarce resources more generally. Modernity sees the solution to scarcity in progress: progress that leads from a past of privations and primitivism to a future of abundance and civilization. Contemporary accounts of prehistory confirm this perspective, but these and their assumptions have been questioned. Malthusian approaches to famine are central to the modernist view and remain influential as the base for commonsense conceptions. Contemporary neo-Malthusians combine optimists (the technical fixers: those for whom technological advances can be relied upon to find the solutions) and pessimists (the prophets of doom).

Famines occupy a central place in the political configuration of modernity. Modern politics is biopolitics: a concern for the regulation and control of populations, which replaces a politically qualified life with bare life—a form of life that can be killed but not sacrificed.[2] Power over life displaces political participation and debate. Even the institutions of politics are technologized.

Two specific representations of famine take place in Ethiopia in 1984/85 and in Ireland one hundred and forty years earlier. These tales are juxtaposed to highlight both similarities between the two accounts and the contending views they contain, and to consider the questions of the modern representation of famine. What controversies arise when famines are at issue within the modern world? How do we see "famine"?

ETHIOPIA

In Ethiopia, seven million people are threatened by starvation. Thousands have already died. The famine, caused by drought, is the worst in living memory. And now the rains have failed again for the third year in succession. The relief organisations are doing all they can, but there just isn't enough food to go around. One of the worst hit areas is in the north of the country where the problem has been complicated by two secessionist wars in Eritrea and Tigray. Forty thousand refugees have converged on the town of Korem, in the hope of getting some food and medical aid. Our correspondent, Michael Buerk, has been back to Korem after four months, and he found the situation far worse.[3]

In October 1984 television pictures of starving people gathered in camps in northern Ethiopia were shown around the world. These were the opening words of the story that accompanied the film when it was shown on the BBC news:

Dawn. And as the sun breaks through the piercing chill of night on the plain outside Korem, it lights up a biblical famine—now, in the twentieth century. This place, say workers here, is the closest thing to hell on earth. Thousands of wasted people are coming here for help. Many find only death. They flood in every day from villages hundreds of miles away, dulled by hunger, almost to the point of desperation.[4]

The piece was shown in the lead spot on the six o'clock bulletin largely by chance. It was otherwise a slack news day, and any one of a handful of fairly substantial stories could have been chosen.[5] In the later bulletin it was the fourth story. It was syndicated to 425 of the world's television networks, reaching a potential audience of 470 million. The Live Aid concert in July of the following year reached an estimated 1,500 million viewers.[6] The publicity produced "an earthquake in the relief world" and a doubling or tripling of aid. In the case of USAID, donations increased thirty-fold from $11 million in 1983 to $350 million in 1985.[7]

This marked the beginning of what came to be known as the Ethiopian Famine. For people in Britain it seemed to rank with the Great Hunger in Ireland in the nineteenth century in terms of its symbolic significance. Fintan O'Toole argues that the Irish famine was the first media famine, "making it the point at which a whole set of assumptions gained a currency that's never quite been lost. A view of famine as a single catastrophic event, based on Malthusian ideas of nature's revenge has echoed down through the last 150 years. We've learned to look only at the last stage of a long descent into horror."[8] The Irish famine had its "Michael Buerks," too, in the form of reports in *The Times* and the *Illustrated London News* and letters from eye witnesses urging relief measures. Here is an example from a letter from Nicholas Cummins:

> The scenes that presented themselves were such as no tongue or pen can convey the slightest idea of. In the first [cabin], six famished and ghastly skeletons, to all appearance dead, were huddled in a corner on some filthy straw, their sole covering what seemed a ragged horsecloth and their wretched legs hanging about, naked above the knees. I approached in horror, and found by a low moaning that they were alive, they were in fever—four children, a woman, and what had once been a man. It is impossible to go through the details, suffice to say, that in a few minutes I was surrounded by at least two hundred such phantoms, such frightful spectres as no words can describe. By far the

greatest number were delirious, either from hunger or from fever. Their demoniac yells are still ringing in my ears and their horrible images are fixed upon my brain.[9]

Images of famines, whether in Africa or Europe, are frequently images of women: often women as mothers, with babies in arms or, more likely, at the breast. Margaret Kelleher has called this "the feminisation of famine": "the representation of famine and its effects through images of women."[10] There is some debate as to whether women actually survive starvation better than men, which could explain why their images predominate. Another explanation sometimes given is that the menfolk have gone in search of work in the cities or employment on public works schemes.[11] A disturbing feature of the use of female images is the voyeuristic and intrusive character of the accounts, with their images of naked women producing "the dangerous configuration of issues of sexuality and charity."[12] The representations of women combine a disgust at the vision of women as beggars or employed moving stone in public works with troubled descriptions of nakedness. Cummins describes an encounter as follows:

> decency would forbid what follows, but it must be told. My clothes were nearly torn off in my endeavour to escape from the throng of pestilence around, when my neckcloth was seized from behind. . . . I found myself grasped by a woman with an infant just born in her arms and the remains of a filthy sack across her loins—the sole covering of herself and baby.[13]

Although the predominant image of famine today seems to be that it is an African problem, there have been and continue to be famines elsewhere, including instances in Europe in the twentieth century—the famines in the Ukraine in the 1930s and the Netherlands in 1944, for example—and in the 1990s in North Korea. "Famine, and a fear of famine"[14] has punctuated history, and accounts that survive from antiquity contain similar harrowing stories.[15]

The images of the camps in Korem prompted a concern with Ethiopia that continues ten years later, as does the portrayal of famine as mass starvation produced by drought. There are people working today in Ethiopia, and no doubt in other African countries, who can trace their commitment and involvement in relief agency work to the influence of those images. And the preponderance of people from Ireland in aid work has been related to the Irish experience of famine. During the Great Famine two million Irish people emigrated to North America. There must be many aid workers with family if not personal experience of famine from other parts of Europe or elsewhere who are motivated in part by that background. Certainly, the nongovernmental organizations (NGOs) as they exist in the 1990s see 1984 as of crucial significance: it is from this period that the tremendous increase in their support and thus their growth as organizations can be traced.

In 1984, the voluntary bodies and Ethiopian government relief agencies regarded the response to the news broadcasts with a certain amount of frustration. For many months it had been obvious to them that a famine, on a massive scale, was happening in the region. The government had blamed the weather and crop failures (rather than its own policies) and had appealed to the international community via the UN. Several films and appeals had been transmitted before the Buerk-Amin broadcast, but with a much smaller response. Furthermore, there was fierce criticism of the manner in which famine victims were portrayed: an extensive period of self-examination by the agencies followed. Although large amounts of funds had flowed into NGOs, there was a sense of guilt because these had been received on the back of very negative stereotypes of Africa. And the Marxist-Leninist government of Mengitsu in Ethiopia was less than wholehearted in its welcome of what at times it saw as Western interference.

For the liberation fighters of the Eritrean and Tigray People's Liberation Fronts (the EPLF and the TPLF), the response might have been equally frustrating. The reports in the news media in 1984 emphasized the situation in camps in towns in Ethiopia, portraying what was by then over twenty years of sustained fighting in Eritrea and Tigray as little more than the activities of a few bandits in the north.[16] At the time, those agencies who were unable to accept the government's assurances that they had access to the whole of the population in need had already grouped together in consortia to undertake a cross-border operation, ferrying supplies of grain from the Sudan for distribution by the relief agencies of the rebel fronts.[17] The continuance of the support the fronts were receiving in this way was dependent on it remaining publicly unacknowledged. Front-sponsored films made at the time contrast starkly with the images from the camps in

Ethiopia: they show resourceful, articulate Eritrean relief workers and officials, extensive field health services, and a participatory, locally run approach to relief.[18]

Criticism of NGOs involved on the government side came from agencies who had problems with the policies of resettlement and villagization being followed by the Ethiopians under Mengitsu. A number of NGOs, it seems, took the view that if they objected to the genocidal policies of the government, they would be unable to pursue their objectives of helping the civilian population with food aid.[19] Others pointed out (then and later) that this food aid itself was being used to promote the government's counterinsurgency objectives and other policies, such as resettlement, which "have become a major cause of death in the country."[20] So although it was recognized in a marginal way that there was a conflict going on in Ethiopia, the nature and scale of the war and the way it could, arguably, be said to have produced what we call the Ethiopian famine was not discussed openly until much later, after the victory of the rebel fronts in 1991. This is often forgotten in academic international relations circles and among NGOs when the Ethiopian famine is renarrated as the first example of successful humanitarian intervention in an internal conflict in Africa.[21]

Although accounts of abuses are accepted now, and it is even fairly widely known that the United States and the European Union channeled relief through the cross-border operation, the media account of the Ethiopian famine has not changed. This was evident when the tenth anniversary was celebrated in 1994/95. The narrative in the West remains focused on an account of the famine as caused by drought (although relief efforts were impeded by conflict) and solved by massive charitable donations.

As part of a commemoration of the tenth anniversary of the famine in Ethiopia, a symposium was held in Addis Ababa in March 1995. The aim was to discuss what could be learned from the famine ten years later.[22] The communiqué issued at the end of the meeting began with the statement that "the 1984–85 famine was in fact a political crisis characterized more appropriately by war than by drought." The discussions covered a number of the contentious areas. The 1995 meeting brought together for the first time officials, activists, and academics from both sides of the relief effort. Discussions became quite heated and emotional at times, with some NGOs and charities facing accusations of complicity in human rights abuses. These were countered by the argument that they had been doing what they could to relieve suffering under difficult conditions.[23]

In spite of the severe differences and the varieties of involvement that participants had had in the events of 1984/85, the closing statement contained a number of points of agreement on how to move forward. There was a consensus that local control by rural people themselves, including women, was crucial. Although important, emphasis on increasing production should not obscure the need for equitable distribution. It was generally recognized that there had been very significant progress in technical and managerial aspects of famine prevention in the past ten years, including putting in place early warning systems involving rural communities and local institutions, building reserves for food security, and linking relief and development. The transitional government of Ethiopia's policy and international agencies had improved their technical response, too.

Despite this, some participants felt strongly that the political aspects of famine disasters needed to be more widely debated within the international community. Famines, they argued, were part of a context of complex or political emergencies in which international humanitarian organizations played an increasing role. Issues of the control of information, the accountability of humanitarian organizations, and their ability to tackle crisis situations needed to be discussed. It was argued that international humanitarian assistance could not be seen as a substitute for self-reliant economic development. Humanitarian aid addressed crises, hopefully managing and containing their symptoms, but it did not resolve or prevent them. In the same way that famine relief was seen in the 1970s and 1980s as not addressing the root causes of famine, humanitarian assistance in the 1990s was seen as an external response that did not tackle the problems of long-term political and social crises but rather institutionalized them.[24] The symposium made a strong call for "collective self-reliance" within the region and within the African continent. The statement concluded:

> On one fundamental point, the majority of the participants were firm in their conviction. While a humanitarian, technocratic approach, based on improved procedures and largely funded by foreign aid could facilitate the prevention of famine in Ethiopia, it is at the same time

necessary to move beyond this approach to a strategy of empowering the people to prevent famine through political accountability of all actors to the people of Ethiopia in recognition of their fundamental political, economic and human rights.[25]

This symposium reflects the move to a reading of famine relief as humanitarian intervention, with the case of Ethiopia and Eritrea seen as originary, and it is interesting for a number of other reasons. First, it firmly characterizes famine not as a natural disaster caused by drought, but as the outcome of, or part of, conflict.[26] Second, it expresses the view that the technical, managerial aspects of famine prevention are not the only factors that should be considered, nor even the most important: attention to political concerns such as accountability, participation, and control of social and economic processes is crucial. Finally, implicit in the meeting is the view that aid or intervention from outside is not the solution and that it can be very harmful, exacerbating the crisis and impeding the prevention of future problems. The meeting itself, in its format, location, and structure, played a part in making the region an active participant in decision making.

Although the Addis symposium was an indication of how the debate had moved since 1984/85, articles commemorating the anniversary of the famine that appeared in newspapers in Britain provide a marked contrast. In the British media, as elsewhere outside Africa, Ethiopia remained more or less synonymous with "famine." For example, a special section in *The Guardian* headed "A Decade of Drought" and flagged as dealing with "famine, and how scientists try to prevent it" appeared on 6 December 1994. It begins: "Ten years on from the tragedy in Ethiopia, people are still dying from severe drought." The article, headlined "Victims of Drought and War," continues:

> Despite the return of peace, severe drought continues to leave Ethiopia in the hands of Western donors. It is now 10 years since the charity single *Feed the World* reached number 1 in the pop charts. The hit single and other fund-raising activities were inspired by Michael Buerk's news reports for BBC television, which brought images of starving children from Ethiopia into British homes.[27]

The account in the article itself places war and conflict, in combination with severe drought, as the causes of the famine. But the graph-

the famine, the dead went unburied, whole families hid themselves away to die, and half-starved dogs consumed corpses or attacked those still living. Here is an example:

> There were houses in this district in which all died of fever and none were buried. Things were so bad at that time that no one cared how the other was. Every household was left to itself and no one would come in or out to it. Families began to die and the rest were so weak and far spent that they could do nothing for them but leave them until the last one in the house died. All in the house died and the bodies lay here and there through it. They were never moved from it. There were many hungry dogs going about; and they say, God save us, that they were going into these houses and eating the bodies. When the fever went by and those who were left after it came to themselves a little, they went to those houses. The door leaves had dropped from the doors; when they went in there was nothing to be seen but people's bones lying about the house. They gathered the bones and buried them together in one grave. Then they burned the house to the ground.[35]

Another explanation for the unwillingness to speak of these traumatic times is linked with guilt: survivors felt they should have shared the fate of those who died. An event of such proportions affects the entire community, too, not just individuals, and leaves scars that take generations to heal. However, a minority of those who remained were not just lucky in their survival. They benefited financially from the disaster of their neighbors:

> There were some of those who shared with their neighbours then and others who rejoiced that all around them were evicted so that they fell in nicely for their places. We have them around here since, people whose ancestors did that—but we must leave it so and press it underfoot.[36]

The view that there has been mostly silence in terms of literary and historical representations of the famine is disputed by Margaret Kelleher. She argues that this silence or repression is overstated. There were fictional accounts of the Irish famine before the recent resurgence of interest, many written by women and a large number in the Irish language.[37] Oblique references have been found in texts where the famine was considered absent, for example, in the discussion of fecundity in Joyce.[38] These literary accounts are notable, in contrast with portrayals of famines on television and in journalistic reports, for their attempts to deal with precisely the questions that we have discussed as leading to silences—questions of how people fought to survive and with what consequences.[39]

In the academic literature on the famine, Kinealy distinguishes two approaches, the traditional nationalist approach and the revisionist approach.[40] The revisionist approach was predominant from the 1930s to the 1980s. In this period, there was little original research and few books were published. Revisionist historians were self-consciously attempting to bring a value-free, objective method to their work, as opposed to what they saw as the politically inspired nationalist interpretations. It was a "conscious debunking of 'nationalist' myths."[41] The revisionist approach comprised a number of key assertions. First, the famine was to be seen not as a major historical discontinuity but as an event that, at most, accelerated existing trends. Second, following Malthus, as a subsistence crisis it was inevitable: "the relationship between population, poverty and potatoes"[42] was a compelling one. As we saw in discussing the Ethiopian famine, this remains a forceful explanation for contemporary writers.[43] Third, the revisionists claim that by the standards of the day the British government did all that it could have reasonably been expected to do to alleviate the suffering and prevent the famine deepening.

The account downplays the political context, both within the British Isles and in Europe more broadly. It fails to examine the effect of Britain's relationship to Ireland in the framework of the Act of Union of 1800, which imposed control on Irish policy from Westminster. Local advice and interventions were largely ignored in favor of the interests of the British politician, economic theorist, and taxpayer. For example, the British government refused to intervene to close the ports to the export of food, an action that the Irish government had taken to good effect in the famine years of 1782–84. Revisionism does not examine the role of racist stereotypes or the attitude of the imperial power to its colonized. Relief was made dependent on participation in public works schemes, which Kinealy describes as "intended to be punitive, reflecting the ideological concerns of the ruling classes."[44] Inevitably, given its depoliticizing aims and claims to a value-free approach, the revisionist account downplays "suffering, mortality and blame"[45] and does not consider issues of responsibility.

As an approach, revisionism draws on the view of the famine that first appeared with the account, written in 1848, of Sir Charles Trevelyan, architect of the British relief effort in his position as permanent secretary at the Treasury. Trevelyan described the famine as "the judgement of God on an indolent and unself-reliant people"[46] and was self-congratulatory about the extent and effectiveness of the government response.

If Trevelyan blamed the Irish victims, the nationalist writers "readily and variously attributed [blame] to the British government, the 'English' Queen Victoria and the Irish landlords."[47] A particular focus for nationalist writers was on the way the continuing export of food indicated how "the demands of the commercial sector were given priority over the needs of a starving people. Economic imperatives triumphed over humanitarian concerns, regardless of the cost in human lives." Although the nationalist narrative of the famine was produced largely outside Ireland in the remaining years of the nineteenth century,[48] it resonates closely with the folk memory and the firsthand accounts that survive, perhaps a reason why historians have felt obliged to avoid using such sources. In one respect, however, the two accounts differ sharply. Contemporaneous accounts and the traditional memory of the famine see it as a visitation of God: nationalist writers dispute this strongly.

Issues of responsibility and blame for the famine are clearly and closely entangled in the politics of the relationship between Britain and Ireland. It is not surprising that this should have had a restraining effect on scholarship and debate about the famine, nor that the climate in the 1990s should see the need for a reexamination as part of a healing process. What remains a subject of concern is the way in which contemporary famines are still accounted for in apolitical terms, with responsibility placed not on God, perhaps, but on an unaccountable nature.

The view of famine as a crisis of food supply and a natural disaster involving mass starvation is so strong, and resonates so deeply, that any other account is liable to go unheard or to be reinterpreted in more familiar terms, as we have seen in both the cases examined here. The next chapter explores how this particular view of famine arose, how it is centrally located in the discourses and the politics of modernity, and why it has such a strong hold despite continuing empirical and theoretical rebuttals.

Famine has become naturalized as part of a scientific framework: it is seen as an object of investigation and resolution by calculation and technology, rather than the subject of political debate and contestation. In this framework, famine and scarcity form the flip side of modernity's promise of progress and abundance. Our understanding of modernity is so constructed that it already contains a place for famines. We expect famines to occur in modern times, but as anachronisms—as reminders of a nonmodern past that has yet to be totally overcome by progress. We regard famines as evidence of a failure, a lack of progress. I argue that famines are a product of modernity and specifically a part of modernity's transformation of political action and participation into biopolitics.

2

The Emergence of Famine in Modernity

A break from classical ways of thought took place at the end of the eighteenth and beginning of the nineteenth centuries. This discontinuity marked the beginning of the modern episteme in European thought and gave rise to the birth of the human sciences and the production, as an object of knowledge, of their subject, "man."[1] At this point and not before, a framework arose within which we could ask the question: Is famine man-made, or is it a natural disaster? At this point, too, a notion of generalized scarcity and the competition for resources in the face of a hostile nature arose. The epistemic shift, or the move to a new form of knowing, was accompanied by a shift to a modern type of politics: biopolitics.

In an archaeo-genealogy of famine, I trace three shifts that bring modern famine into being. First, I examine how the modern scientific episteme of famine arose within a more general epistemic shift that brought the human sciences into being. Second, I analyze how modernity's concern with scarcity and the Malthusian approach inform our specific views of famine and entail a separation of man and nature and how the story of prehistory that supports this view has recently been challenged. Finally, I consider the relation of the modern picture of famine to a specific view of the political as biopolitics.

Michel Foucault examines the epistemic shift in *The Order of Things*. It is a shift that can be traced in a range of systems of thought. Foucault argues that it is a move from a practice of knowledge that looks at representations and their order in a tabulation of events and their similarities to a practice that seeks explanations in terms of a hidden depth, "an interior mechanism"[2] beneath the surface of representations. In other words, it is a practice of referring representations to something beyond themselves:

> The signs whose representations were affected, the analysis of identities and differences . . . the continuous, yet articulated, table that was set up in the teeming profusion of similitudes, the clearly defined order among the empirical multiplicities, none of these can henceforth be based solely upon the duplication of representation in relation to itself. From this event onwards . . . the relation of representation to itself, and the relations of order it becomes possible to determine apart from all quantitative forms of measurement, now pass through conditions exterior to the actuality of that representation itself.[3]

No longer can the analysis of the exchange of wealth consider the value of objects of desire in relation to other objects of desire; they are now considered in relation to the quantity of labor from which they are constituted—something external to the system of objects. Natural beings are no longer characterized in relation to their place among other natural beings in the overall scheme of things through a consideration of their visible attributes, but by reference to an invisible organic structure. The concept of an organic structure of living beings had existed before, but it had not been used as a basis for classification or ordering. In the study of language, the counterpart of this is found: "language no longer consists only of representations and of sounds. . . . It consists also of formal elements, grouped into a system, which impose upon the sounds, syllables and roots an organisation."[4]

This move to a regime of truth is validated in a search beneath the surfaces of the visible for some organizing mechanism beyond and prior to representation is a move away from the thinking that constituted the classical age to a modern vision of what comprises knowledge and truth. We are still within this new episteme. Classical knowledge based on ordering was itself a break with a previous way of thought characterized by a reference to resemblance: an observance of relations of similitude. In the sixteenth century, knowledge consisted of a study of the inexhaustible hierarchy and infinite interplay of similitudes, drawing things together by seeking shared attributes. From the beginning of the seventeenth century, resemblances were referred either to numerical measurement or a placing of elements in a finite and numerable order. Knowledge was concerned not with similitude but with establishing identities and discriminating differences.[5] Previous beliefs based on resemblance were regarded as magical or superstitious, to be replaced by rationality and science.

A modern history of ideas would regard this sequence of beliefs and systems of knowledge as a series of steps on the road of progress from error toward a more perfected system of truth. Foucault contests this view. A key point of his work is the contention that these various systems of thought are not progressive. They are just *different* ways of determining what should count as knowledge or truth, separate resolutions of the problem of how thought should be organized. They are connected to arrangements of power, through the institutionalization of truth. For Foucault, "truth isn't outside power, or lacking in power . . . each society has its régime of truth, its general politics of truth: that is, the types of discourse which it accepts and makes function as true."[6] There are a number of distinct regimes of truth, and Foucault is concerned with the history of these. The goal of Foucault's project is a history of truth, which has an archaeological and a genealogical dimension and which would analyze

> the problematisations through which being offers itself to be, necessarily, thought—and the practices on the basis of which these problematisations are formed. The archaeological dimension of the analysis made it possible to examine the forms themselves; its genealogical dimension [made it possible] to analyse their formation out of the practices and the modifications undergone by the latter.[7]

Thus the shift from the classical to the modern episteme that took place at the end of the eighteenth century should not be seen as the discovery of objects of analysis that were unknown before, or the improvement or rationalization of previously immature or inaccurate forms of knowledge. It is not a question of these forms of knowledge emerging from their prehistory into the light of reason. Rather, what changed was knowledge itself, bringing into view "on the one hand new knowable objects . . . and [prescribing] on the other, new concepts and new methods."[8] We should not attribute this to the advancement of science:

> We must not seek to construe these as objects that imposed themselves from the outside, as though by their own weight and as a result of some

autonomous pressure, upon a body of learning that had ignored them for too long; nor must we see them as concepts gradually built up, owing to new methods, through the progress of sciences advancing towards their own rationality. They are fundamental modes of knowledge which sustain in their flawless unity the secondary and derived correlation of new sciences and techniques with unprecedented objects.[9]

AN OBJECT OF SCIENCE

One of the objects that was brought into being with the rise of the new episteme was famine. Famines, in the modern episteme, are not to be listed or compared or categorized. Famine is to be defined and its underlying causes sought. This brings into play notions of food supply and population and ultimately a vision of the relationship of one to the other in terms of scarcity as exemplified in the work of Thomas Malthus. The concept of scarcity, so specific to the modern episteme, conceals its novelty by the production of an account of prehistory as a long struggle for survival.

But what happened in the shift to modernity was quite revolutionary. Famine was constituted as a subject of scientific enquiry within the human sciences. Famine was technologized. Examining the contrast between other (nonmodern or non-Western) approaches and the view of famine accepted in modernity can help to reveal as strange that which we tend to take for granted as natural and obvious. It demonstrates how historically and culturally located modernity's view of famine is. My contention is that our discussions of famine tend not so much to examine an already existing object of study as to produce that object in a particular way and alongside particular relations of power. Demonstrating how a number of things that we take for granted in contemporary discussions of famine are not pre-given or inevitable can unsettle that object a little and thereby begin to dislodge those power relations.

A feature of modern discussions of famines is the desire to define famine. This seems an obvious step, but it contrasts with the nonmodern practice of the enumeration or listing of famines and their characteristics. In the modern episteme, knowledge is founded on hidden essences, on the structure that is not visible but is found beneath the surface appearance of diversity and resemblance:

> European culture is inventing for itself a depth in which what matters is no longer identities, distinctive characters, permanent tables with

all their possible paths and routes, but great hidden forces developed on the basis of their primitive and inaccessible nucleus, origin, causality, and history.[10]

The hunt for definitions of "famine" has led to much debate and the production of many alternatives. In his book *Theories of Famine*, Stephen Devereux devotes a chapter to such attempts, which he regards as important, first, "for establishing a rigorous definition of the phenomenon under study"; second, to avoid "weak or misleading definitions [that] reflect an implicit theory which is deficient or incorrect"; and, finally, "for diagnostic purposes—a famine has to be identified as such before institutional responses are triggered."[11]

However, this position is not unproblematic. As we have seen, theories do not represent a number of differing approaches to the same problem ("a famine"): famine is constituted by theory. Also, it is not possible to separate the issue of what the *nature* of famines is from issues of what their *causes* are.[12] Theoretical accounts represent alternative ways of producing "famine" as the object of study along with the framework for analysis. In addition, they lead more or less directly to different forms of action. Modern accounts attempt to identify famines as events with a *cause*. Each gives a different account of what famine *is* and derives from this a prescription for policy. Theories are not just abstract ideas. They have concrete results: they are social practices.[13]

Devereux gives us a number of examples of definitions of famines. First, dictionary definitions:

> Extreme scarcity of food in a district, etc.; dearth of something specified (water famine; famine prices; prices raised by scarcity); (archaic) hunger, starvation (die of famine).[14]

Then definitions that reflect theories of famine as food shortage:

> A famine is usually agreed to be a general, acute and extreme shortage of food within a region, which is not relieved by supplies of food being sent in because of inadequate distribution. Famines cause death from starvation and disease, which follow the extreme shortage of food, calories and nutrients.[15]

or as mass starvation:

> Perhaps when a man keels over and collapses from lack of food, then that can be accepted as the dividing line between malnutrition and

starvation. . . . Perhaps when whole families and communities keel over, then it can be called a famine.[16]

and those that look at the behavioral changes that accompany famine:

> Famine is an abnormal event, characterised by a breakdown in social relations, giving rise to epidemic starvation and excess mortality.[17]

> Famine is a socio-economic process which causes the accelerated destitution of the most vulnerable, marginal and least powerful groups in a community, to a point where they can no longer, as a group, maintain a sustainable livelihood.[18]

Finally Devereux turns to what he calls insider definitions. Here he draws on the work of Alex de Waal:

> The concept of famine in Darfur is primarily one of destitution, and not mortality and starvation. . . . Europeans believe that famine implies death by starvation, Africans who are exposed to famines do not.[19]

So, in modern discourses we find a variety of definitions. But do insiders *define* famine? When we begin to look at oral evidence and records, we find rather that they give names to each individual instance of famine, and these then serve as points around which other memories and experiences are collected.[20] Here is an example from Chad:

> We have suffered four major famines during my lifetime. The first was called Amzaytone, meaning "the time we sold our necklaces," in the 1950s. The second, about ten years later, was El Harigue, "the year when everything burnt," when our crops shrivelled under the heat of the sun. The third, in 1982, was Alchouil, "the year of the sack," when traders came with sacks of millet for us to buy. Finally, in 1985, the big famine came upon us. We called this Laïtche, meaning "the year when everyone fled from the area." At other times of difficulty, the men would go and leave the women behind.[21]

Similar "famines which were worthy of names"[22] are found in the list compiled by William Wilde from records in Ireland:

> 1433 There was a famine in the summer of this year; called for a long time afterwards, *samhra na mearaithne* [the summer of slight acquaintances], because no one used to recognise friend or relative, in consequence of the greatness of the famine.

1491 This year was commonly called by the natives the Dismal Year, by reason of the continual fall of rain all summer and autumn, which caused great scarcity of all sorts of grain throughout Ireland.[23]

When famines were remembered in this way as part of oral tradition, they served as markers over many centuries. They were recurrent tragedies and "the terror of their possible, even probable, return . . . kept them alive in myth and memory" and experiences of past survival had practical value.[24]

In the modern episteme, in contrast, what matters is finding a scientific cure for famine. Once a good definition is established, scientists can proceed to study famines in detail, establish their hidden causes, and prescribe appropriate preventative measures. By finding the underlying causes of famines, the specific structure that is assumed to lie behind the appearance of each individual case, famines can be ended.

A second shift can be identified in the transformation and technologization of famines as they were incorporated into the regime of modernity, from an emphasis on prices and price movements (dearth) to a new focus on food production (or food shortage). William Wilde's table of famines gives details of prices of various foodstuffs during past famines—in 1316 there was "a prodigious dearth; wheat was sold for three and twenty shillings the crenoge, oats six shillings . . . so that many died for want"; in 1317 "corn and provisions were exceedingly dear, wheat sold at 23s. the crannock, and wine for 8d., and the whole country was in a manner laid waste by the Scotts and those of Ulster"; in 1497 "there was a great dearth this year through most of Ireland . . . for a peck of wheat, being almost four English bushels, sold for 10s., and malt for 8s. . . . many perished"; 1741 "wheat and oatmeal are excessive dear; potatoes, 4s 4d. a bushel. Many through want perish daily in the roads and ditches"; in 1800 "the price of food has been enormous . . . oatmeal has been a high from May to harvest as from 37s. to 40s. per cwt."[25]

With the rise of modern economic analysis, this changed. The new objects of study included food supply (and food itself) and, with Malthus, population. It was not the cost of a foodstuff that was measured but the quantity of food per head of population. Here is an example:

The central pillar of the Irish diet was the potato. Total acreage of potatoes on the eve of the famine was approximately 2.1 million statute
acres. We can compute the total energy value of the potato crop by
assuming a mean gross output figure of 6 ton of potato per acre. As a
pound of potatoes contains about 317 calories, the total gross output
of calories per annum was about $8,947 \times 10^9$ calories. . . . it is reasonable to assume that the potato crop alone provided the Irish with at
least $4,200 \times 10^9$ calories per year, which is equivalent to 1,400 calories per capita per day.[26]

Modern approaches regard famine as a question of food and generally assume an unproblematic and uncomplicated notion of food.
Food is "fuel for the human machine": what is important is its
calorific and nutritional value. Questions of nutritional status and
minimum needs are addressed and malnutrition is identified.

However, food is not something that exists as a pre-given object,
awaiting analysis by nutritional science. It was produced as an object
of study with the appearance of the science of life that took place in
the late eighteenth or early nineteenth century. In that emergence,
what became important was the study of organs and their function. Although gills in fish and lungs in mammals are dissimilar in form, they
share the function of respiration: this "functional homogeneity . . . is
their hidden foundation."[27] The subject of biology becomes possible,
replacing natural history. The reference to function implies a necessary coexistence of organs in a system and a hierarchy of functions,
some of more importance than others in the overall plan of the organism. We have a distinction between classical "being" and biological
"life" and "the emergence of a certain energy, necessary to maintain
life, and a certain threat, which imposes upon it the sanction of
death."[28] In relation to biological life, food is defined in terms of its
function for the organism that is adapted to capture, consume, and
digest it and measured in terms of the abstract qualities of calorific
and nutritional value.

In other places and at different times

food was not merely considered to be fuel for the human machine.
Rather the sharing of food bound individuals indissolubly together in
spirit . . . it was a condensed symbol of society.[29]

Prior to the modern episteme, the customs and rituals surrounding the consumption and production of food in particular groups are

seen as important, and what counts as food is regarded as socially, not biologically, determined. Overstepping these social boundaries is possible—as in cases of cannibalism reported in famines—but their existence is confirmed by the guilt and remorse that this engenders. The notion of the production of food, firmly lodged in the modern episteme, is quite distinct from the concepts of generations who addressed their prayers to a God "whose gift it is, that the rain doth fall, the earth is fruitful, beasts increase, and fishes do multiply."[30] The idea of trade in food as a commodity like any other, which can be owned by an individual, is set against notions of food as gift, food for sharing, traditions of hospitality and obligation. Again, the failure of these imperatives to survive the exigencies of famine does not invalidate the notion.

In her study of the Bemba in Northern Rhodesia, Audrey Richards shows "how the biological facts of appetite and diet are themselves shaped by the particular system of human relationships and traditional activities which are standardized in a social group—in other words the cultural mechanisms for producing, preparing and dividing food."[31] Levels of food consumption are not dictated by some absolute biological need, but by requirements of labor and its reproduction. This is as true of the diet of the industrialized West as of that of the Zimbabwean tribe that Richards was studying: "we each of us have some kind of theory or belief, based on traditional teaching, childish memories or personal experience, as to what will do us 'good,' suit us, slim us, make our children grow, or 'last' us when at work."[32] Food advertising clearly draws on and embellishes these notions and attributes further qualities to food as well—as an aphrodisiac, for example. In Richard's study, there was a contrast between the Bemba's absorption by and interest in the question of food—a constant topic of conversation—and their lack of willingness to work harder to improve their apparently inadequate diet. For European outsiders it was puzzling that although the Bemba were short of food, they did not work harder and drink less beer;[33] government reports described them as lazy and unenterprising. However, for the Bemba, "to have too little to eat is not a shocking situation . . . and therefore not a stimulus to exert their last ounce of energy to alter an intolerable state of affairs. Living at this particular economic level, other advantages sometimes seem preferable to a sufficiency of food."[34] The Bemba had been a warrior tribe, subsisting on the tribute that their ferocity extracted from others, and fearlessness and bravery were admired more than good gardening. In the past, warrior youths would settle down in middle age to become the cultivators of the village, but this age group was employed as migrant labor in the mines. As laborers their diet necessarily changed, as they put in far more work than the three or four hours customary in the villages.

To the poor of medieval Europe, food, or the lack of food, meant more than energy or its absence. Piero Camporesi contrasts the irrational, dreamlike (or nightmarish) existence of the poorest groups with the rationalist Cartesian model being elaborated by well-off intellectuals. The latter was a world machine "regulated by a coherent mechanical and logical apparatus, a perfectly and inexorably self-adapting system of fittings and attachments."[35] In contrast, the world of the poor was characterized by a different model: "the flight of the ragged and starving masses . . . into artificial paradises, worlds turned upside down and impossible dreams of compensation [which] inspired an unbalanced, incoherent and spasmodic interpretation of reality."[36] Food was central to this distinction, reflected in the contrasting diets of the two groups. The bread of the poor, an object "on which life, death and dreams depend," becomes "the culminating point and instrument, real and symbolic, of existence itself: a dense polyvalent paste of manifold virtue in which the nutritive function intermingles with the therapeutic (herbs, seeds and curative pastes were mixed into the bread), magico-ritual suggestion with the ludico-fantastical, narcotic and hypnotic."[37]

As well as consuming bread made of contaminated grain, the poor suffered from hunger, itself known to bring about altered mental states: "the most effective and upsetting drug, bitterest and most ferocious, has always been hunger, creator of unfathomable disturbances of mind and imagination."[38] Both food and lack of food were productive of a desirable distraction from the unbearable word of poverty and distress:

> If . . . hunger, like mescaline, produces hallucinations and the tremors of dementia, by inhibiting the formation of enzymes which serve to coordinate the ordered working of the brain and by reducing the level of glucose necessary to this organ . . . [then] a huge stratum of the poorest part of the population, suffering from a profound deterioration of will, socially demoralised and without interest in the highest and most

human "causes," lived in a world of squalid intellectual and moral apathy, altered in the relations of time and space: a universe of completely unreal extrasensory perceptions.[39]

The modern view of starvation and hunger as a bodily affliction, then, does not come close to the full horror of famine sufferers or those who are malnourished. Although the use of drugs and stimulants remains very much a part of eating in the everyday life of the modern world, it is perhaps for the most part voluntary and temporary in a way it was not for the poor of earlier times; the converse of this, the altered rationality that results from deprivation and starvation and is neither chosen nor avoidable, is forgotten. In the past poverty-stricken populations suffering from hunger "had not the slightest possibility of organising themselves into revolutions, existing as they did outside of time and space, and beyond any social or political strategy."[40]

In present-day Brazil, hunger produces a condition called by sufferers *nervos* or "nerves." It is treated by tranquilizers or other medication.[41] This could be interpreted as an instance where the modern impulse to technologize, expressed here through a medicalization of hunger, relies on and exploits a broader nonmodern understanding of starvation. The people of the Alto do Cruzeiro now describe their affliction as *nervos* rather than hunger, although in the past they understood that nervousness was a symptom of hunger. It was called *delírio de fome*, the madness of hunger. But now, "where once *delírio de fome* was a popular representation of the tragic experience of the body with frenzied hunger, *nervoso* now represents the tragic experience of tormented and worried bodies with a nervous social and political system."[42] As Nancy Scheper-Hughes argues, hunger has become "a disallowed discourse, and the rage and dangerous madness of hunger have been metaphorised" so that the hungry "see in their wasted and tremulous limbs a chronic feebleness of body and mind."[43] This has political implications: "hunger and other unmet and basic human needs are isolated by a process that excludes them by redefining them as something other than what they are."[44] While the hungry need food, the sick only need medicine:

> The transition from a popular discourse on hunger to one on sickness is subtle but essential in the perception of the body and its needs. A hungry body needs food. A sick and "nervous" body needs medications. A

hungry body exists as a potent critique of the society in which it exists. A sick body implicates no one. Such is the special privilege of sickness as a *neutral* social role, its exemptive status. In sickness there is (ideally) no blame, no guilt, no responsibility. Sickness falls into the moral category of bad things that "just happen" to people.[45]

In other times and places, hunger is placed in this category of neutral, blame-free event, when it is seen as a natural or an economic disaster. Responsibility is removed and political action ruled out in favor of, not medical action, but action by other experts—development specialists, food scientists, agriculturists, or conflict resolution experts—who determine the scientific causes of the problem and prescribe remedial action. In Brazil today, as in the medieval Italy described by Camporesi, hunger is pacified and depoliticized, and the hungry seek solutions in forgetting their misery when action to contest their oppression becomes impossible for them. In the shantytowns of Brazil, doctors are complicit in this. They acquiesce to diagnoses of hunger as nervous disorder and prescribe the food supplements or antidepressants requested by their patients; they attribute deaths to *nervos* that they can see are equally or, more properly, more scientifically attributable to severe malnutrition. Scheper-Hughes points to the role of the intellectual in "the concealment of hunger in the folk . . . and later the biomedical discourse on nervos":[46]

> Increasingly in modern bureaucratic states, technicians and professionals come to play the role of traditional intellectuals in sustaining commonsense definitions of reality through their highly specialised and validating forms of discourse. Gramsci anticipated Foucault, both in terms of understanding the capillary nature of diffuse power circuits in modern states and in terms of identifying the crucial role of "expert" forms of power/knowledge in sustaining the commonsense order of things. In [Brazil] doctors occupy the pivotal role of "traditional" intellectuals whose function, in part, is to misidentify, to fail to see the secret indignation of the sick poor expressed in the inchoate folk idiom *nervos*.[47]

The poor acquiesce in their mistreatment, perhaps because drugs have a magical efficacy: "if hunger cannot be satisfied, it can at least be tranquillised."[48] Medicine captures their imagination, as it captured intellectuals studying the new disciplines of biological science at the end of the eighteenth century. The translation of hunger into *nervos* is a medicalization, part of the process of technologization that is spreading from industrialized societies to other parts of the world. It is a process that has ethical and political implications, and intellectuals as "experts" are complicit in the power structures and oppression it reproduces.[49]

If the notion of food and the medicalization of hunger are specific to the modern episteme, so is the notion of a natural disaster, unprompted by and unconnected to human acts.[50] In past famines—and indeed in the present too—victims regarded their predicament as a "visitation from God." Famine is a sign of God's anger or the victims' transgressions. The answer is prayer and supplication, scapegoating or sacrifice:

> O God, heavenly Father . . . Behold, we beseech thee, the afflictions of thy people; and grant that the scarcity and dearth, which we do now most justly suffer for our iniquity, may through thy goodness be mercifully turned into cheapness and plenty.[51]

In the classical Mediterranean world there was no distinction between secular and religious responses to famine: the two were intertwined and of equal importance.[52] The response to famine or the threat of famine was the scapegoat or Pharmakos ceremony, where, in one description, "two ugly men were selected, one for each sex, and ritually expelled from the city, perhaps with violence, carrying with them the guilt of the community."[53] Human acts brought divine displeasure and famine; the gods had to be appeased or placated or their anger refocused on a scapegoat. If the gods failed to heed supplications, they could face demotion or desertion.[54]

In early China, in the eastern Chou and Ch'in dynasties, the influence of Confucian thought meant that "the ruler and his officials . . . were morally and practically responsible for natural disasters. . . . there was a direct correlation between the human and the natural world, and ill conceived or morally corrupt official actions could bring about an almost immediate response from the natural order."[55] Famines were not distinguished from floods or droughts; all were the responsibility of the rulers. Natural and human disasters could be averted by following the prescribed actions appropriate for each season laid down in the Confucian calendar. If droughts or famines did occur, divinations were made and sacrifices offered.[56]

It was only with the advent of nineteenth-century thought that man could be put "in his ambiguous position as an object of knowl-edge and a subject that knows: enslaved sovereign, observed specta-tor,"[57] and the human sciences became possible. Only then could natural laws be conceived as separable from human acts and

> The representation one makes to oneself of things . . . is the appear-ance of an order that now belongs to things themselves and to their interior law. It is no longer their identity that beings manifest in repre-sentation, but the external relation they establish with the human being.[58]

With the emergence of man as positive subject/object, separated off, knowable, comes the notion of finitude. Natural disaster, man's powerlessness before the laws of nature, is the flip side of his ability to understand nature and gain control through understanding. This ridge is the boundary from which both the power of science to know the laws of nature *and* its own powerlessness before their unchange-able and dispassionate inexorability can be seen. Natural disaster has a scientific cause.

MALTHUS, SCARCITY, AND SURVIVAL

Since the work of Thomas Malthus in England in the eighteenth cen-tury, the debate about famine has been framed in terms of scarcity, whether the focus has been on population, crop improvement, or ecology. Like other theories in the modern episteme, Malthusian theory was an assertion of what famine *is*. Malthus saw famine as a natural phenomenon, where "nature" is distinct from "man":

> Famine seems to be the last, the most dreadful resource of nature. The power of population is so superior to the power in the earth to pro-duce subsistence for man, that premature death must in some shape or other visit the human race. The vices of man are active and able ministers of depopulation [and] sickly seasons, epidemics, pestilence, and plague . . . sweep off their thousands and ten thousands. Should success be still incomplete, gigantic inevitable famine stalks in the rear and, with one mighty blow, levels the population with the food of the world.[59]

Malthus was opposed to the view prevailing at the turn of the nineteenth century that Enlightenment progress could solve prob-lems like famine. This made him an opponent of the introduction of the Poor Laws in England, and Malthusian ideas have had a profound influence on the constitution of poverty and the pauper in welfare discourse.[60] Ironically, Malthus's work was initially an argument against the technologization of politics that derived from the rise of the human sciences. He argued against the use of the social sciences to improve the human condition on the basis of the existence of supervening natural laws. Donald Winch, in his introduction to Malthus's work, writes:

> Malthus described himself as a reluctant opponent of the radical interpretation of the science of politics that was then most readily associated with the French Revolution. . . . According to this . . . politics connoted the activity of human reason operating . . . to improve the lives of individuals and nations. . . . Standing this proposition on its head, Malthus maintained that misery and vice were attributable to a fundamental law of nature that was impervious to institutional change and legislative contrivance. He also shifted the terms of debate from political culture towards biology by grounding his law of nature on the population principle—an ever-present propensity for population growth to outstrip the means of subsistence.[61]

According to Malthus, "population, when unchecked, increases in a geometrical ratio. Subsistence increases only in an arithmetical ratio. A slight acquaintance with numbers will show the immensity of the first power in comparison of the second."[62]

In terms of famine policy today, neo-Malthusian approaches mean concentrating on a number of specific areas. The general ethos is a focus on large-scale, countrywide, or global solutions. Population control is of course important, but so is the increase of food production by improving agricultural techniques and incentives. Food stocks are crucial, and there is concern for food security. Environmental problems must be tackled, too, as it is important to bring an increasing area of the earth's surface into production and to increase the efficient and sustainable use of that already cultivated. Pesticide and fertilizer development and the breeding of new plant varieties is another area of work. In terms of the response to famines themselves, there is a tendency to blame the victim—for breeding too fast or whatever—and relief is sometimes given reluctantly. Food for work programs are favored over free distribution since otherwise the so-called feckless poor will continue to be dependent and lazy. The morality of relief is questioned by writers such as Garrett Hardin,[63] who contend that helping the improvident will only increase the chance of global disaster. Since the carrying capacity of the earth, like a lifeboat, is limited, those who try to clamber aboard to save themselves must be firmly repulsed in the interest of the survival of the whole.

Central to Malthus's approach is the notion of population and the image this produces of famines afflicting entire societies. Aid workers still express surprise that this image is not borne out in practice: it is not whole populations that suffer starvation in famines.[64] Malthus's work produced "population" as an object of study and a corresponding scientific discipline: demography. Although the Malthusian stress on the problem of population growth in relation to famine is not unchallenged in contemporary theory, it nevertheless continues to structure much of the thinking on the problem. Particularly in scientific discourse, the debate is between Malthusian pessimists, who think that a population explosion to levels beyond the earth's carrying capacity is inevitable, and Malthusian optimists, who believe that technology can continue to expand food production to outstrip population needs.[65] A newspaper report preceding the 1994 United Nations conference on population in Cairo appeared under the headline "Overcrowding Points to Global Famine." There was the usual photograph of a third world crowd, despite the reference in the text of the report to the disproportionate consumption of resources by rich countries. The article discusses a report of the Worldwatch Institute (WWI) that argues that "food scarcity, not military aggression, is the principle threat to our future," and concludes "the world's food supplies can no longer keep up with its exploding population growth."[66] Similar headlines followed the publication of the 1996 WWI report.[67] Clearly the "population delusion"[68] is still very much with us.

In the 1970s, after the famines in the Sahel and the oil price crisis, confidence in the possibility of growth and technology solving the problems of the developing world was shaken. The situation was perceived as a world food crisis. The solution was seen as "Ending World Hunger": a global problem with global solutions. Work on the global food regime[69] was undertaken in the context of Malthusian projections and the "limits to growth" discourse.[70] A plethora of publications appeared calling for action to solve the problem or discussing "world hunger."[71]

Malthusian ideas are framed by a specific view of nature. In this view, not only is nature separate from man, but nature is seen as the site of competition over scarce resources rather than as fruitful, plentiful, or cooperative.[72] Such concepts of scarcity, competition, and limits underlie modern economic theory, too. The idea of a battle with a (separate) nature leads to the need to understand and thus control natural forces, which is a driving force behind the natural as well as the human sciences. Environmentalism can be seen as a reassertion of the same Malthusian ideas of limits.[73] The contradiction between a fear of scarcity (the root of the limits to growth argument) and the *need* for scarcity (to drive economics and hence growth) is embodied in the expression "sustainable development" and its politically powerful articulation or linking of these disparate positions. Famine discourse is central to this whole discursive formation because it represents the point at which ideas of scarcity/abundance, culture/nature, food/want, famine/plenty, and life/death converge. Starvation and its skeletal forms depict a living death—evocative perhaps of our image of the limits posed by life-giving nature. As Nicholas Xenos puts it, "televised and printed images of poverty and famine are constant reminders of the precariousness of the human condition."[74] We see such images as confirmation of a general condition of scarcity, not historically specific circumstances.

This notion of a generalized scarcity and its twin, abundance, is peculiar to modernity. If we examine the etymology of the English word "scarcity" we find that its original use was to indicate an insufficiency of supply of anything. The word "famine" was similar. The Lancashire cotton famine was a shortage of cotton, for example. This sense of the word is still found occasionally. By the fifteenth century "a scarcity" had become an insufficiency of supply of necessities, or dearth. Later, it came to mean a *period* of insufficiency or "a dearth." This changed in the nineteenth century "when neoclassical economics made the scarcity postulate its foundation and the term passed into general usage through its transformation into a concept signifying a general condition: not 'a scarcity of,' or 'a time of scarcity' but simply 'scarcity.' . . . Scarcity in the general sense is a modern invention."[75] The promise of abundance accompanies this new concept of scarcity; both are framed by modernity's idea of progress, which provides "a narrative structure within which scarcity and abundance could be accommodated in a single linear frame."[76]

The notion of scarcity and specifically scarcity of food or famine is fundamental to modern economics as it arose in the nineteenth century: "Labour—that is, economic activity—did not make its appearance in world history until man became too numerous to subsist on the spontaneous fruits of the land. . . . What makes economics possible, and necessary, then, is a perpetual and fundamental situation of scarcity."[77] In the period where "what matters is no longer identities, distinctive characters . . . but great hidden forces,"[78] we find Malthus proposing laws of nature whereby the properties of populations are determined. Economics also was to be "related . . . to the biological properties of the human species" and a new "subject" came into being—economic man, "the human being who spends, wears out and wastes his life in evading the imminence of death."[79] It is at this point that economics becomes separated from the discourse of morals—value is analyzed in terms of cost, not need. It becomes depoliticized. And the discourse of limits, imposed by nature's avarice, is embedded in modern thought.[80] In pictures of famine, then, we see our own plight as "economic man." This account shows how firmly a part of the modern, Western episteme Malthusian approaches to famine are.[81]

The Malthusian view of nature and economics has not gone unchallenged. There is the empirical argument that in the two hundred years since Malthus, population has failed to outstrip food supplies. His dire predictions of impending disaster have not come true. Another is that after a famine, it is only a relatively short time before population returns to levels it would have reached had there been no famine. Such empirical challenges have little impact: there are always other statistics—or projections—that can be used to discredit the argument. A number of theoretical challenges have been equally unsuccessful. Ester Boserup has argued that, contrary to Malthus, an increase in population will *improve* food availability. More people is seen as a good thing, not a problem: it means more minds to help solve problems, more technological development.[82] Nicole Ball argues that food scarcity is the product of socioeconomic conditions, not something that arises out of any natural tendency to scarcity or from climatic problems. She quotes accounts of agricultural abundance in sixteenth-century Ethiopia and argues, "That this no longer holds true results directly from changes in economic and political relations within African societies."[83] She links dependency and disaster and argues that it is the relationship between rich and poor countries that creates disasters. Furthermore, she sees that international agencies are unable to break out of the type of responses that make matters worse because of the limitations of their position in the international system.[84] Such arguments have remained on the margins, while the Malthusian view is central.

Modernity's account of famines as scarcity is predicated on a view of "man" continually struggling with an adversarial nature. The companion to the notion of scarcity is an image of an inexorable historical progress toward plenty and abundance. This progress is seen as the fruit of modernity; specifically, it will be the outcome of modernity's increasing control of nature through enlightenment and knowledge. To support this perception, the modern notion of famine has produced its own prehistory. The shift from the classical to the modern episteme identified by Foucault not only affects how we understand what happens now and in the future, but also involves a renarration of the past. When our view of famines changes, as it did at the end of the eighteenth and beginning of the nineteenth centuries, particularly with the work of Malthus, our account of famines in the past also has to change. We have to write another history of the present.

The Malthusian approach has retrospectively written its own history, so it seems remarkable that we still have famine in the twentieth century. This history is a story of economic progress moving beyond primitive societies in which starvation was a recurrent feature of a life of struggle against an inhospitable nature to a modern, technologically advanced world where famines are an anomaly. The Malthusian picture looks at recent improvements and extrapolates these backward. It leads us to "assume that measurable improvements in nutrition and health since the eighteenth century are only the most recent and visible parts of human progress."[85] We also link this with our assumptions about the role of Malthusian checks in limiting growth of prehistoric populations until they were overcome by modern technology.

Three transitions are thought to have taken place in primitive times: the transition from a reliance on large game to foraging for small game and seeds, to settled or farming populations, and to urbanization (what we call "civilization"). Mark Cohen is one of a number of recent writers to dispute the Malthusian assumption that these transitions both improved the quality of diet and reduced the frequency of famine.[86] Although they meant that larger populations were supported and the total amount of food increased, according to Cohen they did not signal improved quality or reliability of the food supply. The new technologies, such as the fishing and trapping equipment and grindstones that accompanied the first transition, "represent a necessary adjustment to declining resources and/or increasing human population density."[87] Rather than producing an improvement in nutritional standards, they avoid a fall, and perhaps accompany an increased level of risk. For example, the storing of food has advantages, but brings with it changing constraints: "Stored food can be, and often is, expropriated by other groups of people: sedentary populations with stored resources face a new, politically induced risk of hunger not faced by their more mobile forebears."[88] This is in addition to the severe risks to health in terms of disease and parasites that settled populations, and the cultivated crops and domesticated animals on which they rely, also face. A similar mix is found with increasing urbanization and the growth of trade. Although this enabled populations to increase the variety of their diet and overcome problems of unreliability and local famine, it brought its own risks. As Cohen puts it:

> Large-scale civilised storage and trade, although potentially powerful in alleviating famine, also imply control by a political elite and the existence of classes of people who exert little economic or political demand in the system. . . . Most people . . . lose control over their own food supplies [and] starvation may become more of a function of political and economic forces than of actual crop failure.[89]

There are some contradictions in the evidence, and the scope for differing interpretation is large, but Cohen concludes that "[n]either ethnographic evidence nor archaeological data support the common assumption that malnutrition or starvation were particularly common among early and/or 'primitive' human groups."[90] Famine was not prevalent in prehistoric times. Cohen argues that Malthusian checks of this type are not the only way of accounting for the implication in the archaeological evidence that the growth of human population in pre-agricultural times was very slow: "We tend to assume that the very slow, early growth of population before the advent of agriculture must represent either extremely low average life expectancy or relatively frequent population crashes resulting from famine or epidemics."[91] An alternative explanation would be that "early human populations were naturally (or by regulation) low-fertility populations with only moderately high mortality."[92] The increase in population growth after the introduction of farming has more to do with an increase in fertility than a reduction in deaths by starvation or malnutrition. Malthusian assumptions, however tempting, are not necessary to explain this change.

David Rindos's work represents a further challenge to a Malthusian prehistory.[93] For Cohen the transition to agriculture was due to population pressure or reduced resources. Rindos gives an account based on co-evolution, "an evolutionary process in which the establishment of a symbiotic relationship between organisms, increasing the fitness of all involved, brings about changes in the traits of the organisms."[94] An increased yield of plants that have adapted to human use by becoming domesticated means that the human population increases. This in turn leads to the destruction of alternative food resources, a reduction in the variability of diet and an increasing vulnerability to the loss of food crops. The attempt to reduce this vulnerability leads to trade and exchange, which in turn produces social change. According to Rindos, agriculture is maladaptive—it is a high-growth, low-stability system—but it spreads, precisely because of these characteristics, at the expense of more stable food systems.[95] As Rindos puts it:

> Fitness and "adaptiveness" may even show a negative correlation. The relative fitness induced in a culture by means of its agricultural behaviour is seen as being simply the result of a higher realised rate of population growth—agricultural behaviours increase the carrying capacity of the local environment for humans and, hence, the proportion of individuals per unit area who will have agricultural modes of subsistence will inevitably be larger than the proportion of individuals with most other subsistence strategies. . . . This will hold true even if agricultural behaviour brings with them a decrease in robustness, a decline in life expectancy, and increase in morbidity and mortality. . . . While all these factors may easily be judged as indicators of decreased adaptation, the higher growth rate of agriculture will nevertheless favour it over other forms of human subsistence.[96]

Increased instability in productivity of an agricultural system will lead to that system's spread "by literally driving out individuals to colonise new regions. Occasional episodes of lowered productivity [famines], induced not by the environment but rather by the plants and techniques of the agricultural system itself, will cause the spread of that tradition to occur at a rate greater than that of other, more adaptive and stable, agricultural traditions."[97]

Rindos's view contrasts both with that of Cohen and that of the traditional, or mainstream, Malthusian-inspired approach to the origins of agriculture.[98] It is supported by the archaeological record, which shows that increased stress, measured by such indicators as skeletal structure, height, and the condition of tooth enamel, occurred with the appearance of developed agricultural systems. This stress, which Cohen's population pressure would predict to be worst during the introduction of agriculture, and Malthusians would see in hunter-gatherer societies, seems to be found once agriculture has become established.[99] Agriculture was not the solution to a food-supply problem, but rather it produced one.

The modern episteme in which the traditional, Malthusian accounts of prehistory are placed relies on the separation of man and nature. This view is extrapolated backward in time to produce an account of the origin of agriculture and civilization in terms of human control over nature. Rindos argues for an account that sees the domestication of plants and animals and the evolution of patterns of human activity occurring simultaneously, and "the increased utilisation of wild plants by an increasingly large human population led *naturally* to an increased yield of food plants"[100] and the rise of sedentary agriculture, with all its drawbacks, including instability and famines.

Narratives of famine claim that subsistence crises—crises caused by insufficiently developed agricultural systems—more or less ceased with the onset of modernity and that present-day food crises in the developed world are concerned with distribution not supply. If agriculture was not an escape from the scarcity that preceded it but rather a system that *produced* scarcity, famines, and stress in human populations, and if the technology of agriculture does not improve food security but leads to the insecurity of a high-risk system, then we have a completely new set of questions.

We are faced with the conclusion that famine is a concomitant of progress, the price that has to be paid for the benefits of civilization. Garrett Hardin's lifeboat is not a prescription for action but a description of what happens: we survive as civilized, settled peoples through the acceptance, inevitably, of the periodic sacrifice of thousands of our fellow humans in famines. Our means of production of food both enables a centralized, differentiated social system and produces the instability that leads to famine. The social system itself gives rise to a situation where the majority of people no longer have direct control of their food supply but rely on powerful elites who are in charge of trade and exchange systems.

Famine is not an anachronism in the modern world; it is the inevitable accompaniment of modernity. The technology of agriculture produces, rather than solves, the problem of hunger:

> Our technology, which we are inclined to view as a great liberating force, appears . . . to be more of a holding action. . . . the present food crisis . . . might be more constructively faced if we realised that it is the prevailing notion of "progress" rather than the contemporary "crisis" which is the historical anomaly.[101]

BIOPOLITICS

I have argued so far that modernity involved a move from a view of food as socially defined (and defining) to food as fuel for the human organism—a biological view. In Malthus this translates into a vision of survival as a battle to conquer scarcity, where human technology is pitted against the laws of nature. In modernity conflict is no longer a question of the resolution of political issues or questions concerning how society should be organized. It becomes a contest between man and nature, and political issues are translated into biological terms; for example, it is a question of resources. This, as Foucault and subsequent writers have argued, is a move to biopolitics, where what is at stake is control of the biological existence of human beings, not their political organization. Giorgio Agamben builds on and extends Foucault's analysis of governmentality and biopolitics.[102]

Agamben argues that since Aristotle "politics" has been founded on a separation between *zoe* (bare life) and *bios* (a politically qualified life). He describes "bare life" as common to all living beings, but *bios* as a form of living proper to an individual or a group, a particular way of life. Originally, *zoe* or bare life was excluded from the *polis* and confined to the home. Foucault analyzes the transition at the threshold of the modern era when bare life was included in the mechanisms and calculations of state power. At this point politics needs a new name, to distinguish it from what went before: biopolitics.

Whereas for Aristotle, man is a living animal with a capacity for political existence, in modernity man has become "an animal whose politics calls his existence as a living being into question."[103] Modernity is the point at which the species and the individual as a simple living body become what is at stake in a society's political strategies. There has been a transition from a territorial state to a state of population—rather than governing territory, the state governs people. For Agamben the concentration camp is the exemplary space of modern biopolitics. The famine relief camp is another site, albeit less appalling, where biopolitics is installed. In the relief camp the authorities' concern for death rates and the bureaucracy of organization obscures any awareness of the refugees' own social and political aims.[104]

With the constitution of the modern sovereign state, life *as such* is reduced to calculability. It becomes bare life, which is "the life of *homo sacer* (sacred man), who *may be killed and yet not sacrificed.*"[105] This figure of *homo sacer* has an essential function in modern politics: it becomes "the one place for both the organisation of state power and emancipation from it."[106] Humanitarianism is an example of how sovereignty is maintained by the very forces that appear to contest it. Humanitarian action is complicit in the reproduction of sovereign politics, since it maintains the very separation upon which sovereignty depends:

> The separation between humanitarianism and politics that we are experiencing today is the extreme phase of the separation of the rights of man from the rights of the citizen. In the final analysis, however, humanitarian organisations . . . can only grasp human life in the figure of bare or sacred life, and therefore, despite themselves, maintain a secret solidarity with the very powers they ought to fight.[107]

Famines in modernity are seen as episodes of mass starvation, where thousands lose their lives for lack of food. Humanitarian aid provides food and the means for bare survival. Life alone, bare life, is what matters, not the continuance of a particular way of life. In a nonmodern view of famine this is not so: preservation of a way of (political) life is vital.

The nonmodern sees famine not as starvation but as social catastrophe. All efforts are directed, not toward the avoidance of hunger, and not even toward minimizing the absolute number of deaths, but toward preserving the wherewithal to regenerate the community and ensure the survival of their way of life. Families will go hungry rather than sell their farming equipment or their herds of animals.[108] In extremity, it is recognized that it is the survival of adults of reproductive age that will enable the community as such to survive: more children can be conceived, and babies cannot survive as members of a community without the adults. This in no way implies that the death of children is taken lightly; many accounts testify to the anguish it brings. Here is an example:

> It was a time when there were no birds singing. They must have died too, I suppose. Vultures drifted high in the air without flapping their wings. They didn't need to since the air rising from the ground was so hot. Cows bellowed from hunger throughout the night and cockerels crowed at strange times. But children didn't cry. That was the worst of it. Children looked their mothers in the eyes, pleading for food, but there was none. I couldn't find any and my breasts were dry. My little girl died on the fifth day without food. I should have died with her.[109]

The dread of famine is the fear of more than death: accounts of famines in history show that they have a greater, more powerful effect than starvation. As we see in this example from Ireland, famines involve the destruction of an entire society:

> It didn't matter who was related to you, your friend was whoever would give you a bite to put in your mouth. Sport and pastimes disappeared. Poetry, music and dancing stopped. They lost and forgot them all and when the times improved in other respects, these things never returned as they had been. The famine killed everything.[110]

In the modern view, famine is widespread starvation; the suffering and death of particular individuals is what counts and what is counted. The greatest famines are the ones where the largest number of deaths occur. In this picture, children and babies are given as much if not more importance than adults. Their survival in orphanages or refugee settlements is a solution rather than a failure. Relief is aimed at *preserving the life of the biological organism* rather than restoring the means of livelihood to the community.[111] Meaning resides in the invisible subsurface of the biological organism and its functions, not in its distinctiveness or its discursively produced relationships. Life, not living, is all.

What modernity's picture of famine produces is bare life, a life that is mere existence with no political voice and no particular way of life. The way "the spectacle of famine" is conveyed through female figures is instructive here.[112] Famine is seen as inexpressible, something that cannot be expressed in language. It is partly a question of the scale and enormity of the tragedy. But there is something more than that—perhaps the association of food with life itself gives rise to "a double fear: both of language's inadequacy and its dangerous power."[113] Images of women unable to feed their children convey a breakdown in the natural order: bare life again. The female/male distinction is aligned with and constituted alongside the dichotomy between nature and culture: "the resulting implication, that famine is a natural rather than a political event, is itself a political message, regrettable but also convenient."[114] It depoliticizes. The discourse on famine moves "away from the political and economic spheres into a moral register" through the way the figure of woman is conflated with nature: "perversions of the maternal ideal, a woman unable to feed her child, who outlives her child, who cannot bury her child, are the dominant features of scenes which are physically immediate but politically isolated."[115]

CONCLUSION

Foucault's characterization of the epistemic discontinuity that occurred around the time of Malthus has been used to sketch a few features of an archaeo-genealogy of famine—an exploration of the incorporation of famine in the modern episteme. Foucault's method is an attempt "to examine both the difference that keeps us at a remove from a way of thinking in which we recognize the origin of our own, and the proximity that remains in spite of the distance which we never cease to explore."[116] Our contemporary thought about famine lies within the modern episteme, constrained and yet enabled by it. By examining those constraints, and in a sense denaturalizing them, we are able to see the possibility of thinking otherwise and to resist more effectively the forces that constrain our reflections and thus our practices. Foucault draws our attention to signs of movement:

> In attempting to uncover the deepest strata of Western culture, I am restoring to our silent and apparently immobile soil its rifts, its instability, its flaws; and it is the same ground that is once more stirring under our feet.[117]

In the case of famine we have found a number of discontinuities and dissonances between what I have very loosely labeled a modern discourse of famine and nonmodern or non-European thought. Particular discontinuities that actually produced our modern notion of famine and constituted it as an object of study surround or are signaled by the work of Thomas Malthus in eighteenth-century England. His work was used in formulating and legitimizing responses to the Irish famine, and it still sets the parameters for debates about famine and food supply today. Malthus's view of famine as a shortage of food for a growing population that leads to mass starvation arose at the end of the eighteenth and the beginning of the nineteenth centuries with the rise of the modern episteme. The contemporary view has a particular notion of food as fuel, of the natural and social worlds as distinct, and of order as arising from hidden structures beneath surface appearances. There is a contrast between this view and alternative pictures of famines, some of which have been described. The modern account also writes its own prehistory. The contemporary view is not unitary or homogeneous, however, and later chapters elucidate debates that take place within the modern episteme and against it. In many senses it is impossible to stand outside the present. However, the hope is that a discussion of these discontinuities may serve to defamiliarize and dislodge some of the notions that form part of the assumptions that we take for granted and show how firmly these are located in the form of knowledge that characterizes modernity. In chapter 4, I examine the role of power/knowledge in the constitution of the subjects of food aid and practices of famine relief and how the modern way of knowing famine leads to methods of relief that discipline and reproduce relations of power. The forms of knowledge of modernity are closely entangled with particular forms of politics.

3

Availability and Entitlement

*The law stands between food availability and food entitlement. Starvation
deaths can reflect legality with a vengeance*
—AMARTYA SEN, *POVERTY AND FAMINES*

Offering food aid to suffering victims of famine was widely regarded
by the international community, donor states, and nongovernmental
organizations (NGOs) as an uncontentious example of humanitarianism until recently. A starving population was assumed to be in
need of relief in the form of food supplies, and this was duly, although often belatedly, offered. This seemingly straightforward response in fact invokes a specifically Malthusian notion of what famines are. The Malthusian approach that I discussed in the previous
chapter arose alongside the epistemic shift to modernity that took
place at the beginning of the nineteenth century. As an approach to
famine, it produces technical responses. Famine is seen as a natural
disaster and famine relief as a question of food supply. Famine is depoliticized. This view has been widely contested.

One of the challenges to this view has been from Amartya Sen.
Sen's approach, first propounded in the late 1970s and early 1980s,[1]
claims that, contrary to Malthusian assumptions, famine is not caused
by food shortages or a failure of food availability. In Sen's view, famine is due to a breakdown in food entitlements. This fall in entitlements, which would typically affect only certain small sections of a

population, could be triggered by a shortage of food in general, but this shortage is only one of the factors that could give rise to this result. A fall in entitlements to food could equally be caused by unemployment, a rise in prices not itself indicative of shortage, or a number of other factors.[2] This would leave the affected groups vulnerable to starvation, and extensive starvation would lead to famines, defined by Sen as "involving fairly widespread acute starvation."[3] Famine is seen as an extension of starvation, which is an acute manifestation of poverty.

Although a powerful denunciation of the picture of famine as a natural disaster, attributable to causes such as drought or pestilence beyond the control of states or governments, Sen's approach retains the notion of famine as a sudden economic collapse, a failure, but this time in the economic system. The remedies advocated include the establishment of early warning systems to detect signs of entitlement collapse, as well as systems of public welfare to provide replacements for those entitlements through public works or, if the process has gone too far, free distribution of food.[4] Through the play of market forces, food would be attracted to food shortage areas as soon as the affected groups have reestablished their exchange entitlements. Sen's approach was widely welcomed as a major advance, enabling detailed attention to be focused on the specifics of the entitlements of particular groups in historical cases, rather than on broadbrush statistics of quantities of food per head.[5] It stresses two crucial points: in any population it is only certain vulnerable groups that are affected by starvation; and famines are man-made—they are not the equivalent of earthquakes, hurricanes, or floods. As such, the remedy is to be sought in the economic system; government intervention can replace lost entitlements through public welfare programs.

However, despite his challenge to Malthusian approaches to famine, Sen remains within its central assumptions, those of the modern episteme. The similarities between Sen and Malthus are more instructive than their differences. Both reflect, to a greater or lesser extent, modernity's view of man and nature and its logic of scarcity. By understanding this we can see how, despite their differences, they both produce a technological, managerial approach to famine as a disaster or failure. Such practices technologize and depoliticize famine, producing particular relations of power between those who suffer famine and those who offer famine relief or humanitarian aid.

Sen's work relies on a number of exclusions, and I argue that these are central to famine; by excluding what he does, Sen excludes the violence implicated in any particular social order.

SEN'S ENTITLEMENT APPROACH

Sen's analysis of the role of entitlements in famine changed the terms of the debate and moved the focus from explanations based on food supply to explanations based on food distribution and the social, political, and legal system on which this was grounded. Famine was not a question for the natural sciences but for the social sciences, and in particular for economics. The importance of the amount of food available per head of population and the efforts directed at increasing food supply were argued to be largely misplaced and in some cases damaging. In the opening words of Sen's *Poverty and Famines*:

> Starvation is the characteristic of some people not *having* enough food to eat. It is not the characteristic of there *being* not enough food to eat. While the latter can be a cause of the former, it is but one of many *possible* causes. Whether and how starvation relates to food supply is a matter for factual investigation. Food supply statements say things about a commodity (or a group of commodities) considered on its own. Starvation statements are about the *relationship* of persons to the commodity (or that commodity group).[6]

This is a marked shift of focus, and the contrast with Malthus is clear. As well as the move away from an emphasis on quantities of food—widely regarded as Sen's most important move—there are other aspects, equally significant. We have the notion of "famines" not "famine"—each situation is different and "a matter for factual investigation." Sen claims to present a framework for the analysis of famines, not a single-cause explanation of famine. Also, he moves away from the notion of population introduced by Malthus toward a focus on persons.

Finally, Sen emphasizes ownership relations, introducing the concept of entitlement relations, relations that legitimize ownership: "starvation statements translate readily into statements of ownership of food by persons." In order to understand starvation, it is therefore necessary to go into the structure of ownership. "Ownership relations are one kind of *entitlement* relations. It is necessary to understand the entitlement systems within which the problem of starvation is to be analysed. This applies *more generally* to poverty as such, and *more specifically* to famines as well."[7] The type of entitlement relations that are accepted in any particular society are specific to the social system (or economy, in Sen's terms). In a private-ownership market economy, accepted entitlement relations include those based on trading items, arranging the production of goods, products of one's own labor, inheritance, and gifts. A socialist society might not accept production-based entitlements, whereas in a capitalist society private ownership of the means of production, and thus production-based entitlements, is central. Neither society would accept ownership of one human being by another, as a slave economy would.[8] It is interesting to note that under famine conditions it is often reported that people are sold into slavery in societies where this would not be accepted under normal conditions. This raises the question of whether the notion of accepted entitlement relations is of any use in exactly those conditions where Sen wishes to apply it.

In a market economy, the set of commodities that people can acquire through exchange is called their "exchange entitlement." According to Sen, people may starve if their exchange entitlement "does not contain any feasible bundle including enough food"[9] and if there are no non-entitlement transfers or charity. In summary:

> The entitlement approach to starvation and famines concentrates on the ability of people to command food through the legal means available in the society, including the use of production possibilities, trade opportunities, entitlements *vis-à-vis* the state, and other methods of acquiring food. A person starves either because he does not have the ability to command enough food or because he does not use this ability to avoid starvation. The entitlement approach concentrates upon the former, ignoring the latter possibility.[10]

Using this approach, an understanding of famines requires "careful consideration of the nature of modes of production and the structure of economic classes as well as their interrelations."[11] Sen illustrates this by a study of four cases of famine, most notably a study of the Bengal famine of 1943.

In Bengal "shifts in exchange entitlements in a general inflationary situation"[12] led to the destitution of certain groups of people. There had been a poor winter harvest, but, as the authorities maintained at the time, this was not sufficiently severe to cause concern in itself. This lack of concern was because of a "disastrously wrong" theory of famines. Although food supply per head was adequate, people in certain occupational groups suffered disproportionately from a rise in the price of rice due to "general inflationary pressure in a war economy," the indifferent winter crop, and panic hoarding and speculation.[13] The occupational groups concerned, mainly agricultural laborers but also other wage laborers and the sellers of certain services, saw a slow rise in wage rates but very sharp increases in the price of rice. Peasants and sharecroppers were not affected by the famine to the same extent: their exchange entitlements were protected by the nature of their situation as rice producers. However, the British authorities based their actions on analyses of food output per head. These figures gave no cause for alarm and "even when the famine erupted in Bengal with people dying in the streets, the government evidently had some difficulty in believing what was happening."[14] The idea that famine was caused by shortages was not challenged. It was argued that the figures must have been wrong, and they were recalculated to show that contrary to earlier statements there had indeed been severe food shortages. The same was the case in reports prepared after the famine. So, "like the Phoenix, the FAD [the theory that famine was caused by a decline in food availability] arose rejuvenated from the ashes, and it can be found today chirping in the current literature on the food crises of the world."[15]

The success of Sen's work in penetrating the debate can be attributed, to some extent, to the way his contribution was presented. His formal development of theory made it acceptable to mainstream economists, but his work was also accessible to nonspecialists.[16] There had been a number of previous attempts to dislodge the view of famine as a natural disaster and to argue that food scarcity was not the sole cause of famines.[17] Nicole Ball, in 1976, argued that "the notion that famine results from non-natural phenomena, although currently gaining in popularity, has been a topic of academic interest for more than a decade" and that the nonnatural causes suggested included "colonial administrative policies . . . forced production of cash crops . . . unequal terms of trade"; in addition, she stated that "socio-political repression and unrest [has been linked] with declining agricultural output and famine."[18] She quotes a number of other writers who at that time attributed famine to socioeconomic exploitation rather than natural causes.[19] Though work in this vein continued, it did not gain as wide an acceptance as Sen's work.

Sen also produced a characterization of Malthusian discourse as FAD: Food Availability Decline.[20] This is often used as a label for this whole category of theory in widely differing accounts.[21] Other concepts derive indirectly from Sen's work—the concept of vulnerability, for example. There has been a good deal of work aiming to identify groups vulnerable to famine and factors leading to their vulnerability.[22] Along with issues of vulnerability, we find the discussion of coping strategies. The emphasis of the entitlement approach is away from large aggregates of people—populations—and figures of food availability per head and toward attempts to understand the individual household and its vulnerability to and coping strategies during famine conditions. The household has become the object of study, and data on household assets and behavior are collected. Coping strategies are enumerated and classified.[23]

Sen's work can be seen as a challenge to the Malthusian type of approach in economics in general, not just in relation to famines. The existence of competitive markets in conditions of scarcity is fundamental to classical economics. Sen's work on famines challenges the notion of scarcity in a manner parallel to John Maynard Keynes's work on unemployment. As Meghnad Desai argues, Sen shows that "just as involuntary unemployment can occur in the face of excess capacity and unsold commodity surpluses, famines and 'unnatural deaths' can occur in [the] face of available food stocks."[24] Jean Drèze and Sen's work argues strongly in defense of public action, along the lines of Keynesian intervention, to eradicate hunger.[25]

However, Sen's work has been incorporated into mainstream discourse, and its subjects have altered. The concept of entitlement is often equated more or less with money, or income, which was not what was intended. In discussions of coping and vulnerability, there is a tendency to return to ideas of food scarcity as well as entitlement failure and for Malthusian concepts of survival, food stress, and the like to reenter the discussion. Contemporary academic theory favors complex, multicausal, eclectic explanations. The solution remains technical, working within (and reproducing) existing structures of (state) power. The more radical implications of Sen's work have largely been sidelined; it has been incorporated into reformist, pluralist types of discourse, arguing for welfare systems, a free press, public works, and so on.[26] Theoretical plurality and multicausality are acceptable: famine is seen as a complex problem, not admitting of simple solutions. It is debatable whether this slight shift in academic thinking away from the Malthusian view of famine as food shortage has had any significant impact, as discussed in chapter 1.

CRITICISMS AND INTERSECTIONS

When Sen's work appeared it was well received on the whole. Singer, for example, writing in *International Affairs*, commented that "even in the short time since publication this book [has] helped to shift the attention of policy makers and international organisations away from excessive concentration on food production to broader issues of 'food security.'"[27] A number of disputes appeared in the literature later, most defending the food availability decline thesis.[28]

The most fundamental and earliest criticism was that of Amrita Rangasami in 1985.[29] Rangasami challenges the novelty of Sen's approach. She claims that the provincial Famine Codes of India and other official documents show that those administering relief in the period from 1880 to 1905 treated unemployment and decline in real wages as critical factors alongside food shortage.[30] In addition, the notion of entitlement had been previously articulated.[31] She puts forward two chief substantive points of criticism. First, entitlement theory treats famine as a "biological" process—a process that essentially leads to starvation. For Rangasami famine is much more than this. It is a "politico-socio-economic process," and, what is more, Rangasami claims that mortality is not a necessary condition of famine. Famine as a process goes through several stages—of dearth, famishment, and morbidity—and "the culmination of the process comes well before the slide into disease and death."[32] Second, entitlement theory considers only the victims of starvation. As Rangasami puts it, famine "is a process in which benefits accrue to one section of the community while losses flow to the other."[33] It is a process with "winners" and "losers," and in order to determine what famine is—which, for Rangasami, is the same as determining its causes—we must look at "the adaptations, manoeuvres, and strategies utilised by both victim and beneficiary [which] can be economic, social or psychological or partake of all three."[34]

Rangasami offers a definition of famine as a "pressing down" or oppression, "a process during which pressure or force (economic, military, political, social, psychological) is exerted upon the victim community, gradually increasing in intensity until the stricken are deprived of all assets including the ability to labour."[35] She claims that accounts of famine focus on the last phase of this long process, the phase of morbidity: "The state as well as the do-gooders, the voluntary agencies, do not enter the arena, until the process is resolved against the victims. The famine accounts we have today, begin even with the moment of state intervention."[36] So-called early warning systems only pick up these final stages, where dislocation and movement of people is already apparent. Assistance, when it comes, may be sufficient to save lives, but it does not replace lost assets.

Sen himself stresses that the entitlement approach is *not* "one particular hypothesis about [famine] causation."[37] It is not a theory in that sense and is suited to interpretative rather than causal analysis.[38] It provides a framework for the detailed empirical analysis of individual famines, and Sen regards the identification of the causes of entitlement failures in historical instances as crucial. However, he concedes that "there is, of course, a very general hypothesis underlying the approach, which is subject to empirical testing. It will be violated if starvation in famines is shown to arise not from entitlement failures but either from choice characteristics (e.g., people refusing to eat unfamiliar food that they are in a position to buy or people refusing to work) or from non-entitlement failures (e.g., looting)."[39]

According to Charles Gore, Sen's positivist approach to law ignores the way legal rules operate in practice and neglects gender biases and "socially enforced moral rules."[40] The result of this is that people are seen "as passive victims of famine. Those who have identified 'coping strategies' of the poor and vulnerable in times of famine have redressed the balance somewhat. . . . But 'coping' essentially means acting to survive *within the prevailing rule systems*."[41] The moral economy literature,[42] which looks at the way food entitlement is determined by conflicting rule systems when people are starving, is useful in showing that:

> The assertion of entitlements also involves negotiation of the rules, confrontation and struggles, in which "unruly" social practices of various kinds are brought to bear. . . . it is possible to view entitlement relations as an *active process*. . . . A second important insight is that . . . in a famine situation entitlement shifts can occur because the

dominant rules of entitlement change. . . . famine "twists" routine moral and social arrangements. [Thirdly, long-term] transformations in the rules of entitlement take place. . . . changes occur through the active negotiation of rules at particular historical moments. . . . the negotiation of moral rules is bound up with power relationships and based on particular discursive strategies.[43]

This approach is a view of famine as a dynamic social and political process, not a technical problem.

Ben Fine arrives at a similar conclusion by a different route. He argues that a simple causal view of entitlements "preempts the socio-economic processes by which endowments are created and in which entitlements play a causal role." As Fine puts it, "the exercise of socially determined power is crucial."[44] In particular, he argues that state power should be examined: "If underlying class and property relations are a cause of famine through entitlement failure, then these relations have to be examined as such rather than as the source of individual attachment to entitlements."[45]

The work of Alex de Waal at the end of the 1980s challenged Sen's work and prompted a thoroughgoing reappraisal of entitlement theory[46] while attempting to avoid a return to Malthus. According to Jeremy Swift, in the introduction to a special issue of *IDS Bulletin* on famine in 1993, "it is now fashionable to be critical of entitlement analysis."[47] In De Waal's work on the famine in Dafur in the Sudan in 1984/85, he claims to develop an approach based on entitlement theory but takes a different view of what famine *is,* one based on listening to people who experience famines.[48] This new account "places the coping strategies of the affected population at its centre."[49] De Waal argues that people try to avoid destitution and the loss of a way of life first and foremost, not starvation. Only when social disruption or collapse or external violence makes this impossible do they begin to sell vital assets to buy food.

Like Gore, de Waal points to the way entitlement theory sees famine victims as generally passive. It focuses too strongly on the asset-less wage laborer, stressing the lowering of the incomes of the poor rather than the threat to their assets. It is overly economistic, ignoring social disruption, migration, and disease, and it has no place for war. Finally, it "does not take account of the historical processes leading to the vulnerability of all or part of a population to famine"[50] or changes during famine. De Waal's criticisms arise from two sets of observations. First, during a famine, people would "choose to starve" in order to try to preserve their way of life:

> Right at the nadir of the famine, people were spending only a proportion (sometimes as little as one tenth) of their income on food. Although they were hungry and many people around them were dying, nevertheless they could buy food; instead they were spending their money on maintaining their animals, buying seed for their farms, hiring labour, etc. Their potential income from selling assets was even higher, but they chose not to sell assets whenever possible.[51]

Second, de Waal argues that famine mortality is disease driven: people die as a result of the disruption brought about by the famine, which leads to greater risk of epidemic and disease. In some cases, a famine can occur without any increased level of mortality at all. This is why in Dafur the famine of 1984/85 was called the "famine that kills": as far as people who experience them are concerned, famines are of many types. Some kill, some don't.

Thus the causal links between impoverishment, starvation, and death that are given primacy in entitlement theory are called into question.[52] A reduction in entitlements cannot be related directly to starvation: people may choose not to use their exchange entitlements to procure food in a particular situation. Similarly, a failure of entitlement can lead to starvation and increased risk of death, but the relative contribution of starvation and disease to mortality is an empirical question. The new account of famine that de Waal proposes "places the coping strategies of the affected population at its centre."[53] De Waal argues that we must abandon the conception, held since Malthus, of famine as necessarily involving mass starvation unto death. He suggests instead the distinction between famine where coping strategies enable society to survive (the majority of famines in Africa) and those where social collapse occurs: coping strategies break down and mass starvation accompanied by violence occurs. He argues that implicit in entitlement theory there is "a positivistic conception of famine as a natural kind,"[54] which he rejects.

If this is the case, it then becomes necessary to ask whether we should continue to call this event a famine: "We have to choose between redefining the word 'famine,' and altering drastically our usage of the word. . . . On the grounds that usage is logically prior to definition, the current usage of 'famine' should stay, and the definition should change. The Sahel did suffer famine." What de Waal is suggesting is the graft of new meaning upon the old term "famine." This is not an easy thing to do: discourse is a complex articulation of terms and traces. It is not just a question of pointing to contradictions or illogicalities in current usages and choosing a more correct terminology.[55] In his challenge to the scientism of Malthus, de Waal retains a belief in the efficacy of scientific forms of discourse and rationality; this serves to undermine his own position. He himself is within the episteme of modernity that he attempts to challenge.[56]

What do the apparently opposing theoretical views of Sen and Malthus have in common? What does the argument that famine is caused by a shortage of food share with the argument that famine is a problem of lost entitlements? There are two points: famine is seen as a failure, and famine has a causal explanation. Famine is a disaster with a scientific cause. It is the equivalent of a technical malfunction of a mechanism: once the cause of the problem is identified, it can be solved by prompt, expert action and the machine returned to working order.

Both Malthus's food shortage and Sen's entitlement theories see famine in this way: as a *failure*. It is a disaster, whether of a natural or an economic kind, whether it leads to death or to destitution. It is undesirable and preventable: for Malthus, by control of human fertility or by increasing food production; for Sen's followers, by putting in place a mechanism to replace lost entitlements (for example, through cash for work schemes). Neither Malthus nor Sen see famine as produced by the normal run of things; it occurs only exceptionally. Malthus sees famine as benefiting nature, but neither approach attaches importance to famine as benefiting particular groups of people. There is "a prevailing consensus that famine situations are extraordinary and that they should be met by extraordinary means."[57]

The constitution of famine as a disaster has certain power effects, as Barbara Hendrie points out. Narrating famine in this way produces it as an event and "enables it to be detached from its embeddedness within a set of historically specific and locally based economic and political processes."[58] This decontextualization is what I am calling depoliticization or technologization. The specificities of time and place can be bracketed out and famine can be removed into "the realm of regulation and control by humanitarian institutions."[59] Or rather, because the regime of truth of modernity is based around a scientific form of knowledge that seeks generalizable, universal laws, famine, in all its specificity and with all its "disturbing implications"[60] must inevitably be seen as a disaster if it occurs in modernity. The alternative, as I have argued, is to regard it as anachronistic and not part of the modern. Either way, famine is technologized.

Famine as failure, as disaster, produces victims. Victims need welfare provision or aid, not a political voice. Vulnerable or at-risk households are produced as subjects on whom data can be collected. They are then controlled by administrative mechanisms of food distribution or food aid.[61] The process depoliticizes famine and constitutes it as a site for intervention and control.

The "famine as failure" narrative has a role in the reproduction of the international system. It is deeply enmeshed in the third world/first world discourse. The solution to the problems of Africa, for example, is seen as coming from the benevolence of the economically rich countries of the North. Africa is produced as a region that is almost depoliticized by virtue of its status as a recipient of advice, concern, and aid, and existing global structures of power are buttressed.

Famine is technologized. Neither food shortage nor entitlement theories provide a historical account nor explore the processes of change that occur during a famine. Preventing famine, as a technical malfunction, favors expert knowledge and expensive (and profitable) technological solutions. It is linked with the centralization of power/knowledge in international organizations or research institutes. In Foucauldian terms, the science of famine produces the starving subject as a subject of knowledge within a regime of truth produced by the institutions and practices of development studies. The coping strategies of households in famine situations are studied; victims of famine and refugees from famine are interviewed, categorized, and counted. The numbers that died in a particular famine are counted, though how this is possible when conditions in famines are often such that there is even no means of burying the dead, we are left to imagine.

A second point of intersection that food shortage and entitlement theories share is that they both see famine as *something with a cause*. The problem of famine is situated as a question suitable for theoretical investigation by, in a broad sense, the scientific method. The modern episteme is characterized by its reliance on separation of subject and object, theory and practice, and its choice of quantitative methods. This way of thinking produces a discourse that distances the emotional, humane response and prioritizes the search for causation over the need to respond. Theorizing and empiricizing famine make it the terrain of the expert, the agriculturalist, and the development specialist, just as war can become the terrain of the defense expert, the strategist, and the military commander. Only the experts can tell us how the problem can be tackled and what mechanisms are at work.[62] The reliance on experts produces institutions devoted to the production of knowledge about famine within the framework of progress-oriented discourse. Hard facts are sought, and famine is excluded from political debate. As Kirsten Hastrup points out, this reliance on experts and technical solutions represents a gendered approach.[63] When famine is looked at in scientific terms, any connection with pain, suffering, or the body is taken away. The relationship between persons is removed. Other approaches, as we shall see in the final chapter, locate famines precisely in this relationship: a relationship between winners and losers. They move beyond the view of famine as a failure and look instead at the functions of famine and those who benefit from it.

EXCLUSIONS AND DEPOLITICIZATIONS

One of the chief criticisms leveled at Sen is that, as a theory of famine, "entitlement theory has no place for violence."[64] I explore this claim by looking in some detail at Sen's work as presented in *Poverty and Famines*. I shall take a deconstructive approach that looks for the marginal, the deferred, and the excluded in Sen's account. What is put to one side as irrelevant to the matter under examination can be more instructive than it might appear. The separations that are made, and the oppositions and hierarchies that form the often unspoken basis of the argument, can help in the analysis. I argue that the exclusion of non-entitlement transfers and the exclusion of deliberate starvation are central to understanding what Sen is doing. I relate this to Jacques Derrida's work on the "Force of Law."[65] Sen uses the exclusion of non-entitlement transfers to define the existence of entitlement and legality.[66] His argument also relies on separating the economic and the political and placing them in a hierarchical opposition.[67]

Drawing boundaries by exclusion, which places something outside and thus defines an inside, is a process that is typical of logocentric analysis.[68] In this mode of analysis, the process of differentiation places the risk of an accident or failure outside.[69] If this is the case, then what is deferred or excluded can be called a constitutive outside,[70] an outside that is *necessary* to constitute or form the inside. Derrida asks: "Is that outside its inside, the very force and law of its emergence?"[71] In other words, is what is excluded effectively essential? Logocentric analysis does not admit this possibility. As soon as it recognizes it, it denies it. Logocentric analysis

> consists in recognising that the possibility of the negative . . . is in fact a structural possibility, that failure is an essential risk of the operations under consideration; then, in a move which is almost *immediately simultaneous*, in the name of a kind of ideal regulation, it excludes that risk as accidental, exterior, one which teaches us nothing about the . . . phenomenon being considered.[72]

If this is what logocentric analysis does, then what Derrida suggests is another approach—deconstruction. In a deconstructive analysis we would need to ponder what follows if "a possibility—a possible risk—is *always* possible, and is in some sense a necessary possibility. [And] whether—once such a necessary possibility of infelicity is recognised—infelicity still constitutes an accident. What is success when the possibility of infelicity continues to constitute its structure?"[73] Thus we need to take seriously the role of what is excluded when something is constituted by the process of drawing boundaries. A deconstructive reading does just this, looking for precisely that which is deferred or regarded as accidental by the account that is being studied.

Returning to Sen, we see that, from something he is going to call "entitlements," he wants to exclude instances when a person starves deliberately (or is deliberately starved) and instances where extralegal means are used to obtain food. These are regarded by Sen as parasitic, as abnormal, and can be excluded from a theory of starvation and famine:

> The entitlement approach to starvation and famines concentrates on the ability of people to command food through the legal means available in the society, including the use of production possibilities, trade opportunities, entitlements *vis-à-vis* the state, and other methods of acquiring food. A person starves *either* because he does not have the

ability to command enough food *or* because he does not use this ability to avoid starvation. The entitlement approach concentrates on the former, ignoring the latter possibility. Furthermore, it concentrates on those means of commanding food that are legitimised by the legal system in operation in that society. While it is an approach of some generality, it makes no attempt to include all possible influences that can in principle cause starvation, for example illegal transfers (e.g. looting), and choice failures (e.g. owing to inflexible food habits).

Ownership of food is one of the most primitive property rights, and in each society there are rules governing this right. The entitlement approach concentrates on each person's entitlements to commodity bundles including food, and views starvation as resulting from a failure to be entitled to a bundle with enough food.[74]

Sen proposes "leaving out cases in which a person may deliberately starve."[75] He also sets aside the notion that starving may be an act of "deliberate harming."[76] De Waal challenges Sen on the former deferral, arguing that in famines people often choose to go without food rather than sell assets.[77] Sen accounts for this with a straightforward extension of the theory. It is a rational decision to choose to safeguard entitlements in order to avoid starvation in the future, as against avoiding hunger now: "people sometimes choose to starve rather than sell their productive assets, and this issue can be accommodated [by] taking note of future entitlements."[78]

However, choosing to starve has more significant ramifications than this. It can be a political act, even part of a violent struggle. Starvation has been used as a weapon by those who have no other weapon available to them; Irish prisoners in the 1980s are one example. Bobby Sands was the first of ten Republican prisoners who deliberately starved themselves to death in a campaign for political status in British prisons.[79] These actions were "following an international political legacy that had gained moral legitimacy since the time of Ghandi [and] reinterpreting and enacting the cultural model of the Christian sacrifice."[80] In these cases, the act of fasting was a political act intended to influence relationships of power. Sen's omission of deliberate starvation omits a relation that demonstrates the entanglement of hunger and the political. Fasting also has other implications, particularly in its connection with the sacred and the emotive; for Sen, however, understanding these instances is not necessary "in order to understand starvation."[81]

Sen also sets aside the notion that starving people may be a deliberate act. He makes a distinction between starvation and famine, but
he wants to make this without "attribut[ing] a sense of deliberate
harming to the first absent from the second."[82] This ascription is
commonly made, as Sen acknowledges. He quotes a passage from
Bernard Shaw's play *Man and Superman* about the Irish famine that
draws attention to the deliberate harming implicit in the word "starvation": "When a country is full of food and exporting it, there can
be no 'famine' only deliberate starvation."[83] Sen concedes that the
word "starvation" still carries the meaning of causing death through
lack of food and that "the history of famines as well as regular hunger
is full of blood-boiling tales of callousness and malevolence,"[84] but
then he proceeds to set aside any notion of intentionality behind famines and strip "starvation" of its transitive quality. For the purposes
of Sen's analysis, "starvation is used . . . in the wider sense of people
going without adequate food, while famine is a particularly virulent
manifestation of its causing widespread death."[85]

Setting aside the intentionality behind starving and being starved
makes it possible to regard famines as accidents—failures of the
natural or economic system. This is what complex emergency approaches are combating. Famines, they contest, have winners and
losers. Setting aside intentionality is also part of a structuralist analysis that argues that famine is not a failure, but a product of the capitalist economic system.

Sen's second deferral is the exclusion of non-entitlement transfers.
As far as entitlement theory is concerned, transfers that are extralegal—looting and raiding for example—do not count. They are seen
as quite distinct from activities that involve the upholding of legal
rights in the face of starvation.[86] Sen does see this exclusion as representing one of the limitations of the entitlement approach:

> While entitlement relations concentrate on rights within the given
> legal structure in that society, some transfers involve violation of these
> rights, such as looting or brigandage. When such extra-entitlement
> transfers are important, the entitlement approach to famines will be
> defective. On the other hand, most recent famines seem to have taken
> place in societies with "law and order," without anything "illegal"
> about the processes leading to starvation. In fact, in guarding owner-
> ship rights against the demands of the hungry, the legal forces uphold
> entitlements; for example, in the Bengal famine of 1943 the people

who died in front of well-stocked food shops protected by the state were denied food because of *lack* of legal entitlement, and not because their entitlements were violated.[87]

Clearly, "entitlements," in Sen's use of the word, does not reflect in any sense a concept of the right to food or a concept of what people might be entitled to as a human right or as a question of justice. The legitimate violence of the state can be employed to uphold the ownership rights of one section of the community against the demands of another. This is seen by Sen, in this section of the book, as unproblematic. However, in the final sentence of the book, he returns to the central conundrum that this entire approach produces: "The law stands between food availability and food entitlement. Starvation deaths can reflect legality with a vengeance."[88] The fact that Sen's theory, which purports to provide a framework for understanding starvation and famines, excludes any adequate understanding of precisely those conditions that obtain *whenever there is a famine*—the denial of access to food *by force* employed on behalf of those who possess food—is a clear cause for concern. Further, this exclusion indicates more than that the theory is defective in certain cases. It returns our attention to the role of the force of law in relation to justice.

Law itself is inextricably bound up in complex, internal relationships with force, power, and violence. One relationship is entailed by the phrase "to enforce the law," when an existing system of law or a legal code is enforced:

> Law is always an authorised force, a force that justifies itself or is justified in applying itself, even if this justification may be judged from elsewhere to be unjust or unjustifiable . . . The word "enforceability" reminds us that there is no such thing as law [a legal code] that doesn't imply *in itself, a priori, in the analytic structure of its concept,* the possibility of being "enforced," applied by force. There . . . is no law without enforceability, and no applicability or enforceability of the law without force, whether this force be direct or indirect, physical or symbolic, exterior or interior, brutal or subtly discursive and hermeneutic, coercive or regulative, and so forth.[89]

Another relationship involves the state and state formation and invokes the performative violence of the founding moment of the law. This founding moment, "the very emergence of justice and law, the founding and justifying moment that institutes law implies a performative force."[90] As we have seen, law has to be *enforced*. It does not have any effect without enforcement. In the very founding moment of law itself, there is a performative force, a "violence without ground": "violence is at the origin of law."[91]

This founding violence is closely linked with the state. The foundation of a state takes place alongside the institution of a new law, and "it always does so in violence. Always, which is to say even when there haven't been those spectacular genocides, expulsions, or deportations that so often accompany the foundation of states."[92] However, this founding moment is outside time: "it always takes place and never takes place in a presence."[93] In the foundation of the state, discourse will "justify the recourse to violence by alleging the founding, in progress or to come, of a new law. As this law to come will in return legitimate, retrospectively, the violence that may offend the sense of justice, its future anterior already justifies it."[94] The founding moment of the state is outside time in that, until the state has already been founded, its foundation is in question, and, as a state, it does not exist. In retrospect, it will seem as if a certain act constituted the moment of foundation; at the time when that act takes place (could such a time exist) the violence that accompanies it cannot be legitimized. These moments are terrifying—they involve sufferings, crimes, tortures—and they are also "in their very violence, uninterpretable or indecipherable."[95] The terror arises in part because the founding moment is one in which the social and symbolic order no longer holds sway.[96] These moments are the unspeakable—that of which we cannot speak, that which is outside all language, all discourse.

Here we can return to famine, and that which is the unspeakable of famine—that which does not get any acknowledgment from theories of famine causation or from discourses of relief and intervention. The link between famines and complete social catastrophe is not often made. In firsthand accounts the horror of the absence of social ties, the degradation and inhumanity of starvation deaths, and the "madness of hunger"[97] occasionally appear. More often, eyewitnesses and survivors are silent in the face of the unspeakable trauma they encounter. It is perhaps this which impels theorists to tame famine, to refer to its harshest aspects only in nonemotive terms, and to confine themselves to "hard facts."[98]

Such approaches confine themselves to a technologized view.[99]

This is limiting and denies engagement with justice.[100] Law and justice are distinct:

> Law is the element of calculation . . . but justice is incalculable, it requires us to calculate with the incalculable; and aporetic experiences are the experiences, as improbable as they are necessary, of justice, that is to say of moments in which the decision between just and unjust is never insured by a rule.[101]

This is so because "each case is other, each decision is different and requires an absolutely unique interpretation, which no existing, coded rule can or ought to guarantee absolutely."[102] A decision in a singular, particular case has to go through what Derrida calls the "undecidable."[103] At the point when the decision is made, it is not a question of the straightforward application of a code of law. There is something more involved in each particular instance, and this is where the notion of justice can arise. Before the decision has been made, there can be no claim that justice has been achieved. After the decision has been taken, it is seen to have followed a rule, whether that rule is one produced by the decision or not. So, justice is impossible: "There is apparently no moment in which a decision can be called presently and fully just."[104] Although the ordeal of the undecidable must be gone through, it cannot be overcome, and "the undecidable remains caught, lodged, at least as a ghost—but an essential ghost—in every decision, in every event of decision. Its ghostliness deconstructs from within any assurance of presence, any certitude or any supposed criteriology that would assure us of the justice of a decision."[105] We cannot even know that a decision has taken place, and we cannot say whether it was just.

Does this leave us with an acknowledgment of the violence inherent in all attempts at a legal system, but with no ethical message, no way of distinguishing different kinds of violent acts? Drucilla Cornell raises the question of whether the intervention of deconstruction comes to an end with its exposure of "the nakedness of power struggles and, indeed, of violence masquerading as the rule of law."[106] She claims that, on the contrary: "the undecidability which can be used to expose any legal system's process of the self-legitimisation of authority as myth, leaves us—the us here being specifically those who enact and enforce the law—with an *inescapable responsibility* for violence, precisely because violence cannot be fully rationalised and therefore justified in advance."[107] Cornell is arguing that Derrida's notion of undecidability and the process of decisioning inevitably leads us back to the notion of individual (ethical) responsibility. The process of decision cannot follow a code of law and is not calculable. As such it entails responsibility that cannot be evaded by an appeal to the law. This means that the actions of agents of the state in forcing people to starve by protecting food stocks in shops cannot be justified by reference to the law or legitimacy as Sen claims. The law itself is produced and reproduced in particular decisions. What happens cannot be legislated for in advance—it has to be the subject of a decision—and enforcement of the law in any case contains within itself the violence of the law. Sen attempts to exclude instances of violence outside the law. The exclusion of the violence of the extralegal in Sen's constitution of entitlements returns to haunt his account in the violence of law itself— both its foundation in the state and its enforcement.

Finally, I look at two other exclusions, distinctions, or deferrals that Sen makes: the exclusion of food supply, by considering food as a commodity (where *having* is opposed to *being*), and the exclusion of the prescriptive, in which Sen shares with Malthus a view of famine as having a cause, a scientific or managerial solution, and the question of the technologization of famine and relief.

In the opening sentences of *Poverty and Famines*, Sen sets aside the Malthusian assumption that formed the foundation for much theorizing about famines prior to his work. This is the assumption that famine is caused by, indeed, is characterized by—in other words, famine *is*—a lack of food. Sen proceeds by distinguishing a particular notion of what starvation is. It is "the characteristic of some people not *having* enough food to eat"; it is not "the characteristic of there *being* not enough food to eat."[108] Sen proposes that this contrast is the difference between statements about a commodity "on its own"—there being not enough food—and statements about the "*relationship* of persons" to a commodity.

Sen argues that this is a contrast between "the [Malthusian] tradition of thinking in terms of what *exists* rather than in terms of who can *command* what."[109] However, in what sense does food exist? Surely we all know what food is, and clearly food, essential to maintain physical existence, the difference between life and death for millions of people in famines throughout the world over the centuries, has to be something that exists. And yet, is not food socially defined?

It is not possible to read accounts of famines and the hardships and inhumanities to which people are driven during such periods without coming across accounts where things are eaten that under normal circumstances would in no sense count as food.[110] During famines, people search the land for wild fruits, berries, etc., which serve as famine foods. If circumstances become more extreme, bark is stripped from the trees, grass is eaten, even the dirt is consumed, and, finally, people may resort to eating each other's children or even their own children. Such practices of cannibalism are well documented.[111] They appall the imagination and make one wonder precisely in what sense food *exists*.

Sen contrasts not *having* enough to eat with there *being* not enough to eat: who can *command* what with what *exists*. He regards the former as having to do with relations—relations between people and a commodity—whereas the latter, food supply, is merely statements about a commodity. For Sen, ownership is privileged over existence: in the hierarchy having/being, having is the more valued. Questions of existence are deferred. But what *counts as food* in any given situation is in any case socially constituted—in much the same way as is ownership or having.[112] And, moreover, it is only if one disregards those very circumstances Sen claims to be considering—circumstances where people facing starvation consume foods that are unimaginable—that one can accept Sen's version of starvation. In this precise sense, *having* food and there *being* food are both statements to do with relations between people.[113]

Sen attempts to bring questions of relations between people into economic consideration, but such discussions in the economic realm arguably must, by definition, exclude consideration of social relations. As Karl Marx showed, in capitalism social relations become relations between commodities.[114] To adopt a position where economics is seen as quantifiable and scientific and separate from values and politics is to adopt a discursive stance that *cannot see* relations between people as such—these are fetishized as relations between things (commodities).[115] Thus, although Sen's work advocates a relationship-based approach, I argue that this does not translate into any meaningful consideration of the *social* nature of relations—these are deferred at each step of the way. The entitlement relations at the heart of his approach are relations of people to food, and the dependence of this on relations between people is deferred as secondary.

The final point I want to consider is Sen's deferral of the prescriptive. For Sen, a number of things—rising prices, loss of employment or food supply problems—can lead to a "decline in exchange entitlements," and this is what Sen counts as the cause of starvation. Which of these triggers applies in a particular case of starvation is "a matter for factual investigation." This emphasis on "factual investigation" and "cause" puts the study of starvation firmly in the realm of economics and social *science*: the answers to be sought are not in the form of *reasons* for actions (why one group of people allowed another group to starve to death or perhaps why they killed them), but the form of *causal explanations*. Answers do not lie in the realm of the study of *relationships between people,* but on the *relationship of people to commodities.* There is to be no history or narrative of famine, no account of what happened in a particular case in terms of who did what. Instead, there is an account in terms of cause and result, an account that is quantifiable.

This point is closely linked to the fact/value distinction that Sen makes when he introduces entitlement relations: his "interpretation of entitlement relations . . . is descriptive rather than prescriptive."[116] He is concerned not with who *should be* entitled to own what, but who *is* entitled to own what. The word "entitlement," which carries overtones of human rights (food for the starving, for example), turns out to do solely with buying and selling, ownership and legality, under a market economy. It is through the exclusions Sen makes that we begin to grasp what his argument might be.

CONCLUSION

I have shown that Sen excludes, sets aside, or defers certain aspects of famine. These are ones that the critical approaches discussed in chapter 6 regard as central: questions of deliberate acts of starvation and extralegal transfers of entitlements, both involving force and violence. These aspects haunt Sen's notion of entitlements and famine in that the law is based on a founding violence and depends on the threat of violence for its enforcement. This violence is seen when famines occur in states under the rule of law—in China, for example, in the Great Leap Forward of the early 1960s, where there were some thirty million excess deaths.[117] It is also seen when famines occur in states under the democratic rule of law—in Britain, for example, during the Irish Potato Famine in the 1840s,[118] or in Bengal, again under British rule, in the 1940s, where around three million died.[119]

I have also argued that Sen's analysis can lead to a particular practice of famine relief—one that technologizes suffering. Although Sen strongly distinguishes his approach from that of Malthus, in this important respect it is similar. Both lead to a view of famine as a failure, a disease, that can be cured or prevented by intervention by the state or the international community.

These theories of famine reflect a specific regime of truth, that of modernity, which "is centred on the form of scientific discourse and the institutions which produce it."[120] Famine is produced as a disaster with a scientific cause. It is a failure in either the economic or the natural system. The discourse produces victims and areas of the world that are dependent on the benevolence of others.

It is partly in the course of separations of this sort that the power of the Malthusian approach arises. As discussed in chapter 2, this discourse produces the subject of famine within the exclusions, divisions, and ways of ordering that constitute the human sciences within the modern episteme. Arguments about whether famine is natural or man-made reflect this discursive position, which is not open to question. Although these things are constituted within discourse, this does not mean that they can be changed by just describing things differently. Attempts to do so may result in not being heard: Sen's arguments were diluted in order to be co-opted into the existing episteme. Certainly, assertions or reasoned argument may be ineffectual.

In Sen's work, famines are treated as a particular case of starvation, which itself is a particular instance of the more general phenomenon of poverty. He does not look at the role of political struggle or conflict, but, like Malthus, sees famines as an instance of a "disastrous phenomenon."[121] The distinction between Sen's work and the Malthusian view of famines as a failure of food supply, nature's "last, most dreadful resource"[122] in the face of an inexorably expanding human population, is that, as Sen says, "the entitlement approach views famines as economic disasters, not just as food crises."[123] This approach means that famine is still a problem to be solved by technology and management (as is development itself). *Famine itself has been excluded.* The risk (of famine) has been set aside as something accidental, something that teaches us nothing about the economic, social, or political system being studied, even though the competitive market economic system relies on the concept of a certain scarcity.[124] To see famine as either a natural disaster, in the work of Malthus, or as an economic disaster, in the work of Sen, ignores the way some people benefit from famine.

In effect, the problem has been reduced to one of theory.[125] Famine is seen as a breakdown of liberal economic theory, which leads to the question: How can we have such a thing as famine in the modern world? An alternative would be to ask what is in the texts of economics that could have made famine possible and even now continues to justify it. There is also a historical reductionism, which sees the problem of famines as one of causes, as some sort of "a residue or a sequel of the past."[126] Seeking a cause makes the problem seem like a sort of *disease* that we can either prevent (by development) or cure (by relief).[127] If we see famine negatively, as a disease, an *accident*—what in deconstruction has been called the constitutive outside—this enables us to retain the preexisting categories of economic thought. We see famines as obstacles on the road to modernization: Africa's lack of development or specific economic difficulties are to blame. The solution is technical or managerial.

We should be considering not how to solve the problem or cure the disease, but "what use is [it], what functions does it assure, in what strategies is it integrated?"[128] We should treat famine as a "positive present."[129] What matters is not the search for the origins of famine, but understanding its function in the here and now, in a particular narrative and specific relations of power and conflict.

4

Practices of Aid

With one hand they offered the poor an alms, with the other they opened a prison.

— GUSTAVE DE BEAUMONT

The concepts of famine produced with the shift to the episteme of modernity have generated specific practices of aid. These practices are variously presented as global food aid, emergency famine relief, and development programs. These distinctions play an important role in negotiations between donors and implementing agencies. Agencies rely for their identity on particular constructions, each having concern and legitimacy historically in a particular area. The distinctions can be crucial in policy making and when matters of power and control are disputed between the different agencies involved.[1] However, the disciplinary processes are similar, whether it is food aid, famine relief, or development that is the legitimizing discursive framework.

Practices of aid, like famines themselves, benefit some groups at the same time that they make victims of others.[2] Powerful groups exploit those less powerful. Particular aid practices, such as food for work programs, produce and reproduce these power relations. Food for work (FFW), in which food aid is distributed not as a gift but as a payment for work performed, has grown up as part of the food aid process. Here the priorities of the implementing agencies (internal and external) and the donor and recipient governments are inscribed

67

on the bodies and in the work of those employed on the schemes. The "failure" of food aid programs is central to their "success"— they produce and reproduce relations of dependency between first and third world states and within those states. Foucault contends that the failure of prisons to rehabilitate offenders is best seen as part of their achievement.[3] Prisons produce political consequences, disqualifying a whole range of political action by redefining it as criminal. The failure of food for work programs to improve agriculture or the environment ensures their continuation as a disciplining process.

According to Mark Duffield "relatively little attention has been devoted to the study of relations of accountability and power in relief operations."[4] This chapter begins to remedy this, looking at the workings of aid from a Foucauldian perspective in terms of discursive and disciplinary practices.[5] I discuss global food aid discourse before turning to famine relief in Ethiopia and Ireland and food for work practices in Eritrea.

GLOBAL FOOD AID

Discourse is socially embedded and institutionalized in its interactions with other social practices. Foucault was interested in exploring why, irrespective of what grammatically *could be* said at certain periods, certain things and not others *were* said, and how the limits of things said were transformed from one era to another. This is distinct from a notion that treats discourses as groups of signs referring to signifieds. Discourses do more than use the signs of which they are composed to designate things, and "it is this *more* that renders them irreducible to the language and to speech" and makes them instead "practices that systematically form the objects of which they speak."[6] At a particular period in time, for a specific social group, there are rules that define the limits and forms of the sayable and the conservation, memory, reactivation, and appropriation of discourses.[7] Certain things *can be said* in specific domains of discourse (scientific, literary, etc.), and certain things said will be remembered and reiterated while others will be forgotten or repressed. Some things said in the past will be regarded as valid and not others, and these things will be reconstituted in different ways. Prescribed individuals and groups will have access to particular discourses, and relations of authority will be defined; there is a struggle for control of discourses. This approach runs counter to the traditional study of discourse as "a pure surface of translation for mute objects; a simple site of expression of thoughts, imaginings, knowledges, unconscious themes."[8] It negates the view that supposes "that all operations are conducted prior to discourse or outside of it, in the ideality of thought or the silent gravity of practices; that discourse, consequently, is no more than a meagre additive . . . a surplus which goes without saying, since it does nothing else except say what is said."[9] On the contrary, discursive practices are bound up with other social practices and together constitute relations of power/knowledge. Specific power relations make possible particular forms of discourse:

> Each society has its régime of truth, its "general politics" of truth: that is, the types of discourse which it accepts and makes function as true; the mechanisms and instances which enable one to distinguish true and false statements, the means by which each is sanctioned; the techniques and procedures accorded value in the acquisition of truth; the status of those charged with saying what counts as true.[10]

The discursive background that produces and legitimizes food for work practices is found in the food aid debate. This centers on questions of whether and how food aid should be provided—is it effective in helping third world countries and what are the arguments in its favor? There is a great deal of academic literature that looks at these questions.[11] The debate has been particularly prominent in the United States, where the Agricultural Trade Development and Assistance Act (Public Law 480) in 1954 began a program of food assistance to poor countries. Food aid, as distinct from foreign aid in general, was seen to have a number of overt purposes: for surplus disposal and overseas market development; as an instrument of foreign policy in the Cold War context; and to provide basic needs via links to human rights programs. These purposes were often contradictory. However, food aid, in contrast to foreign aid, received wide support in the United States from the public and Congress.[12]

Nevertheless, a number of controversies have surrounded food aid. Opponents in North America argued that surpluses generated by U.S. agricultural policies were avoidable and that food aid was merely designed to fit U.S. farm policy. In addition, according to Theodore Schultz, food aid, far from benefiting the recipient countries, was having harmful effects on their agriculture,[13] the so-called disincentive hypothesis. The energy and food crises of the 1970s moved the debate away from issues of agricultural economics into concerns of the ethics of food aid, involving writers such as Garrett Hardin and Peter Singer.[14] It also led to a popular debate about food aid, which, following Theodore Schultz, questioned the impact of development project food aid on the recipients and looked at concerns about resource scarcity and environmental degradation. More radical critics saw structural causes for third world poverty and hunger and argued that the rhetoric of food aid was serving to obscure these.[15]

In a special issue of the journal *International Organisations* in 1978, conceived in response to what was perceived as world food shortages in 1973/74, Hopkins and Puchala addressed the chronic problems of the global food system and its institutions.[16] They identified a global food regime, by which they meant something more than just the global food system.[17] Although they stressed the importance of decisions about production, distribution, and consumption, they adopted a largely Malthusian view of the crisis. Global food shortage was the problem, and the modernization of agriculture, by and large, was the solution. However, the regime failed to tackle chronic hunger: "regime norms facilitated global humanitarianism and enhanced survival during shortfalls and famines . . . but contributed to huge gaps in living standards between richer countries and poorer ones."[18] The failure is attributed to the way that "the political forces shaping norms of the food regime are largely divorced from the majority of people most severely affected by problems in the global food system. These are the rural poor of the third world. Food trade and aid, investment and information do not affect these people significantly since they are simply not part of the modern interdependent world."[19]

In the 1980s much work focused on how effective food aid was in the context of development programs. Structural adjustment programs, international food stamps, and EEC policy were debated.[20] According to Vernon Ruttan, despite the arguments favoring development over aid, it has become generally accepted that "food aid has been important in meeting emergency food needs, in meeting the subsistence needs of poor people, and in providing budgetary support for fragile governments."[21] The international epistemic community agreed that food security was a central goal of food aid, which should be targeted to countries categorized as food insecure on the basis of caloric intake and income criteria. Hopkins argues that "the evolving consensus about the uses of food aid has stemmed from academic studies and from the experience of officials administering programmes in donor and recipient states." He claims that this represents a shift in approach from emergency aid to aid more oriented to development and achieving food security. According to Hopkins, "motivation for change has come principally from a development-orientated epistemic community of food aid specialists. Nevertheless, commodity groups, grain traders, farmers, shipping firms, marketing managers in LDCs, and other interest groups seeking specific economic gains have also made proposals to shape food aid practices."[22] This epistemic community can be distinguished from another, "a more critical, leftist community" of "radical critics of food aid," but they are outside the agenda. The basic rationale underlying the priority given to food security goals rests on links forged between population growth, food, and the environment.[23]

Hopkins's interpretation is contested by Peter Uvin, who argues that in the international food regime there are two competing principles: the neo-Malthusian principle (hunger is caused by too little food or too many people) and the "hunger is caused by poverty" principle. These lead to different norms and solutions. The distinction Uvin makes reflects the discussion in chapter 3 where Sen's work was contrasted with Malthusian approaches. The Malthusian approach is dominant because "it pleases . . . financing institutions . . . donor governments . . . third world governments and . . . elites [and] industrial and commercial interests," whereas "important political processes militate against the operational translation of the poverty principle on an international level."[24]

In the discursive practices surrounding food aid, we find the Malthusian approach dominant. Even in Hopkins, despite his assertion that the regime has moved away from emergency food aid to development, the primacy of food and *agricultural* development is undisputed. Famine and third world poverty can be solved by the provision of food aid or by the development in the third world of self-sufficiency in food through agricultural modernization. In addition, the role of expertise is unquestioned: the problems of the third world are to be solved by the West.[25] The discursive practices of food aid are institutionalized under the control of "economic development specialists, agricultural economists and administrators of food aid."[26]

Interestingly, the institutions of the food aid regime have managed to take over the entitlement argument—initially aligned with the radical critics—by a rearticulation that links poverty with population growth and shortages with the environment. As Hopkins describes it, there is "a growing consensus among development experts that population growth, food needs, and pressures on the environment are linked."[27] Amartya Sen's entitlement argument claims that famine and starvation are not caused by a general shortage of food but by lost entitlements. It is not that there is no food, but that people do not have access to food. If lost entitlements can be blamed on environmental degradation, which threatens food security, then projects to remedy this can be seen as projects to replace lost entitlements. The crucial move is to regard the fertility of the land as part of the entitlement bundle of third world peasant farmers. Food aid thus needs to be reoriented toward environmental improvement, rather than feeding programs. This could account for the predominance of environmental projects in food for work programs: it is through a reference to the environment that the relief (food shortage/ emergency) and development (distribution problems/long-term poverty) can be linked. Environment is a Malthusian monster, a scarce resource; environmental sustainability represents the aim of a modernized agriculture. Food for work programs are the site at which the linking of Malthusian and entitlement discourses takes place. They are a way of replacing lost entitlements (by providing employment on public works) while at the same time combating environmental degradation (implicitly caused by overpopulation) and providing sustenance (needed because of failure of the food supply).

Despite the changes in the food aid discourse that we have charted, the predominance of the development and food security approaches has to be continually maintained and reproduced. The Ethiopian famine, and the enormous public response it generated, is seen by many commentators as having shifted the balance back again from development aid to immediate relief: "despite the unresolved debate concerning the cost effectiveness and morality of food aid, few voices were raised in 1984/85 against a mass mobilisation of emergency food to Ethiopia."[28] In the 1990s, this trend has continued, with increasing amounts of money spent on expensive, high-profile, and dramatic humanitarian relief efforts, many involving food aid and centered on relief to starving populations. The U.S. contribution to

Operation Restore Hope, which was around $1.6 billion, represented five times the total U.S. development assistance to Somalia over the preceding three decades.[29] Following 1984/85, development NGOs argued that the emphasis on relief had been unhelpful.[30] In the 1990s they seem to have accepted the public commitment to relief. They are now arguing for the linkage between the two in a discourse of a relief-development continuum. The concept is expressed in a variety of ways: "linking relief and development,"[31] "the interface between relief and development," "relief-development strategies," and "famine mitigation."[32] In this way, resources that the *donors* want to regard as relief can be used by the *recipients* for development or rehabilitation purposes. As I argued in chapter 3, the discursive practices of both Malthusians and entitlement theorists lead to the vision of famine as a disaster—a natural disaster in one case, and an economic disaster in the other. There are two approaches to solving the problem, once it is identified in this way. The first is rapid relief—the provision of food, cash, or whatever—by humanitarian agencies. This disaster relief seems to attract immediate public support.[33] The second response is one that aims to avoid a recurrence of the disaster by reducing what is perceived as the vulnerability of the population. This involves development, and it brings into play a completely different set of organizations and approaches. During the late 1980s and early 1990s, disaster relief was carried out largely independently from development practitioners. Development was being marginalized in terms of resources and public support.

In this context the attempts of development professionals to press their claims is unsurprising: "[With] diminishing bilateral development resources . . . the need to incorporate developmental objectives into relief and humanitarian aid planning takes on a new dimension of importance."[34] Stressing the linkage between relief and development is one way of doing this for agencies fearful of loosing their place:

> The linking debate is primarily an argument over resources, a defensive move by an institutional interest which fears for the object of its existence: stable societies that can sustain socio-economic improvement. The shift in aid flow towards emergency spending has accentuated this crisis. Developmentalists have been forced to argue their centrality in a space that, in the past, was willingly abandoned to relief.[35]

An example of this linking discourse can be found in an article by Gayle Smith, where she argues that what is in effect a new concept—the "relief to development continuum"—is now gaining currency in discussions about disaster preparedness and prevention.[36] She sees this as bringing together the two approaches that were mistakenly separated in the past: disaster relief and development aid. These were, and indeed still are, the province of distinct institutional groups. The separation was, according to Smith, based on the constituted distinction between a disaster, seen as something sudden, unpredictable, and often attributed to natural causes, and underdevelopment, which requires longer-term approaches. Underdevelopment is seen as a lack of economic growth or modernity; the solution is one that, according to Smith, requires technicians, economists, and other experts.

Governments in recipient countries (Eritrea, for example) perhaps saw in this trend an opportunity to gain control of the huge amounts of relief they were still able to command. By supporting the notion of a relief-development continuum, they could argue for the translation of much of the food aid funding into development projects controlled by the state. In a paper setting out their arguments, the Eritrean Rehabilitation and Relief Agency asks donors to "allow Eritrea to use food aid in a rational way."[37] Inflexibility, with food aid allocations made only for particular purposes set down by the donor governments and an unwillingness to allow local agencies such as ERRA to monetize the donations at a reasonable sale price, was described as obstructing the achievement of food security and self-sufficiency for Eritrea, which could be achievable with the rational use of food aid. What is proposed is increased food monetization, that is, selling food that has been provided as part of a food aid package by donors. The food would be sold at local market prices. The paper attempts to establish monetization as one of three possibilities in the use of food aid alongside free distribution and food for work.

In this same paper, food for work programs were seen as a means of moving away from relief and the free distribution of aid to all toward a system that allowed the distribution of food in exchange for labor for development projects.[38] Food monetization and food for work are claimed by ERRA to be a rational part of "a total mandate for the recipient country to use food aid in the way it deems fit but with the aim of food security for the general population."[39] Such a mandate is necessary "for a population that has been depending on emergency food aid" in order to "empower" it to develop food security: "It seems the ultimate test of donors' sincerity to help recipient countries to emancipate themselves from a state of chronic dependency is to show flexibility on the issue of food pricing during monetisation."[40] This argument attempts to articulate into the food aid discourse notions of empowerment, flexibility on the part of donors, and the achievement of food security by Eritrea: "if the ultimate aim is food security and self sufficiency of locally produced food, then donors should allow recipients to use [emergency] food aid in a flexible manner."[41] The so-called risks inherent in emergency food aid are acknowledged—they include dependency—and this is set against the desire for food security. The aim in the paper is not to separate food aid from emergency food aid—it is emergency aid, after all, which is likely to continue while foreign aid in general is cut—but to remove the stigma of dependency that is attached to food aid, rearticulating it instead with rationality, flexibility, and food security.[42]

As Gayle Smith puts it: "the new approach mandates relief aid to reflect not only immediate emergency aims but also longer-term rehabilitation and development goals. . . . This approach would require a simultaneity of relief and development goals that is altogether new."[43] It means "redefining the primary cause of disaster as chronic vulnerability . . . to the whims of nature and of man." She identifies practical problems arising from the way the institutional structure reflects the split between relief and development, but points to initiatives by USAID, the UNDP, and the UN's Department of Humanitarian Affairs that all address the origins of crisis—including political causes—and ways of disaster prevention. However, in her assessment change "will require considerable political will, widespread institutional change and, above all, patience."[44]

FAMINE RELIEF
Eritrea

The discursive practices that provide the backdrop for famine relief and food for work programs are a key site around which aid discourses have been rearticulated. They bring together otherwise contradictory positions—those based on food scarcity and those based on lost entitlements. The relief and aid programs, as social practices that produce power/knowledge, have consequences beyond those prefigured in the food aid discourse. Famine relief can in practice be used in a number of ways to aid particular political aims. Food for work practices have implications in terms of the subjectification and disciplinary practices they embody. They are an instrument of control and subjugation.

In Eritrea in 1995 the shift from free distribution of food aid to food for work was well underway at the same time that discussions with donors about monetization were proceeding. The transitional government in Eritrea was run by members of the Eritrean People's Liberation Front (EPLF), the same people who had been in control of relief operations in large areas of Eritrea during the war with Ethiopia. In the short term, the 1984/85 famine had been, potentially, a disaster for the rebel fronts in Ethiopia. But in the longer term they were able to "turn the . . . people's experience of famine into an asset."[45] The scorched earth policies of Ethiopian government militia and their conscription from rural areas made the peasants increasingly hostile and raised the level of support for the EPLF. The fact that the rebel fronts operated their own food distributions was most significant. Food aid and famine relief had been used by both the Ethiopian government and the rebel fronts as part of their respective strategies. Aid solicited from donors as humanitarian and nonpolitical was used with quite clear political and military results.[46] The Ethiopian government had refused to allow safe passage for relief supplies to territories in the north. The British government agreed with this stance because to do otherwise would "confer recognition on the rebels . . . and thus condone their activity."[47] Eritrean officials of the EPLF saw it the same way: "As soon as Ethiopia accepts safe passage, they are admitting there is a popular movement and that large areas of their territory are not under their control."[48]

The international community did not force Ethiopia to move on this question. The solution was an enlargement of the cross-border relief operations that had been established some years earlier. These were organized by consortia of Western NGOs working largely in secrecy to bring food and other aid supplies to areas of Eritrea and Tigray by routes that bypassed territory in government control. They had been going on quietly since before the famine became international news.[49] In 1984/85 the quantities of relief being handled in this way increased. The distribution system was administered by the Eritrean Relief Association (ERA) and the Relief Society of Tigray

(REST), and operated through village councils at a local level in the rural areas controlled by the TPLF and the Eritrean People's Liberation Front (EPLF). These activities were not publicly acknowledged because of their political sensitivity and out of respect for Ethiopian sovereignty, though there was some support through the U.S. government from mid-1985. Operations took place at night to avoid the threat of air attack. So although the sovereignty of Ethiopia was formally accepted and the large areas of the country outside government control were officially regarded as inaccessible to relief, unofficially large quantities of aid were being distributed in those areas through ERA and REST.

In 1991 the rebel fronts finally overthrew the Ethiopian government and Eritrea became independent, a position that was recognized by the international community after the UN-supervised referendum in May 1993. During the conflict, funds for rehabilitation projects in Eritrea, essentially a "national recovery programme,"[50] had been provided by international NGOs. This led to "a gradual metamorphosis of the military struggle [and] the crystallisation of a countergovernment with an active social programme."[51] Aid from NGOs assisted this process. In Ethiopia relief and rehabilitation had been administered by Western aid agencies, but in Eritrea, by virtue of the military situation, it was organized by ERA. This helped to produce "a new [national] identity based on common experience," and "the altruistic commitment and effectiveness of the ERA . . . won much support for the country's independence, and . . . created a positive image around Eritrean nationalism."[52]

In Ethiopian-controlled areas the use of the relief food aid was controversial, as discussed in chapter 1. Western aid agencies administered the relief under the direction of the Ethiopian government of the day, the military regime led by Mengistu with its Marxist-Leninist allegiances. The agencies' freedom of movement was very restricted, and the government controlled the location of feeding stations and determined which people should be admitted. The government was also in charge of the flow of information—both to the agencies about the needs of the rural areas and to the famine victims about their options for relief and resettlement.[53] In rebel-controlled areas, the rebel fronts had similar control of information flow.[54] At that time, at the height of the cold war, agencies were pleased to be able to operate at all in a communist-controlled country and "complied with all these restrictions without complaining or drawing attention to the constraints." As Clay and Holcomb describe it, "there was an air of grateful surprise," and the stand the agencies took was supported by the media and governments. There was no attempt at independent research and "few Westerners raised questions."[55] Even later, when reports about the conflicts with the rebel fronts began to emerge, "the issues of how the wars had contributed to food shortages and famine and how food assistance was used as a weapon were not clearly spelled out."[56]

It has become clear since that the government used food aid as part of a large-scale forced resettlement program. Accounts of this, based on interviews with people who had escaped resettlement by fleeing to camps in neighboring Sudan and those who became refugees when they were displaced from their own areas by new settlements, were published at the time but were disputed.[57] These accounts claim that the resettlement program contributed to many thousands of deaths, for example, on overcrowded transport and through the spread of famine to other areas of the country.[58] Food aid was used both to entice people to cities where they were captured for resettlement and to bribe peasant associations to put people forward for resettlement before they were given a quota of aid to distribute.[59] Clay and Holcomb argue that this program of resettlement was not a policy specific to the communist government but one that had been used over many years to consolidate the control of the central government of the Ethiopian empire. Ethiopia was made up of a number of diverse groups, brought together under central state control by authoritarian policies that included the regular displacement of peoples from the north to areas in the south of the country. This forced movement was used politically as a means of undermining any resistance from minority groups and consolidating the power of the central state.[60] Despite evidence that the productivity of settlement areas was generally low, resettlement had been proposed as a means of solving the food crisis before Western intervention in late 1984.[61] The availability of food aid from the West and transport in the form of trucks from the Soviet Union made implementation of the politically motivated program easier. Peasants from the areas of Tigray and Wollo, where much of the resistance to the Mengistu regime was located, were targeted.

Accusations and counteraccusations of the abuse of food aid

curred in "a country which, despite concurrent economic problems, was at the centre of a still-growing empire and was an integral part of the acknowledged workshop of the world."[65] Kinealy has no doubt that had these considerable resources been used, the consequences in terms of starvation of even a series of years of potato blight could have been averted. The government policy was to refuse to help unless and until all local resources had been exhausted and distress was evident and widespread. This inevitably meant that much food aid would arrive late. Despite detailed information and a sufficient administrative machine, the government response was cautious. According to Kinealy, "it became apparent that the government was using its information not merely to help it formulate its relief policies but also as an opportunity to facilitate various long-desired changes within Ireland."[66] The covert agenda included population control and the consolidation of land ownership and property. This was achieved when many people emigrated, smallholdings were eliminated, and large estates, which had gone bankrupt, sold. The famine was used to bring about social changes that benefited the ruling classes and consolidated their control; this was achieved by a policy of minimal intervention justified by economic theory. The prevailing economic orthodoxy "decreed that ultimately [poor] relief was damaging and that genuine improvement could be achieved only through self-help. . . . [It] denied any government responsibility for the alleviation of distress."[67] Ultimately interference with the invisible hand of the free market would cause more harm than good and should be avoided: "Short-term suffering appeared to be a small price to pay for long-term improvement, especially if the theoreticians did not have to participate directly in the experiment."[68]

However, Kinealy claims that relief policies were chosen pragmatically for their influence in bringing about desired ends while appearing to relieve suffering. Their success was measured by the changes brought about, not by the number of deaths averted. Although economic dogma was influential, it would have been dismissed if it had not suited the wider aims of policy. Contemporary examples elsewhere show that it was used selectively and that "the policy of noninterference was employed with determination by a government which used it to achieve aims beyond mere provision of relief."[69]

The famine provided the British government with an opportunity to bring about long-term reforms of a structural nature in the agrarian economy of Ireland. These reforms had not been possible previously and were covert. The government could not admit that it was using distress and suffering to bring about social and economic change. The aim was to establish a more commercial set of farming practices involving changes in both the laboring and landlord classes. This hidden agenda was increasingly important from the autumn of 1847 onward. Effective relief would have perpetuated the existing way of life; all that was necessary to ensure change was to maintain the pressure while deflecting requests to do more: "To achieve its ultimate aims, the government's strategy was based on two underlying principles: that of issuing the minimal amount of relief consistent with political acceptability; and that of imposing the maximum possible burden on local resources to force a restructuring of Irish agriculture. . . . This approach, far from observing *laissez faire* principles, was closer to a model of opportunistic interventionism."[70] As inspecting officers employed under the Temporary Relief Act were instructed, there were two objectives:

> to afford relief to the greatest number of the present really destitute population under the most economical arrangements, and with the smallest amount of abuse . . . and to encourage such principles of feeling and action as shall prospectively tend rather to improvement of the social system and, consequently, of Ireland itself.[71]

A transfer of relief to the Poor Law after 1847 was accompanied by new legislation to restrict access to relief and to facilitate the transfer of properties. One example of the new legislation was the Gregory Clause, which stated that owners of more than a quarter of an acre of land were not eligible for relief. Although it was recognized that the evictions that ensued were harsh, a member of the government stated:

> It is useless to disguise the truth that any great improvement in the social system of Ireland must be founded upon an extensive change in the present state of agrarian occupation, and that this change necessarily implies a long, continued and systematic ejectment of smallholders and of squatting cottiers.[72]

Kinealy concludes that "the response of the British Government to the famine was inadequate in terms of humanitarian criteria and, increasingly after 1847, systematically and deliberately so [because] the government pursued the objective of economic, social and agrarian reform."[73]

The assumption that governments, and everyone else, are acting to alleviate suffering leads to instances of inaction, as in Ireland, or inappropriate action, as in Ethiopia, remaining unseen. Or if they are discovered, they are assumed to be the outcome of a lack of administrative capacity, of development, of infrastructure, or of expertise about famine. They are not seen as deliberate acts. But famines have beneficiaries, and it appears that quite often these beneficiaries are the very governments that are supposed to be acting on behalf of the people who are starving. In some cases, communist governments are to blame, as in Ethiopia and in China in the Great Leap Forward of the 1950s; in others it is democratic governments like the British government in Ireland or in Bengal in 1944. Zygmunt Bauman's remarks about the Nazi Holocaust are apposite here: "Modern genocide is genocide with a purpose. . . . The end itself is a grand vision of a better, and radically different, society."[74] For Bauman "arguably the most crucial among the constituent factors of the Holocaust [was] the typically modern, technological-bureaucratic patterns of action and the mentality they institutionalise, generate, sustain and reproduce."[75] This parallels the argument here about the role of technologization and depoliticization in famines and famine relief practices, and it was seen directly in the case of the Irish famine.

FOOD FOR WORK

In Eritrea in the mid-1990s the food for work program was formulated through a number of government institutions. In April 1995, when the present research was carried out (figure 1),[76] the food for work program mainly involved the Ministry of Agriculture and the Ministry of Local Government. As we have seen, it was presented as a program of reform, one which would avoid dependency and promote reconstruction and self-sufficiency. The main projects of the Ministry of Agriculture were "conservation of surface water; control of land degradation and environmental restoration, combating desertification and improvement of ecological balance."[77] This translated into 80,000 km of hillside terracing to be built and 13,380 to be maintained; 250 microdams; 130,000 km of stone bunds and 110,000 km of soil bunds to be built and 70,000 km maintained; 18 new nurseries

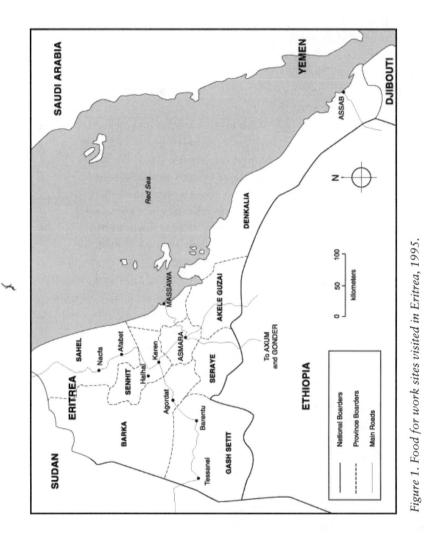

Figure 1. Food for work sites visited in Eritrea, 1995.

and 20 maintained, giving a capacity of 27 million seedlings annu-
ally; and 20 reservoirs to be constructed for tree nurseries. The total
budget for the Ministry of Agriculture for its Food for Work and
Cash for Work schemes for 1995 was 29.57 million Birr (approximately $4.66 million or 4.25 million days of work).[78] The Ministry of
Local Government undertook construction of feeder roads, but its
crucial role was in mobilizing the people for the various projects implemented through other ministries in rural areas.

In this part of the chapter I discuss and analyze a number of features of food for work programs, relating them to Foucault's account
of disciplinary practices. The first aspect is the public nature of the
works carried out and how this is involved with what is seen as a
process of reform. This accounts for the function of food for work as
opposed to the free distribution of food aid and makes this practice a
disciplinary one. The visible nature of the public works is linked
with the need for supervision and control, another part of the disciplinary process, and one that produces as subjects those whom it
documents. These processes of selection and control are embodied in
institutions.

This account from Ireland in the 1840s, reveals many similarities
with Eritrea in the 1990s, one hundred and fifty years later:

> Women and girls worked with the men too, digging, wheeling bar-
> rows, carrying loads of earth and breaking stones, sometimes carry-
> ing helpless children on their backs. Many people objected to the type
> of works undertaken. In general they consisted in the building and re-
> pairing of roads. While the policy of the government was not to pro-
> vide works irrespective of their utility, it became necessary as the use-
> ful roads were completed to build others less useful. The inability to
> supervise properly the selection of schemes meant that many almost
> useless schemes were undertaken.[79]

Moving stones and rocks, largely by hand or with only limited
tools, still formed a major part of food for work programs in Eritrea
in 1995 (figures 2 and 3). The work was very similar whether the
project was one of road construction, stone bunds in farmland, hillside terracing, or the construction of microdams. All involved large
groups of people moving quantities of earth and stones by hand into
rows or lines of one sort or another. In some areas of the country
women seemed to be the major participants. The type of work

Figure 2. Carrying stones for road building. Degasse, Barka.

undertaken did not generally seem to reflect the needs of the community, but seemed to relate more to the requirements of the work as part of a process of reform and rehabilitation—so-called development—despite a rhetoric of participation. In one of the villages visited, people (women) were spending several hours each day on a camel journey to collect water. Construction of a well for the village was presumably a high priority, but road construction was the program being implemented.

The product of the operation has to be both visible and measurable. The work process itself has to be public and available for inspection by visiting teams of monitors from donor agencies or internal ministries. Visiting consultants are looking for large groups engaged in obviously productive and intense labor under good local supervision and with a clearly defined purpose. This has parallels with the form of work in prisons, where, according to Foucault, work "is a

Figure 3. Using hand tools in road construction. Degasse, Barka.

principle of order and regularity; through the demands that it imposes, it conveys, imperceptibly, the forms of a rigorous power; it bends bodies to regular movements, it excludes agitation and distraction, it imposes a hierarchy and a surveillance. . . . The prison is not a workshop; it is . . . a machine whose convict-workers are both the cogs and the products."[80] In food for work programs, the regular lines of peasants working on terracing or road building and the manual, repetitive actions involved are expected to produce the same appearance of organization and purpose. As Patrick Webb and Joachim von Braun express it: "Food for work is not just about providing work, it is also about putting labour to useful effect."[81] It produces "participants" whose involvement validates the program. To what extent these participants are in fact the main beneficiaries is debatable. Foucault's description of prison work evokes images of silence, organization, and obedience, the smooth functioning of a mechanism. He concludes: "What then is the use of penal labour? Not profit; nor even the formation of a useful skill; but the constitution of a power relation, an empty economic form, a schema of individual submission and of adjustment to a production apparatus."[82]

Figure 4. Workers on road clearance site. Agordat.

Food for work projects in four provinces of Eritrea in operation in 1995 varied considerably in scale—and some were more convincing than others. The itinerary of the inspection visit included the provinces (at that time) of Senhit, Gash-Setit, Barka, and Sahel.[83] At Degasse, near Agordat, a group of women were moving stones by hand to place them at the side of a road that was being built. Some men with hand tools were also moving stones (figures 2 and 3). This road would disappear when the rains came. It seemed possible that work at another site, at Agordat (figures 4 and 5), where women, many carrying children, were making a small wall at the side of a road, had been organized especially for the benefit of the visiting inspectors, who were encouraged to take photographs. At another, some 150 women were working to clear a tract of scrub land on the outskirts of the town of Tessanie, close to the Sudanese border. They were working in groups of twenty, each group under a team leader, with supervisors overseeing. The work involved uprooting, chopping, and burning scrub—thorn bushes and the like (figure 6). The project had been requested by the local Ministry of Health as a program to eradicate malaria. There were larger-scale, more convincing

Figure 5. Placing stones at the roadside. Agordat.

Figure 6. Scrub clearance workers. Tessanie.

projects, too. At a site at Halhal 45 km from Keren, a dam of 300,000 cubic meters capacity was being constructed by five hundred men on national service—including postwar returnees to Eritrea from exile in other countries such as the United States—and three hundred peasants from local villages. In conjunction with the dam there was an agroforestry project in the catchment area of the dam and corresponding tree nurseries to provide seedlings. In this case, small hand tools were being used, and there was a supply of wheelbarrows (figure 7).[84] However, there was a problem with this project, too: completion before the rainy season was unlikely, so in all probability the work would be destroyed.

Obviously there was much opposition to the idea of food for work replacing the free distribution of food aid. There was also a willingness to exploit the system. Workers constructing roads that would be destroyed when the rainy season began would presumably rebuild them the following season in return for more food for work. Road building remains a common use of food for work. It has advantages both for those who are implementing the FFW program and those who benefit. In the case of road building and maintenance, the product of the process itself (the road) enables the supervisors of

Figure 7. National service workers at a microdam site. Halhal.

the program to reach the site. Roads do not only "herald . . . improved access to food and medical care,"[85] they also bring areas within the control of central administration and open them up to outside commercial interests.

In Eritrea, the selection of projects for food for work began with proposals from the Woreda (district) level. These were coordinated by each provincial administration and approved. Consultations with the ministries, involved as experts, took place during this process. Administrators saw the decision as theirs, though the proposals were copied to the elected provincial council or baito for comment. In the town of Nacfa, a provincial administrator's office was one of the first buildings to be rebuilt, at a cost of 4.5 million Birr ($800,000). This magnificent structure stands on the hillside with a panoramic view overlooking the town, which lies in ruins (figure 8). The idea that communities participate in the choice of projects and ultimately own the assets produced by the programs has problems. Studies in Ethiopia have shown that participants were not consulted about their wishes before or during the planning of the projects.[86] Often what little consultation there is takes place at a community council level: this presumes that the mechanisms for

Figure 8. The new provincial administration building overlooking the ruins of Nacfa.

consultation between the council members and the people are in place.

The practice of food for work emphasizes the need for input and commitment from the participants. Despite this apparent openness, there are limitations on the type of work that qualifies for FFW projects. It helps if the work undertaken comes within the category of improving environmental sustainability. It is assumed that the recipient population is largely unskilled and ignorant of modern, environmentally friendly farming techniques. They are presumed responsible for the state of desertification with which they are faced. This argument relies on a narrative of a period of environmental degradation. This can be problematic. Melissa Leach and James Fairhead describe how development experts and environmentalists believed that forest-savannah was being destroyed by local farming practices in an area of Guinea in West Africa. After careful research, Leach and Fairhead found that the experience of the villagers and the evidence of archival and air photographs showed that the islands of forest were the result of human management, *created* around villages in savannah by their inhabitants. Vegetation cover had been *increasing* during the period when policy makers believed the opposite.[87]

Training the workers is an important part of the reform or development process: "hay-making . . . was new to pastoralists, who therefore learned the benefits of hay-making and storage in advance of the long dry season, while at the same time earning food for their labour."[88] To what extent these new skills were appropriate to nomadic groups of pastoralists is another question. There is clearly a tension if such groups wish to maintain their lifestyles within a modern state, and food for work can be used to bring pressures on nomads to settle.

Some of the enthusiasm for food for work programs on the part of donors arises from the assumption that otherwise people would sit around doing nothing. Participants are constituted as unemployed and in need of reform. Activities they engaged in beforehand are not acknowledged as work. Simon Maxwell comments on the possibilities if the food aid to Ethiopia were to be translated into food for work programs: "Ethiopia has typically received one million tons of food aid . . . enough to pay for over three hundred million days of work at standard work norms. A work force of this size could build 167,000 km of access road or 417,000 km of artificial waterway or 2,700 earth dams, all in a single year. These are assets which would not otherwise be built and which could contribute to more secure livelihoods and lower vulnerability in the future."[89] Issues of trade-off, feasibility, and institutional development are constraints, Maxwell concedes, but the image is one of a pool of idle (and presumably ignorant, helpless, feckless) individuals, doing nothing until the FFW program swings into action.

In a similar way work in prison is seen not only as a reparation for the crime, but as one of the instruments of reform. According to Foucault, the debates that took place about penal labor throw light on how it is conceived. The question of wages was debated: if prison work was paid then it was not part of the penalty; paid workers in prisons would be in a favorable position in relation to the unemployed outside. The official response was that prison work had no overall effect on the economy because of the small scale involved and that it was useful as part of the process of rehabilitation. Jean Drèze and Amartya Sen discuss critiques of the "excessively punitive" nature of food for work programs, but argue that "a vulnerable population can gain greatly from the discrimination that can be achieved through the insistence on work requirement which would prevent resources being squandered on the privileged . . . famine victims often prefer the status of being employed rather than being mere receivers of charity."[90]

In Eritrea, work norms were set by ERRA for each different type of work. For example, for the construction of soil bund in farmland, which was the responsibility of the Soil and Water Conservation and Irrigation Development Department of the Ministry of Agriculture, the expected rate of work was 100 man days per kilometer; for the construction of stone bund it was 200 man days per kilometer. For road construction it was 2500 man days per kilometer, for road maintenance 700 man days per kilometer. These norms were for the provinces of Denkalia, Semahar, Barka Gash, and Sahel; in the remaining provinces, the work norms were 70 to 75 percent less. This difference is due to differences in climate. Payment depended on the activities undertaken and whether the payment was to be in the form of cash for work or food for work. The cash range was between 6 Birr ($0.95) and 8 Birr ($1.26) per day, with higher rates (10 Birr and 12 Birr) for nursery workers and site guards in Denkalia Province. Although "FFW rates compare unfavourably with local daily wage rates . . . it must be remembered that FFW is not intended as a substitute for other means of local employment and should never compete with the local labour market—FFW is only an alternative use of food aid."[91]

The visibility of public works can be linked to the need for super-

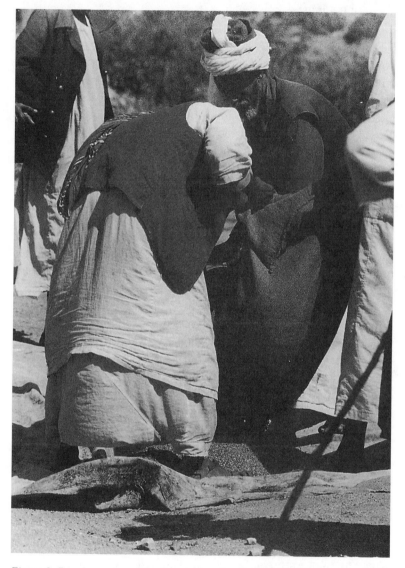

Figure 9. Pouring out a sack of grain for distribution. Nacfa.

vision and control that is part of the disciplinary process. Administrators prepare returns showing the numbers of people involved, the
hours worked, and the amount of construction accomplished: how
many kilometers of road have been built, how many kilometers of
stone banks to retain water, what capacity of dam to provide water
to irrigate what area of land. Books are kept in which the activities
are listed and recorded; these are then used in the process of food
distribution that takes place at a later stage (figures 9 and 10). They
are available when visiting consultants arrive to monitor food for
work on behalf of donors. This style of record keeping in terms of
quantities meets the requirements of food aid donors but does not
help ensure effective projects. Similarly, the monitoring visits by
ERRA and the ministries comply with reporting obligations laid
down by donors, but on the whole this is limited to the monitoring
of deliveries of food or to the extent of work completed—by the kilometer. Consultants engaged on the monitoring and reporting process
spend a limited length of time in the field: one report on food for
work in four provinces was prepared after a period of less than six
days in the field, which included a traveling time of almost thirty-six
hours; another, which took fourteen days, reported on six locations

Figure 10. Grain distribution. Nacfa.

in different provinces. The informants that consultants speak to are very largely ministry and ERRA officials and community leaders. The cursory nature of the visits can be exploited by officials, who can put on a show for the benefit of the visitors.

What is the purpose of these monitoring visits? The potential for misunderstandings is high given the language difficulties, the stressful nature of the visits, and the speed with which the interviews take place. The nature of the information collected is often useful only for statistical returns and does not help improve the FFW programs. I argue that, like any inspection, its purpose is to reproduce the power relation that exists between food aid donor and recipient. Participants are expected to be doing what they are supposed to be doing, *but in addition,* they are expected to demonstrate commitment and participation in the development process constituted by the food for work program. They are expected to play the part of partners in development.

However, it is clear that people in food for work programs participate with a certain amount of detachment. It is debatable to what extent that means that they contest the process that produces them as subjects of a particular type: as recipients of aid or as partners in development. For these people, the failure of food for work programs ensures that they continue as a way of obtaining subsistence— admittedly on certain terms. These terms perhaps entail the adoption of a certain role as subject. However, their participation in the social practice is what is important; a cynical detachment does not help: "they know very well what it is they are doing, but they carry on doing it."[92]

The norm of grassroots participation means that the selection of workers for FFW is largely handed over to local community organizations. In theory, those judged to be the most needy should be employed, but the selection process is felt by many to be unfair, and claims of favoritism and corruption are often reported: "In one case the team questioned the giving of free food aid to an apparently wealthy household with a baito member, who was able to explain very satisfactorily that the household in question was supporting two other households."[93] And in another report:

> Recruitment was managed by village leaders and a ministry foreman, based . . . on "ability to work" coupled with undefined criteria set by the foreman. Seventy-two percent of the non-participants had applied

but had been rejected according to the latter "criteria." All 72% claimed that registration was unfair, referring to bribery, kinship and personal connections as the real criteria guiding selection.[94]

However, it is in nobody's interests to listen to these claims: donors need to be reassured that aid is being channeled appropriately. Drèze and Sen see self-selection as most appropriate where large-scale food for work or cash for work programs are available.[95] The vulnerable will select themselves.

In Eritrea, free food distribution had been confined by the transitional government to certain categories: the needy and the nutritionally vulnerable. The latter included "children under five, disabled persons, people living in arid zones and the aged." It was also extended to war-disabled, orphans, returnees, ex-fighters, war victims, and female-headed households. Fifty thousand ex-fighters, including 13,000 women, were given free food for a year; 400,000 returnees would receive three months' food supply.

In addition to providing work for the participants, food for work schemes create an administrative and advisory superstructure. Agricultural experts, consultants, administrators, and academics are required to initiate, monitor, organize, and comment on the food for work practices. According to Maxwell, "the incremental costs over and above relief will include professional staff for the design of works, tools, supervision, non-food inputs and administration, both locally and centrally," and these can be estimated at 40 percent on top of wage costs.[96] As well as the size of the institutional structure that food for work produces, there are conflicting sites of power. Food for work administration tends to bypass local government structures. Although this does not seem to be the case in Eritrea, where ERRA, a strong indigenous NGO, has a history of controlling relief and development work during thirty years of war. Elsewhere there is conflict, with NGOs wanting to manage projects themselves.[97]

The practices of food aid, as they have been produced in institutions on the ground, are quite different from the discursively legitimated version of food aid discussed in the first section of this chapter. The relationship between ERRA and one of its donors, the European Community, was perhaps an example of the sort of setup common in food aid programs. In 1995, ERRA was beginning to find its own role as a local relief organization. It had become in many ways a semicommercial organization. It already had a commercial offshoot in the form of the Red Sea Corporation, which, as ERRA's trading arm, was involved with buying and selling grain, currency transactions, and so on. ERRA owned a fleet of trucks worth several million dollars. It was not only a question of the role of individual NGOs. Issues relating to the commercial nature and value of food aid in general can be raised.[98] There were profits to be made in the buying and selling of grain as part of food aid programs. For example, ERRA (through the Red Sea Corporation) was involved in trading in grain.

The involvement of donors such as the European Union is complex. NGOs for a long time had had a role in lobbying the EU on behalf of the Eritrean government (or ERRA). By 1995, it seemed that Euronaid was an intermediary in this process. Originally set up by a consortium of European NGOs but by then an autonomous body, Euronaid handled the purchase of food aid and organized its transport on behalf of the EU. They apparently had no responsibility for EU-funding decisions, although it did not appear so to recipient governments who lobbied donors such as the EU via Euronaid through friendly—and, they hoped, influential—NGOs. Some NGOs appeared to be acting as paper handlers, producing bids to the EU in an acceptable form on the one hand, and giving their seal of approval to the FFW projects in the monitoring process on the other. Agencies might ask an NGO to lobby on their behalf if they were competing for an EU contract, for example, to transport food aid. This clearly gave NGOs a position of great power. The transport of food aid was big business, with contracts going out to tender internationally. Contracts for internal transport were competed for by large international organizations, who might well have been familiar with EU requirements and in close contact with the European bureaucracy but who would have had no idea of the nature of the situation on the ground in Eritrea. They would take their percentage, but the job would be handled by a local (African) company as subcontractor.

In Eritrea, to the EU's concern, the situation was somewhat unusual because of the virtual monopoly of transport ERRA had. The purchase of grain also went to tender. In 1995 grain used for FFW in Eritrea was grown in Eritrea, purchased in Eritrea from the Red Sea Corporation, and relabeled "Gift of the European Union" with special stamps sent from Asmara for the purpose—three different stamps were needed. The grain was sold to Euronaid, who then gave it to

ERRA for distribution—after a quality assessment carried out by analysts from France. Local purchase was undoubtedly good for farmers as it helped to stabilize prices, but the European Union was clearly keen to have its recipients' gratitude. It was argued that the continuation of the food aid program was assured because there was such good business in "buying and selling food and moving it around." For Hopkins, parties with interests in FFW include "commodity groups, grain traders, farmers, shipping firms, marketing managers in LDCs, and other interest groups seeking specific economic gains."[99]

CONCLUSION

> In the wake of the 1985 famine, the Ethiopian government launched an ambitious program of environmental reclamation supported by donors and NGOs and backed by the largest food-for-work program in Africa. Over the following five years, peasants constructed more than one million kilometres of soil and stone bunds on agricultural land and built almost one-half million kilometres of hillside terrace. They also closed off more than 80,000 hectares of hillside to most forms of use to foster the regeneration of naturally occurring plant species, and planted 300,000 hectares of trees, much of it in community wood lots.
>
> Today, in retrospect, it is clear that most of this effort was wasted or counterproductive.[100]

Very soon after prison institutions had been set up in 1820–1845, criticisms began. Prisons do not reduce the crime rate; they lead to reoffending; they cause delinquency by the type of existence they impose on inmates; they encourage the association of criminals; criminals who are branded as ex-convicts can't find work and so reoffend; it impoverishes the inmate's family. The response to these criticisms is a return to the same techniques: "For a century and a half the prison has always been offered as its own remedy."[101] Foucault poses the question: "Is not the supposed failure part of the functioning of the prison? Is it not to be included among those effects of power that discipline and the auxiliary technology of imprisonment have induced in the apparatus of justice, and in society in general?"[102] The prison system has remained and survived for so long because it is functional in some way. But if so, what is its role? The answer Foucault gives is that the prison system produces and differentiates a group of "delinquents"; this gives rise to a disciplinary knowledge called "criminology"; moreover, by producing a class of individuals called "criminals" the prison system makes impossible certain forms of political protest—by labeling them "criminal."

The same sort of criticisms can be made of food for work practices: they increase the food needs of vulnerable populations by forcing the participants to work; they are excessively punitive; they create dependency and do not improve the lot of the rural poor; the public works programs fail in what they set out to do; they create enormous logistical and administrative requirements; they do not lead to development; they produce dependency; and so on. Following Foucault's question about prisons, we can ask: what is the role of food for work?

In the same way that the penitentiary concerns itself with the whole life of the delinquent, the specialism of "development" concerns itself with the life of the "vulnerable." The details of day-to-day coping strategies are studied; farming practices, community structures, inter-household distribution, all become the subject of knowledges constituted around practices of relief-development. The distribution of free food can be seen as an emergency response, without strings, but when development takes its place, it is necessary to inquire into causes and solutions. The vulnerable are the subject of the development discourse, and reform of these delinquents is the agenda of food for work: "It falls to [the] punitive technique . . . to reconstitute all the sordid detail of a life in the form of knowledge, to fill in the gaps of that knowledge and to act upon it by a practice of compulsion. It is a biographical knowledge and a technique for correcting individual lives"[103]

Foucault argues that the processes of the penitentiary supported what grew up at the turn of the nineteenth century as a "myth of a barbaric, immoral and outlaw class which . . . haunted the discourse of legislators, philanthropists and investigators into working class life."[104] Crime is no longer regarded as a potentiality of all but as the activity of a specific social class, the bottom rank or the social base. It became accepted that there were two classes, and that "in the courts . . . a social category with an interest in order judges another that is dedicated to disorder."[105] The outlaw becomes a criminal, and political acts of disorder or contestation become crimes.

Again, it is not difficult to draw the parallels with food for work. We have seen the way work is used as part of the process of reform—

or development as it is termed in the context of food aid. What is the function of the continual failure of development itself? It is not just the differentiation of a specific social class of outcasts. Undoubtedly food for work practices do produce as subject the vulnerable peasant who alone is susceptible to famine and in need of our employment safety net. Famine is no longer the stranger waiting outside every door.[106] It waits only outside the door of the improvident, lazy, or vulnerable. These people are not in need of a political voice but require help and training programs. Their participation is limited to a role as grateful recipients of development aid. In addition to this, food aid produces a whole category of countries, third world countries, specifically African countries, as vulnerable, food insecure, and worthy of the attention of development economists, agricultural specialists, and other academic experts. In doing so, it *maintains* the relations of power that exist in international politics between first and third worlds but depoliticizes them.

In the Irish famine, food aid and food for work were seen in a similar way as stabilizing a political power relation:

> The poorest and most ignorant Irish peasant must, I think, by this time, have become sensible of the advantage of belonging to a powerful community like that of the United Kingdom, the establishments and pecuniary resources of which are at all times ready to be employed for his benefit. At any rate, the repeal of the union will not be seriously demanded while so large a proportion of the Irish people are receiving union wages and eating union meal.[107]

I have argued that food for work practices, as part of food aid, are a means by which "the social enemy [is] transformed into the deviant, who [brings] with him the multiple danger of disorder, crime and madness."[108] The third world and Africa the dark continent have been transformed into the underdeveloped countries. The international community is constituted as the benefactor, the contemporary provider of "union wages and union meal" to whom the most ignorant African peasant must surely be grateful, as the Irish peasant was expected to be by Trevelyan.

A Foucauldian analysis suggests that food aid processes can be seen in terms of a power dynamic that produces the control and disciplining of peasants and returnees within Eritrea and their subordination to government agencies as well as the subordination of those agencies to Western donors and NGOs. The constitution of the developed and the developing worlds is reproduced through dividing the practices of aid and food for work programs. These techniques of discipline fail to produce development, their apparent aim. However, they succeed in producing a vulnerable group, who are seen to be in need of not justice or political representation but help and assistance. The form this help takes ensures the establishment and continuance of a system that produces profits for the supposed donors and debts—of gratitude and obligation as well as monetary—for the recipients. It is a system that relies on technologization and depoliticization for its operation, that enables a need for political change to be viewed as a call for improved agricultural technology, and that allows a paternalistic imbalance of power to be seen as a participatory relation of partnership between expert and trainee.

Response and Responsibility

There is something about hunger, or more specifically about the spectacle of hunger, that deranges the distinction between self and other.
— MAUD ELLMANN, *THE HUNGER ARTISTS:*
STARVING, WRITING, AND IMPRISONMENT

Despite the depoliticization of hunger that the modern concept of famine produces, and despite the technologization of aid and its translation into disciplinary practices of control and oppression, we still find that, when faced with pictures of hunger, people respond. That response is often a call to ethico-political action that goes beyond the technical, depoliticized practices of aid. How might we account for personal responses to famine and other international humanitarian crises? As an example, I discuss responses to famines in Ethiopia that culminated in the Band Aid and Live Aid events in 1984 and 1985.[1] In some of those responses we saw, however briefly, action that acknowledged and accepted ethico-political responsibility. This later became routinized and formed the basis for calls for an international humanitarian system based on rules and codes. At the time, public involvement and participation was denounced by development experts as a short-term, unthinking, emotional response, unhelpful to longer-term work. This can be seen as an attempt to re-technologize and again depoliticize famine.

This fleeting moment of ethico-political response to images of suffering and calls for help was superseded by the recommencing of a process of institutionalization and professionalization of humanitarian intervention and by a move to reinstate the preeminence of developmentalism. In the subsequent analysis, these two—humanitarian intervention and developmentalism—are brought together under the rubric of "complex emergency." In some instances, this rubric even becomes "complex political emergencies." The implication is that the emergence of politics itself is what constitutes a failure—a failure of control.

In this chapter I explore how humanitarian responses or responsibility can be linked to accounts of the constitution of subjectivity and the social or symbolic order. First, the impulse to intervention in humanitarian crises can be seen as a response to trauma—in this case, other people's suffering. Second, the role of the international community is constituted through humanitarian response: Why has this notion risen to prominence? Why do national politicians continue to address the international community, although they know that such appeals may well be ineffectual in practical terms? Third, the role of desire in the constitution of subjectivity clarifies why images of hunger or starvation might be so powerful. The link between consumerism and responses to humanitarianism is explored. Hunger, and responses to other people's hunger, have very specific connotations in terms of desire and the political. Depoliticization and technologizing are (necessary) ideological processes. If this is so, is any form of repoliticization possible? There is an extensive literature posing and answering questions concerning responses to humanitarian crises.[2] This chapter focuses on the responses of persons. It does not look at government responses nor responses of the state or nongovernmental organizations (NGOs).[3]

A number of approaches to the question of humanitarian response have gained currency. There is the argument that discounts humanitarian responses as emotional. As such they are unhelpful because they are not based on any knowledge of the objective causes of the problem, and they can even obscure these deeper causes. In the case of famines, this is the argument of developmentalism.[4] Things must be left to the professionals; emotional involvement can lead to mistakes about aid. Even some of those who support the aid-causes-famines argument (discussed in the next chapter), which was intended as a critique of the expert-centered, technologizing approach of developmentalism, might regard emotional involvement as something to be avoided. The emotions identified are those that we normally associate with the feminine: caring, sympathizing, helping. There is no mention of emotions such as anger, hatred, or rage.[5] The devaluing of emotion is similar in other accounts that technologize famine:[6] the emotions expressing connections—caring, compassion, sympathy, guilt—are regarded as unhelpful, and detachment, suspicion, and distrust are seen as objective.[7] A further objection discounts emotional responses on the basis of a variation of the false consciousness argument: Emotional responses arise when people are misled by the media; feelings of guilt are seen as ideologically or religiously grounded and hence invalid.

Another approach to humanitarian responses studies questions of moral agency. It takes a social constructivist line and examines questions of intervention in terms of responses to the other. This "other" is a person whom "we" already know is not "one of us"; what is considered is whether "we" should stand by while this "other" is suffering or whether "we" have a duty to help.[8] Some studies of responses to the Holocaust provide examples of this approach.[9] What individual characteristics did people who risked their lives to help those fleeing persecution have, and how can we make these more widespread? Among the questions raised is the legitimacy of putting national armed forces at risk in pursuit of humanitarian aims.[10] This approach, despite or perhaps because of its social constructivist claims, is based on an assumption that subjects—self and other— exist *before* the question of humanitarian response is considered. The questions it raises have to do with the way others are to be treated. It will, for example, discuss how "Jews" are labeled in particular ways without in any way questioning the existence of Jews as an identifiable group prior to such labeling. Taking a Lacanian approach, I argue that the *relation* between the self and the other, and the self and the social group, is constituted *at the same time* as self, other, and social group, *not later*. It is not, as constructivists claim, something that is constituted afterwards, through intersubjective social processes.

The approach to humanitarianism advocated here is distinct from both the objectivist and the constructivist positions. It has many points of convergence with other writers in critical international relations literature, in particular the Derridean approach seen in the work of David Campbell[11] and the critique of complex emergencies in the work of Mark Duffield, Alex de Waal, and David Keen. It shares much with approaches that emphasize performativity,[12] which draw on the work of Judith Butler[13] and focus at the level of the state or on performances of state leaders. They do not look very much at the responses of persons who are outside the incident, who have no reason to be involved. The Derridean approach argues that whether or not to respond in situations of human suffering is a decision that has to be taken in a particular instance. No abstract knowledge can avoid the ethical and political responsibility involved. An interminable process of decisioning and questioning in the face of what Derrida calls the "double contradictory imperative" has to take place.[14] This is an ethico-political process and will be elaborated in chapter 6. The present chapter accepts this argument and attempts, through the use of Lacanian ideas of subjectivity developed by Žižek, to elaborate on the impasse at the heart of the decisioning process. It also looks at the person and subjectivity as implicated in the social. Campbell's work looks at the collectivity; the addition of a Lacanian view enables us to see how the collectivity is produced in the constitution of subjectivity.

How does this relate to the argument about technologizing? Lacanian notions of the subject recall the idea that modernity entails a hunger for certainty and completion, an impossible hunger, that drives responses to famines.[15] This hunger is at the root of subjectivity. Moreover, it is this hunger that leads us to take a technologizing approach, one that conceals the futility of our desire for wholeness in a finite world where existence is ultimately limited. For Lacan, the subject is the subject of a lack before it is interpellated into a social order, and the social order itself is not complete. This must be concealed for life to "go on," as Ashley puts it.[16] The trauma of events such as those that call for a humanitarian response brings us face to face with the lack at the heart of our own subjectivity.

BAND AID/LIVE AID

On 23 October 1984, the Ethiopian famine finally became a major news story in Britain and around the world.[17] This is now seen as a turning point in terms of the growth of media involvement in raising money for charities;[18] the aid that they produced is narrated as the first example of humanitarian intervention in a conflict situation.[19] The cycle of media coverage of suffering, then a public outcry in the

West, followed by military or humanitarian intervention, is a familiar one in the post-1989 international order.

October 1984 was not the first time that this particular Ethiopian famine had been shown on television. There had been a news item and a documentary shown the previous July that had produced a good response, above expectations. However, this response was nothing compared with what followed the later transmission. The film shown in the October broadcast, shot by Mohamed Amin, was exceptionally moving, according to many accounts. For example, the head of the Ethiopian relief organization, Dawit Wolde Giorgis, saw the videotape in London and said, "It had a chilling effect even on me, who had been there."[20] The film opens with a scene of people, wrapped in pale clothes, seated or lying, mostly still, only an occasional movement visible, spread out over a vast area in the dawn sunlight. Then a close-up of a baby—a tiny body, but a large head, and its mouth open wide in a silent cry. It is held close to its mother's face. She shields it with the cloth that drapes them both, drawing it to her, and looks down. The infant's silent anguish, eyes closed, mouth wide, screaming, continues (figure 11). Finally, the mother tries to

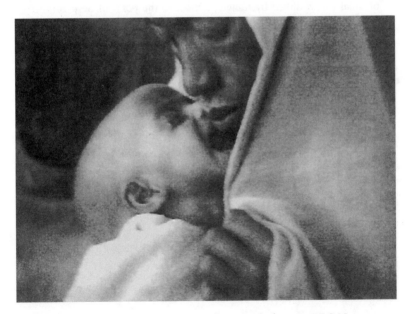

Figure 11. Mother and baby at Korem famine relief camp. BBC News, 23 October 1984.

nurse it. Next is a close-up of a child's swollen knees, then his head, as he turns toward the camera; mouth set, open slightly, he raises his eyes to look at the lens. His head continues to turn and his gaze moves past. He turns back, and again his gaze meets ours briefly, goes past, then returns and looks full at the camera (figure 12). The shot cuts to a bundle—a dead child in a parent's arms—carried along past people seated on the ground. Then the video cuts again, this time focusing on the face of grief of one of those seated in the crowd, moving closer. There are scenes of people carrying bodies shoulder high, again in the beautiful dawn light, of processions of mourners in biblical clothes, and the film ends with shots of these same processions winding their way into the distance.

The images used by the commentary in the BBC news broadcast are interesting. Michael Buerk's words are quoted in chapter 1, but here they are again:

> Dawn. And as the sun breaks through the piercing chill of night on the plain outside Korem, it lights up a biblical famine—now, in the twentieth century. This place, say workers here, is the closest thing to hell on earth. Thousands of wasted people are coming here for help. Many find only death. They flood in every day from villages hundreds of miles away, dulled by hunger, almost to the point of desperation.

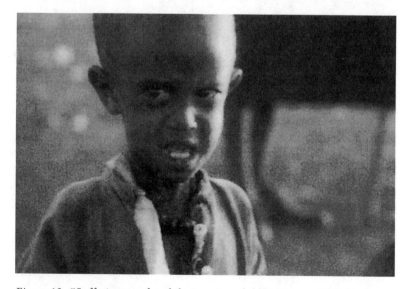

Figure 12. "Suffering, confused, lost . . .": a child at Korem. BBC News, 23 October 1984.

We are given a glimpse of a strange land, a biblical scene. The biblical vision continues in the evocation of a cold, chill night— remember the film was shown in late October, during what is called in Britain "the run up to Christmas"—set against the dramatic appearance of light. This appeal to Western (Christian) charity was repeated later in the words of the Band Aid single "Do They Know It's Christmas?" Of course, this use of references to Christmas is deeply ironic in the context of Ethiopia as one of the sources of Christianity. When Bob Geldof visited Ethiopia, he was first taken to the churches at Lalibella, before any visits to feeding camps, to "show him that we did know what Christmas was."[21] Other pictures reinforce the presentation of the subjects of the film as helpless, dependent victims. They are depicted as anonymous hordes of people who "flood" in, in a state of "desperation," looking for "help," "dulled by hunger." There is no mention that they might have been driven to Korem by the war rather than by a natural disaster. When the religious metaphors continue with the description of the camp as "hell," we are led to ask whether the people are being punished. Is the famine somehow their fault? It is the workers at the camp who speak: the people themselves are speechless. The whole situation is presented as an anachronism—a "famine . . . in the twentieth century." In the modern world of progress and enlightenment (and abundance) such a thing represents a catastrophic failure.

The coverage led to a widespread response.[22] People who saw the news programs were appalled by the level of suffering shown and by the lack of action by their governments. It was felt that the people in Ethiopia should be helped, irrespective of the political leanings of their government. The broadcast led to large donations to charities, some rather fruitless pressure on governments, and to the Band Aid/ Live Aid/Sport Aid movement. Initially apparently motivated by a direct emotional response, the movement later became more explicit about what came to be called the "politics of starvation."[23]

At the same time, both the television news coverage and the Band Aid events generated an enormous amount of criticism.[24] The images were negative; they showed the people caught up in the famine only as victims.[25] No African aid workers were shown, only white Europeans, giving the impression that the West was coming to the rescue of the incompetent Africans. People were not allowed to speak for themselves—the voice-over of a commentator replaced interviews. The use of such negative images, portraying Africans as passive victims, was little short of racism.[26] Some emphasized the adverse effect of Band Aid and its successor, Live Aid, the concert staged simultaneously in Britain and the United States: "[Bob Geldof's] efforts may have hampered considerably the ability of others to change things in the future by whatever means. . . . we have gone backwards. . . . when famine returns . . . the way will be open for a public perception which has Africans responsible for both the problem and the solution."[27] There were many criticisms of Live Aid and other charity-type events from the beginning. At a conference held in Montreal at more or less the same time as the Live Aid concert, criticism was particularly strong.[28] The event was patronizing; it was charity not politics; the involvement of millionaire rock stars was nothing but hypocrisy of the worst sort.

However, others saw the events differently. They questioned whether the reactions of so many people should be written off. If populism or grassroots development in the third world was fine, why was popular feeling discounted in the industrialized North? It seems that people in the North have to be educated, whereas those in the South can be listened to.[29] Stuart Hall and Martin Jacques argued that Live Aid represented a new form of politics. One of the features of Live Aid was "its ability to transcend national frontiers. . . . By using global networks of rock music and television, the movement was able to be, at once, both national and international. For a movement where the key issue is about the relationship between the First and the Third Worlds, this was not only appropriate but added significantly to the power of the appeal."[30] Despite the global television coverage, the movement was still focused on London and Philadelphia.[31] However, with Sport Aid, which followed a year later in May 1986, "Africa was not just an object of a movement in the developed world, it was also, at last, one of the subjects."[32] The Sport Aid events were timed to take place just before the UN General Assembly debate on Africa and included a program of worldwide activities. A ten-kilometer run was staged at the same time in 274 cities in 78 countries. Unlike the Live Aid concerts, it involved up to twenty million people as participants, not spectators.[33] It was a move that, Hall and Jacques argued, actually *challenged*, rather than reinforced, the hegemonic ideological discourse where the image of Africa was as a victim, linked to the charity of the West. It also contested the hegemony of traditional politics.[34] Famine was, temporarily at least, repoliticized through a social movement that arose from outside the formal channels of political expression.

These debates surrounding the Live Aid events are central to the analysis in this chapter. The argument was between those who discounted the outpouring of sympathy and support that the 1984 broadcast and subsequent events elicited as hypocritical, emotional, apolitical, and manipulated versus those who saw it as something positive that might lead to a new form of politics. Why were the disagreements so bitter? To participants in Live Aid, for example, the criticisms seemed "sacrilegious"[35] and were strongly felt. These participants were caught up in the constitution of a new symbolic order, based on a reinscription of a world community. This, although initially accepting ethico-political responsibility and the need for personal action, quickly moves to tame famine by a response constituting donor, victim, and international community. The critics of Live Aid, who appeared to take a more objective, realistic, or even cynical stance, were claiming that there was no need for a constituency of compassion. Instead, the problem should be left to those development experts who could solve it on the basis of *knowledge*. This tames famine by technologizing it and by denying the violence it implies. Both responses can be read as ways of responding to the trauma of *facing the real* and experiencing the nonexistence of what Lacan calls the master signifier.

THE GAZE OF THE VICTIM

This is what it looks like when tens of thousands of people are dying for no good reason . . . these are people, like you or me, who have lost everything and everyone near and dear to them. You are watching them die before your very eyes . . . what are you going to do about it?

— MOHAMED AMIN, "A VISION OF THE TRUTH"

Media accounts present famines as natural disasters, paralleling the academic accounts discussed in earlier chapters. Reviews and critiques of media accounts point out how the natural disaster is the focus of the lead paragraphs, and discussion of political or other facets is relegated to subsequent, less important paragraphs.[36] The focus is on the dramatic and visual aspects and "media . . . typically emphasise the uncontrolled wrath of nature and promote the value of 'social order' . . . by emphasising either the efficiency of rescue and relief operations in the restoration of order or its tragic absence."[37]

Media critiques also point out that accounts of disaster relief have an underlying folk narrative form;[38] the central character is a roving hero—an Oxfam field-worker, a foreign correspondent—and there is a villain or, more often, a lack or misfortune. Another central character is a donor who provides the hero with a magical agent or magical helper—Western abundance and technology in the case of famine narratives. Even factual news programs have this narrative structure. There are political implications behind this treatment, of course. In some sense, the media create a disaster when they give it coverage, and a disaster does not have political or structural causes: emergencies are aberrations, occurrences outside the normal.

Certainly, the portrayal of famines as disasters promotes a depoliticized, technologizing approach. This stress on disaster reflects a fascination with what Žižek calls the sublime and, at the same time, a need to tame and domesticate an encounter with the Real. The distinction between nature (raw, uncontrollable, traumatic) and society (ordered, under control, calm) is a distinction between the Real and what we call social reality. This distinction is central to the process of constituting social reality and subjectivity. Hence media interest in stories where this contrast is featured would not be surprising: they deal with something central to what we call existence itself.

The experience of disaster as an encounter with the Real is one that, like the gaze of the victim, forces us to confront the impossibility of social reality, the void at its heart. The Real is that which cannot be symbolized. The symbolic or social order is always incomplete or impossible. It can only be constituted by the exclusion of some (nonsymbolizable) kernel—the Real. The literature on trauma and post-traumatic stress[39] emphasizes that not only those caught up in a disaster experience this shock of an encounter with the Real, but also those who witness it. Whole communities can be caught up in it; indeed, those who share a traumatic experience of this type feel themselves both part of a new community of a special type (a community made up of those who share a revised view of the world, produced by trauma, that they must continue to bear witness to) and apart from all usual social links.[40]

However, for witnesses of disaster the traumatic element is not so much the encounter with the Real as the encounter with "the gaze of the helpless other—child, animal—who does not know why something so horrifying and senseless is happening to him."[41] It is not, as might be supposed, the gaze of a hero, willingly sacrificing himself, that is so striking to observers of tragedy, but "the gaze of a perplexed victim,"[42] the passive, helpless casualty. It is this gaze that gives rise to the compassion felt by outsiders. It is not, as we might think, the outsiders in distant countries who are the passive ones in cases of humanitarian disasters, who do nothing, who do not want to get involved. Rather, it is the people caught up in the events themselves. They see the horrors that are engulfing them but cannot understand how such horrors are possible and are unable to act.[43] Their gaze, the gaze of the uncomprehending victim, is unbearable and gives rise to guilt in witnesses to distant disaster. It is to avoid the pressure of this gaze that we feel compassion toward those in trouble. This compassion can be related to the reflexive nature of human desire, which is always desire for a desire. Compassion is "the way to maintain the proper distance towards a neighbour in trouble."[44] By giving, we present ourselves so that we like what we see when we look at ourselves from the position of the victim. By responding compassionately, we present ourselves as that which is desired by those who are suffering. This account does not in any sense invalidate compassion; on the contrary, it shows why it is so important and necessary. The reaction of the subject of compassion, the victim, is a separate matter.

In the Ethiopian famine, we saw that the images that provoked an immediate reaction and a strong response were those that portrayed perplexed victims, children in particular, and specifically those that portrayed their passivity and bewilderment.[45] It was precisely that picture of passivity that formed the basis of so many of the subsequent objections to the media coverage. However, the mediated nature of the image, the fact that it was an image seen on television, leads to another account of the response to disaster.

When we watch a television program, we do so from a disembodied space *outside* and beyond the reach of the scene we are viewing. We ourselves are invisible to the people we are watching. We are not *there*, they cannot see us, yet we can see them. The same is the case with a theatrical drama on stage, except that there the distance is fictional or posited by convention and can be broken by audience participation or by applause. In a theater, too, people are part of an audience, not alone. When we witness scenes of suffering on television, our subjectivity is suspended. We are like ghosts. *It is as if we were already dead.* We cannot intervene, and we cannot be harmed by what is going on. Yet, in an important sense we are not passive. As (apparently) the focus of the victim's perplexed gaze, the viewer is placed in the position of the master signifier, the place of the subject who is supposed to know. This is the place the analyst occupies in psychotherapy.

The symbolic or social order can never be complete. It constitutes itself around a lack, a paradoxical element that halts the shifting of signifiers in a "non-founded founding act of violence."[46] This paradoxical element is the master signifier and provides the reference point that holds the symbolic field together. It conceals the void by occupying it and thus enables the social order to be constituted. However, the "master" is always an impostor—anyone at the place of the constitutive lack in the structure of the symbolic order will do. The character of master is produced by the position the figure assumes. It is by reference to the master that the symbolic order acquires meaning and purpose, and its emptiness is concealed. The lack, the empty place at the heart of the symbolic order, cannot be abolished—it is constitutive—it can only be rendered visible as empty. As witnesses of distant suffering on our television screens, we are placed in that empty place, the void that has to be concealed for the social order to come into being. We are the ones who are supposed to be able to answer the perplexity of the victims about the purpose of their suffering. This is an impossible position to hold. The imposture of the master signifier is usually concealed; however, in this case, we ourselves are interpellated into this position, and we *know* we are impostors. We know that what we are part of is not real. We cannot help. We cannot answer the appeal. According to Žižek, the accepted interpretation in media studies is that our perception of violence in a modern society of spectacle is aestheticized by media manipulation—we no longer see reality as such, but reality as spectacle, pseudo-reality. Žižek argues that this is not the case: "The problem of contemporary media resides not in their enticing us to confound fiction with reality but, rather, in their 'hyperrealist' character by means of which they *saturate the void that keeps open the space for symbolic fiction.* The symbolic order can function only by maintaining a minimal distance towards reality, on account of which it ultimately has the status of a fiction. . . . if it is to function normally, symbolic order

Figure 13. "International Community." Copyright Steve Bell 1994; all rights reserved. Reprinted by permission of Steve Bell.

is not to be taken literally."[47] We are not part of what we see: we cannot take on the role demanded of us.

We are watching, helpless to prevent, yet implicated. Not only are we unable to stop the tragedy, we are unable to comfort its victims. We feel the full impact of the ambiguity and ambivalence—the undecidability—that is the metasubject. From this empty place we are summoned by the perplexed gaze to provide answers, to respond to the questioning of the victims who cannot understand the horror they have been caught up in. *It is not a place we can occupy.* There are no answers we can give. There are only (impossible) decisions to be made. Here we see what Žižek means—the space for the symbolic fiction (the master signifier) has been removed. The scene is the impossible one pictured in a Steve Bell cartoon (figure 13), which shows the living room of a modern home in semidarkness. Seated on the floor is a figure, its eyes closed and the television set cradled in its arms. On the bright television screen we can see a body lying curled up on a road somewhere. We can just make out what looks like a figure holding a gun in the background. The title is "International Community."[48]

This is what Žižek describes as an experience of the sublime. Such an experience takes place when we "find ourselves in the face of some horrifying event whose comprehension exceeds our capacity of representation; it is so overwhelming that we can do nothing but stare at it in horror; yet at the same time this event poses no immediate threat to our physical well-being, so that we can maintain the safe distance of an observer."[49]

We are forced to traverse the fantasy, to face the traumatic void at the heart of the social or symbolic order. We experience the nonexistence of the big Other, that is, the social or symbolic order. What do we do after we have traversed the fantasy? Is this moment, when the symbolic order no longer exists and we experience our own nonexistence as subjects, no more than a gap between two orders—a fleeting, vanishing mediator, "an enthusiastic intermediate moment necessarily followed by a sobering relapse into the reign of the big Other,"[50] like a revolution followed by a return to a more repressive regime? One response to this question is a move to produce an *alternative* social order, one based on a *different* master signifier. Another response is a return to, or reassertion of, the previous symbolic order. The first leads to an international community of affect, based on compassion, and a humanitarian practice. This claims a neutrality derived from universal basic human values or rights. The second produces a return to developmentalism, which is founded on the scientific search for objective causes of events and a belief in rational, technical solutions. It claims a value-free truth founded on the certainty of objective method. A third response, to which I return later, is the possibility of "tarrying with the negative."[51] Žižek's Lacanian work allows us to see the various responses in relation to a desire for (impossible) completion, for an overcoming of the lack inherent in *la condition humaine* as such.

RESPONSE

The social order does not preexist the subject; it is brought into being at the very moment the subject is brought into being. This moment establishes the social or symbolic *and* establishes the subject. There is a great similarity between Derrida's notion of decisioning and this idea of what is called the "moment of concluding" in Lacan. In both, there is no way of telling in advance what will happen and no way of knowing whether a different conclusion would have produced a better result. However, Lacan's version brings in the social explicitly. It looks at how the combination of separate moments of decisioning can work. The need for the anticipatory gesture by which we become what we are is explained by "the *inconclusive* character of the causal chain: the symbolic order is ruled by the 'principle of insufficient reason': within the space of symbolic intersubjectivity, I can never simply ascertain what I am."[52] So, we can unpack the decisioning process, or what is called "performativity," and give an account of the social. According to this account, the social functions "precisely and only in so far as its status is irreducibly undecidable, lacking any guarantee."[53] Its temporal structure is important: the social order is "a hypothesis which never directly 'is,' it merely 'will have been.'"[54]

To explain this Lacan distinguishes three moments of logical time, each of which implies a different mode of subjectivity. The first moment, the "instant of gaze," implies an impersonal, neutral subject. The second moment, the "time for understanding," involves intersubjectivity in the form of a transposition into the other's reasoning or an ability to take the other's reasoning into account. The third moment, the "moment of concluding," is when the subject is constituted. There is a shift from "the void of the subject epitomised by the radical uncertainty as to what I am—that is the utter undecidability of my status—to the . . . assumption of symbolic identity."[55] This third moment involves a "double delay and a hindered interrupted gesture."[56] Individuals need to see (in advance) that everyone is going to respond before deciding to respond themselves—for example, to the suggestion "Let's go!" Only after this delay, when the tentative gesture of rising to leave has been observed in everyone, can anyone move in the confidence that everyone—the whole group—will follow suit.

What is important is that the social or symbolic order only arises in this third moment, the moment of concluding; in Žižek's words:

The first time (the "instant of looking") involves a solitary subject who immediately "sees" the state of things; in the second time (the "time for understanding"), the subject transposes himself into the reasoning of the other—we are dealing here with the mirror-relationship to the other, not yet with the big Other. It is only with the third time— when by means of the gesture of precipitate identification, of an act *not covered by the big Other's guarantee*, I recognise myself in my symbolic identity mandate (as a Communist, an American, a democrat . . .)—that the dimension of the big Other becomes operative. The big Other is not "always-already here," ready to provide a cover for my decision: I do not merely fill in, occupy, a preordained place which awaits me in the symbolic structure—on the contrary, it is the very subjective act of recognition which, by means of its precipitate character, *establishes* the big Other *qua* atemporal-synchronous structural order.[57]

In the third moment of logical time, the moment of concluding, which corresponds to Derrida's notion of the undecidable, there is a move from undecidability to the assumption of symbolic identity. The social order and the subject are simultaneously constituted through this process of precipitate identification.[58] A symbolic mandate, which could be called a "subject position," only comes into existence when the subject assumes that it already exists. A subject cannot find out in advance what he or she is; or, in Žižek's words: "'objective' social identity is established by means of 'subjective' identification. . . . If we simply wait for a symbolic place to be allotted to us, we will never live to see it—that is to say, in the case of a symbolic mandate, we never simply ascertain what we are, we 'become what we are' by means of a precipitate subjective gesture."[59] At this point, in the third moment, a different symbolic identity can be assumed. If the disaster we have witnessed was seen as produced or at least condoned by the existing social or symbolic order, a resumption of the previous symbolic identity would be difficult. What is needed is a new, untainted master signifier. In Geldof's words: "to expiate yourself truly of any complicity in this evil meant you had to give something of yourself. I was stood against the wall. I had to withdraw my consent."[60] This withdrawal and resubjectification produces not only a new symbolic identity, but a new symbolic order, a new master signifier. It is a gesture at once social and individual.[61]

The question is, in what way is the social to be reconstituted? What master signifier is to be produced? In Live Aid, we see the constitution of a new social or symbolic order based around the concept of an international community of people. "We are the World" became the slogan of the movement. This symbolic order replaces that based around notions of national identity. Dick Hebdige recounts the Live Aid movement as a form of popularism centered not on the nuclear family of Thatcherism, but on the larger family of man:

"Whereas Thatcher addresses the nation, Geldof interpellates the entire world."[62] For Hebdige, the value of Band Aid lay in "providing an alternative version of—a means of yearning beyond—the appetitive and paranoid versions of human motivation and human worth carried in the Thatcherite and Reaganite visions."[63] In the critics we have a response that "is unable to engage or to engage with the symbolic community—the transcendental 'we'—the 'better half' of all of us—which Geldof and the rest managed to relocate during the Aid campaign."[64]

The critics of Live Aid had an alternative way of reconstituting the social order. They advocated a reconstitution of the epistemic community of developmentalism. For them, a return to objectivity and expert knowledge and a recognition of the problems engendered by emotive appeals would reinstate existing agencies, sidelined by Band Aid, as central to the relief effort.[65] For them, the master signifier is modernity's regime of truth centered on the form of scientific discourse. This could be called "scientific absolutism" because it replaces other forms of authority or master signifiers. In a sense they take on the godlike position, the position of the master signifier itself, to which the media accounts interpellate viewers.[66] They argue that we should move as soon as possible to distance ourselves from the shallow, emotional response associated with the popular famine movement and return to a proper consideration of the root causes and the fundamental scientific explanations for the Ethiopian famine. The relief funding should be translated as soon as possible to funding for longer-term development projects. Aid agencies should take the money, but repudiate the hype.

FAMINE AS SYMPTOM

12:46, 13 July 1985 . . . I stood stock still, my hand raised above my head, my fist clenched in unconscious salute. In front of me stood 80,000 people. Somewhere, invisible, behind them, another billion people all over the world had joined us. Together we held our breath. . . . Throughout Africa on this day people were starving. And, for me, at this particular moment, the threads of a lifetime were uniquely gathered, all there in that one uplifted hand. . . . Something special was happening today; it seemed epitomised in this moment. I stood and looked, tracking my gaze from one side of the auditorium to the other as if to fix each individual with my eyes. I wanted to make contact with them all, and draw them in. . . . at that moment there was no difference between the man on the stage and the audience, none at all. We were all part of some greater purpose, all attempting an understanding of one another and all part of something completely outside ourselves. . . . Today was not about a single continent. Today was about a single world.[67]

If facing images of distant hunger is an experience of the traumatic real, what follows, in the response that we make, is the reconstitution of subjectivity and community through a reinstatement of what we call social reality/social fantasy. For Žižek, social fantasy is to be seen as an escape from the traumatic real, a way of concealing antagonism and the impossibility of the social order. It produces the master signifier and masks the "nothing" behind the curtain. Critics point to the role of the ideological in Live Aid. The discourse of charitable response to disaster, the narrative of the West as rescuer, performs the ideological role of concealing the "true" causes of famine and suffering that lie in the dominance of the West and its exploitation of Africa. For these critics, famine has deep causes, for example, in the effects of colonization and structural inequalities, and the Live Aid narrative is ideological in that it provides a way of avoiding the need to confront these truths. This view of famine as a disaster with a scientific cause—whether the science in question is Marxist economics or natural science—leads to a detachment from disaster relief in favor of a search for further knowledge, which alone can provide a reason to act. It contrasts with the humanitarian approach that calls for action without knowledge to save lives in the immediate future without waiting for a political analysis. This approach is validated by a different detachment or objectivity, one that in its own way equally repudiates involvement and empathy with suffering. It is based on a strict separation of humanitarian and political actions, on an assumption of neutrality, and on a valuation that holds the preservation of human life to be above and distinct from any political aims.

However, ideology does not work solely or even largely by concealing the truth of exploitation.[68] There are two other aspects: "the way in which—beyond the field of meaning but at the same time internal to it—an ideology implies, manipulates, produces a preideological enjoyment structured in fantasy";[69] and "in a given ideological edifice, the element which represents within it its own impossibility,"[70] that is, the symptom. The symptom is not external to the social order. It is the point within that order where its truth erupts: "going through the social fantasy is . . . correlative to identification with the symptom."[71] In the Live Aid record, we have precisely such an identification. In Michael Buerk's commentary in the first news broadcast, the incongruity of "a biblical famine—now, in the twentieth century" was pointed out. The image of famines is an image of food scarcity, want; starvation is a result of hunger unsatisfied. The twentieth century, in contrast, is the century of technological progress, the conquest of nature, abundance and plenty. However, the economic ideology on which that notion of abundance is based is free market economics, a system based on concepts of scarce commodities, competition, and demand or lack. In other words, the economic system of modernity is a system of scarcity par excellence. The symptom, which prevents closure of the social system, the point at which the antagonistic character of the system erupts, is famine— that is, the point at which the truth of scarcity erupts. Famine is thus truly man-made: famine is the element within the social system based around property, scarcity, and impersonal monetary exchange that represents the impossibility of such a system. It is the truth that has to be concealed for the social to constitute itself. As Amrita Rangasami has argued, we all benefit from famine.[72] Through our acceptance of a system of law that regulates ownership through violence, forgetting the violence at the root of the law, we are all complicit in starvations and famines.

This is why Live Aid was potentially so subversive. Live Aid, Hebdige argues, succeeded precisely through its exploitation of those features of the social system so reflective of the apparent plenty and abundance of the twentieth century—communications, media, and technology. The Band Aid team worked "precisely through 'exploitation' and 'manipulation': through the *dedicated* exploitation of their own positions as public figures, through their *passionate, convinced* manipulation of hyper-promotional techniques and marketing strategies learned in the course of their careers in the media."[73] It "wrested technology's sword from the hand of the war lords" as well, using the satellite technology of the superpowers as the medium for the famine movement.[74] Band Aid traversed the fantasy by identifying with the symptom—through enjoyment. To the extent that it could maintain this position, the third position mentioned above, it was arguably "tarrying with the negative."[75] This is why it was subversive, at least initially.

In the case of Band Aid, buying records, sending donations, and enjoying rock music constituted, however briefly, a new politics and a new community. This was the international community, but constituted as a community of people, not states. Ideology is located not just in the knowing but also in the doing—people know what they are doing, but they continue to do it.[76] In supporting Band Aid and Live Aid, even when they knew that this type of aid was problematic, people were participating in the production of the social fantasy, the new humanitarian international community. We see this in the comments: a television producer, who had made a program critical of food aid and the way it conceals structural inequality, still donated to the appeal. He said, with a shrug, "I made the programme, but I still sent a donation."[77] Žižek argues that belief is externalized in social activity. In capitalism, people no longer believe (they see themselves as free, rational beings), but things (commodities) believe for them. The Band Aid phenomenon involved the purchase of a record as something that speaks for us in this way: it was an externalization of ethical commitment.

HUNGER, CONSUMPTION, AND DESIRE

Live Aid was just about having a good time. We all knew why we were there, but the fact wasn't forced down anyone's throat, you know.

— LIVE AID ATTENDEE

I return to the point that hunger, and responses to other people's hunger, have very specific connotations. The relations between hunger and desire and between hunger and consumerism can account for the centrality of the motif of famine, starvation, and hunger in providing the impetus for humanitarian action. They can also account for the taboo against discussions of hunger identified by Josué de Castro.[78] This taboo is seen in operation, I argue, when processes of technologizing take place: when famine is treated as something that can be solved by better techniques of relief and food aid.

There are parallels between pornography (consuming "sex," so-called sex tourism, and the like) and famine imagery—"consuming hunger,"[79] which has also been called "disaster tourism."[80] Why are these terms used? Both share the notion of voyeurism. Drucilla Cornell argues that heterosexual pornography creates a rigid fantasy scene that limits women's sexual expression.[81] She calls for action to free space for women's imaginary. A woman should be allowed to create her own imaginary domain: "If we are to have bodily integrity . . . we must be able to project our own images of our own bodies. That is, I project an image of who I shall have been for whom I might become. This process takes place in the future tense of the anterior since it can never be completed. When I have thrust upon me a fantasy of my body that completely undermines my own image of bodily integrity, I am at that moment harmed."[82] The encoding of woman in a "heterosexual masculine symbolic" as "bodies which are not only violable but there to be violated"[83] dominates the public space. This is perhaps paralleled by the encoding in the world's media of Africans as helpless bodies, bodies that are there to be helped, for us to help, in a Western symbolic. We are the charitable Christians, they, the heathen awaiting conversion: "do they know it's Christmas?" in the title of the Band Aid record. These issues, as we have seen, were at the center of some of the debates and the acrimony over the Band Aid/Live Aid events.[84]

Famine images, like the sexual images they parallel, embody the lack that must be concealed if the subject is to be constituted. Hunger as *desire* is at the root of the constitution of subjectivity. Famine itself can be read as a symptom: a point of overdetermination, of condensation of different strands of meaning. In that sense, there is a fantasy space reserved for it. I looked at the relation of famine and scarcity to market economics in chapter 2. To explore this further, I look at Žižek's account of the role of desire in late capitalism.

For Žižek, late-capitalist liberal-democracy has an impasse at its heart centering around the role of desire. In Lacan's work desire is not something that can be satisfied as such. As Žižek expresses it, "desire is sustained by lack and therefore shuns its satisfaction, that is, the very thing for which it 'officially' strives."[85] Desire is sustained by the unattainability of its object and by the gap between its official motivation and its actual function, which is to provide a way of accommodation with a primordial lack, a lack inherent in the human condition as such. In Lacan, an empirical object fills out the role of the primordially lost Thing and becomes the object-cause of desire. Whereas Freud might argue that the obstacles of convention that are put in place to prevent the attainment of the object of desire—the sexual object, for example—serve to heighten desire, in Lacan's account these obstacles are there precisely to avoid the possibility of the discovery that the object is unattainable *as such*: "*external hindrances that thwart our access to the object are there precisely to create the illusion that without them, the object would be directly accessible*—what such hindrances thereby conceal is the inherent impossibility of attaining the object."[86]

In late capitalism, the immediate satisfaction of desire through superabundance, permissiveness, and accessibility of objects threatens to suffocate desire. We are approaching a position where for *some* of us the attainment of all possible empirical objects of desire is conceivable in practice. This will become even more so, Žižek claims, with the advent of so-called virtual reality. Superabundance threatens desire by supplying the means for its satisfaction; the function of the object-cause of desire is thwarted by this. Although officially desire exists to be satisfied, in Lacanian terms desire provides a means of transcending a primordial lack; it exists precisely because it has to be insatiable. By providing an impossible object, the impossibility of fulfillment itself is sublimated.

However, this superabundance is not without its opposite: scarcity and deprivation. For Žižek, drawing on Hegel, *universal* abundance is impossible, since in capitalism "abundance itself produces deprivation."[87] Excess and lack are structurally interdependent in a capitalist economy. The system produces both together. Some live in abundance and plenty while others live in scarcity and deprivation. Superabundance goes hand in hand with its opposite.

This does not mean that notions of desire are irrelevant in the context of a world where for large numbers of people the necessities of life itself—food, water, shelter, and freedom from violence—are hard to come by. On the contrary, Žižek's account of notions of desire as a concealment of an inherent lack and the need to sustain desire in conditions of superabundance can help us to understand some of the paradoxes of responses to events such as famines and the sight of incredible suffering in these and other disasters.

The object of "Ending Hunger" functions as just such an impossible or unattainable object-cause of desire in the Lacanian sense. *Here we have the irony of a desire sustained by the object of removing the very thing—deprivation—that is indissolubly linked with the superabundance that threatens desire.* Rather than the question of "Why, when there is such an abundance of food, do so many people starve?" the question becomes "Why, when we are so well provided for with an abundance of everything we can possibly desire, do we desire the one thing we cannot have, that is, a world without others who are deprived?" At least part of the answer, I argue, can be found in the Lacanian account of desire.

Not only do we desire the thing we cannot attain, but we put obstacles of convention in the way of attaining it. These obstacles are seen in arguments of developmentalists that portray famine as complex: it needs further research, we have to act carefully and take into account the feelings of those we want to help, and so on.[88] Thus in famine we have an answer to Žižek's question: "So the big enigma is: how, through what kind of limitation of access, will capitalism succeed in reintroducing lack and scarcity into this saturation?"[89] Lack and scarcity are reintroduced as *someone else's* lack and scarcity—as hunger, the stranger that waits outside *some other* door. For those of us who live in an excess of abundance, desire becomes the (impossible) desire for a world free from scarcity: a hunger for a world free from hunger.[90]

CONCLUSION

The tenth anniversary of the famine and the Live Aid concert was celebrated in 1995. The Live Aid concert was replayed on BBC2, accompanied by a film of a return visit by Geldof to Korem in Ethiopia.[91] A conference was held in Addis Ababa, bringing together aid agencies who had helped on the Ethiopian side during the famine and those who had been involved in the cross-border operation into the then rebel-held areas of Eritrea and Tigray.[92] A new account was produced, and the events of 1984/85 received, retroactively, their meaning. For developmentalists, the 1984/85 aid operation has been renarrated as an instance—probably the first instance—of humanitarian intervention in what are now called "complex emergencies." While the Addis conference emphasized the need to find a new way of delivering aid in conflict situations and acknowledged the terrible mistakes made by NGOs working in Ethiopia in 1984/85—the abuses of aid by the regime at that time, in which Band Aid too must have been implicated, are now well known in the aid community—the

Geldof film concentrated on an account of how ordinary people were alive in Ethiopia today as a direct result of the help received from the viewers responding to the Band Aid appeals.

Geldof's return could be seen as an accommodation, although not a return, to science. Once the trauma has been faced, the moment of traversing the fantasy has passed. Holding the place of the hole in the symbolic order perhaps cannot be sustained: a new totalizing master signifier has to be produced.[93] In fact Band Aid, as de Waal points out, became just as much part of the problem as the other agencies: arguably in part because of their inability to take an African perspective, they returned to the position of the prevaricating experts that initially they had been keen to sidestep.[94] The legacy of the Band Aid movement, however, is perhaps more apparent in the rise of humanitarianism and humanitarian intervention by the international community in parallel with, and as a justification for, depoliticization and technologization.

The political entails a never-ending process of decisioning. Justice is impossible: it can only be *to come*, never here.[95] I argue in chapter 6 that a Derridean approach would contend that whether or not to respond in situations of human suffering is a decision that has to be made in a particular instance. But there may be something else involved here. In the last words of *Tarrying with the Negative*, Žižek argues that "our very physical survival hinges on our ability to consummate the act of assuming fully the 'non-existence of the Other,' of tarrying with the negative."[96]

What has to be explained about the social order is how something emerges that is perceived as *not just a collection of others*. Why do people posit the existence of something called "society," something that is not just a sum of individuals but something of a different order?[97] What happens is that the social is what is *posited* by individuals by their social activity, and *simultaneously* an independent *foundation* of that activity. Lacan avoids opting for either of the logical alternatives: the social substance preexists as sui generis, in other words, in-itself; or it is produced by individuals positing it. Instead, Žižek argues that there is another solution to this impasse or impossibility:

> Lacan asserts that *it is this very impossibility which links an individual to his spiritual substance*: the collective substance emerges *because* individuals can never fully co-ordinate their intentions, become

transparent to each other. . . . The very surplus . . . of the *collective* over the mere *collection* of others, thus bears witness to the fact that others forever remain an impenetrable enigma. In short, *impossibility is primordial, and the spiritual substance is the virtual supplement to this impossibility.*[98]

In this respect Lacan gives us an account of the social that parallels Derrida's account of the metaphysical. Both make crucial use of the notion of undecidability or impossibility or, in other words, of the limits (or irrelevance) of the knowable. Without these limits, a community founded on rational argumentation would suffice. This leads to the picture of the social order as a symbolic fiction or a semblance of one that exists merely as a presupposition by each of the individuals of the already existing coordination of all other individuals.[99] My argument is that we saw such a gesture of precipitate identification in Band Aid.

The international community comes into existence not as the result of some successful search for a common denominator, some set of basic values, humanitarian or scientific, that we can all subscribe to, but by the presupposition of the common denominator as already present. However, the price to be paid, according to Žižek, is that future is confused with past; what is to come is confused with what is already here. This is where the precipitate, performative gesture, the declaration, comes in: "the declaration sets in motion a process which, retroactively, will ground it."[100] If we wait for the international community to appear before we act as if it exists, we will be waiting for a very long time.

In examining responses to distant suffering, we can distinguish an international community based on the scientific episteme (knowledge/abstract/objective) and an international community based on humanitarianism (neutrality/common humanity/universal rights). The latter translates to a claim to common humanity through suffering and trauma, the former to a regime of truth based on a scientific epistemology. In the end neither tells us what to do, though both claim the authority to do so. Neither is based on responsibility, involvement, or subjectivity. Both lead to a neutrality that conceals the decisioning process or the political moment. This moment is not a moment *in time*; it involves "tarrying with the negative." The question remains as to whether, and *in what time*, such an impossible solution might be possible.

6

Complex Emergency
and (Im)possible Politics

The incorporation of hunger into the discourses of modernity gave rise to a depoliticized, technologized approach to famine theorizing and famine relief, as I discussed in chapter 2. A brief challenge from Sen's entitlement approach became depoliticized, as did the flicker of repoliticization that arose with Band Aid and the famine movement in the mid-1980s. At the end of the previous chapter, I argued that there might be a way of maintaining a more avowedly political stance in relation to suffering and disaster, one that acknowledges the need for a continual process of involvement and decisioning and does not try to set up principles or regulate practices according to abstract general rules, and one that does not succumb to modernity's hunger for certainty.

I examine some recent attempts to do this—to repoliticize famines—particularly those that introduced the notion of famine as a complex political emergency. Much of this work began as an endeavor to reintroduce an explicit consideration of violence and the political missing in Sen's work. As I argued in chapter 3, violence is always already present in the violence of the law and the state even in the absence of military conflict. Efforts to repoliticize run the risk of constituting no more than a struggle to reverse the view of relief or humanitarian aid as a solution to famine. Such a reversal is problematic because it does not move outside the frame of modernity. It lays itself open to a further technologization, and I will discuss how that is taking place. What is needed is a displacement or resituating of the problematics of humanitarianism and aid. Humanitarianism can be a deeply conservative activity in the face of the emergence of new political formations, or it can be an emancipatory move. Which it is depends on the specific configuration in which it is located and the political substance with which it is articulated or linked at any particular moment. These articulations can be contested: they are not natural or given.

Sen's analysis leads to a practice of relief that relies on technical and managerial solutions. Despite their radical contention that relief can be a cause of famine, there is a risk that theories cast in terms of complex emergency and those who draw on this work will retain a reliance on experts—this time experts in other fields: conflict resolution and prevention, for example. We should take a much broader view of the role of force and violence, eschewing easy dichotomies between peace and conflict or famine and plenty in favor of a questioning of connections and relationships. This would lead to a more critical approach to specific situations in which decisions must be, and are, made. Rather than seeing famines, conflicts, and poverty as problems that call for technical solutions from experts, or codes of practice and principles of action, what is needed is political and ethical engagement that produces a climate where responsibility for decisions about intervention and aid is inescapable.

The struggles to articulate and rearticulate theories of famine can be seen as continuing attempts to reinscribe the political—attempts to rewrite what counts as needing ethical or political decisions—and hence to situate the boundaries to what will be accepted as the terrain of the expert or the professional. In part the debates reflect struggles between different disciplines for the ear of policy makers and the funding that goes with it. Is famine a question of food supply, to be tackled by greater agricultural production, new varieties of seed, and advanced farming methods, in which case it is the province of the agriculturalist? Or is it a matter of poverty and vulnerability, to be tackled by a welfare safety net, public works programs, and early warning systems? Or is it a question of an emergency situation calling for action by the relevant nongovernmental organizations? Further, if it is the latter—if it is an emergency—is it a question of humanitarian relief, military intervention, or conflict resolution? In what is seen by some writers as a new (dis)order emerging in a post–cold war world,[1] the old disciplinary boundaries are being renegotiated. The debate over whether resources should be concentrated on relief efforts or on longer-term development projects, and the so-called relief-development continuum, has been revived by some[2] and considered irrelevant by others.[3] Development specialists saw their assumptions challenged in cold war crises and witnessed the balance swing in financial terms to massive funding for high-profile relief operations.[4] The result is that "with declining resources for development and sizeable resources devoted to complex emergencies, agencies are packaging programmes in order to capture humanitarian relief dollars."[5]

The term "complex emergency" originated in the late 1980s, in relation initially to conflicts in Africa and the Gulf, where for the UN it meant "a major humanitarian crisis of a multi-causal nature . . . a long-term combination of political, conflict and peacekeeping factors"[6] It is a contentious term.[7] The term's widespread use in describing conflicts may be due to the way it diverts attention from any possible political connotations, instead blaming the complexity of the causal picture, and excuses the absence of solutions.[8] For Joanna Macrae and Anthony Zwi, complex emergencies are "intentionally created and . . . sustained in order to achieve their objectives of cultural genocide and political and economic power . . . a potent combination of political and economic factors driving and maintaining disaster-producing conflicts."[9] Duffield shows how complex emergencies are distinguished from natural disasters:

> So-called complex emergencies are essentially political in nature: they are protracted political crises resulting from sectarian or predatory indigenous responses to socioeconomic stress and marginalisation. Unlike natural disasters, complex emergencies have a singular ability to erode or destroy the cultural, civil, political and economic integrity of established societies. . . . Humanitarian assistance itself can become a target of violence and appropriation by political actors who are organic parts of the crisis. Complex emergencies are internal to political and economic structures. They are different from natural disasters and deserve to be understood and responded to as such.[10]

The notion of complex emergencies still draws on notions of food shortage or stress.[11] In that sense, its repudiation of the image of a natural disaster is unsuccessful. For writers like Larry Minear and Thomas G. Weiss, complex emergency refers to "situations that may be triggered by natural disasters such as droughts or floods, by intercommunal violence with roots in ethnic or religious tensions or exclusionary politics, by economic or environmental stress, or by some combination of these factors."[12] The danger of this is that the political or military conflict that characterizes such emergencies is seen as secondary and as complicating efforts to provide relief. Assistance is assumed to be well intended and politically neutral. Complex emergencies are still seen as natural and hence as a failure of an otherwise benign social and political system. Viewing them in this way has important implications for policy and still leads to solutions of a technical or managerial nature. A new object of analysis has been produced and new disciplines enabled, but these take place within the same discursive practices, those of modernity's regime of truth.

David Keen, Mark Duffield, and Alex de Waal are three writers whose work draws on their experiences of famines in the Horn of Africa. There are considerable similarities in their initial approach; however, they end up advocating different positions. Not only is there a split in their views, there is significant divergence in the way their work and that of others like them has been used or appropriated. Although they represented a challenge—a repoliticization—in the form of an attempt to move away from modernity's view of famine, like other moves before them the outcome of their work has been the introduction of new objects of study and analysis and the production or interpellation of different technologies. These include the analysis of famines as complex emergencies, the notion of techniques of aid that do no harm, the use of conflict resolution procedures, the localization of action and the withdrawal of international aid, and the move to elaborate principles of humanitarianism. This has led to much controversy over the aims and methods of humanitarian aid, producing strongly held and deeply divided positions.[13]

In the conclusion of this chapter, I examine attempts to analyze this process as an example of the power of the framework of modernity. If that framework is to be challenged it is important to understand how it works and where its strengths (and its weaknesses) lie. This book has attempted to contribute to that understanding in the case of famines. In the end, the aim should be perhaps not to escape from the limits of modernity (since it is in any case an attempt that inevitably fails), but to continually disrupt and challenge modernity and the power relations that it installs. Modernity's search for closure is bound to continue, but it is also bound to flounder. Similarly, challenges to modernity will not succeed in replacing it (since they operate within it), but they cannot fail either, since modernity's strength lies in a fantasy. The foundations it claims are illusory, and their establishment as the taken-for-granted reality within which we operate is a political process like any other.

CHALLENGES TO SEN'S PICTURE OF FAMINE

While Sen examines how legal structures can prevent access to food by those without legitimate entitlements, theoretical approaches developed in response to famines in the Horn of Africa in the 1980s emphasize the role of the extralegal, namely, war and conflict. This has led to a situation where debates about complex emergencies and the humanitarian intervention that claims to respond to them are replacing talk of famines and famine relief. According to this view, not only may relief not solve the problem as it may never reach those it is intended to help, but, in addition, it may actually produce or exacerbate famine. Famine is seen as a product of conflict, and donations of food in this context can increase the benefits to the winners. Famine is once more a political issue.

David Keen, Mark Duffield, and Alex de Waal all distinguish their work from Sen's entitlement theory of famine.[14] As witnesses and analysts of relief operations in conflict zones in the Horn, they each developed an alternative analysis. They are collectively described as "intellectual originators of [a] novel paradigm."[15] Initially their work was focused on loosening famine theory from its links with entitlements and vulnerability, to stress instead the active response of victim communities and the view of famine as a process over time. De Waal, in his analysis of famine in the Sudan, argued that relief operations do not take into account or support the coping strategies of victims, who see famines not as disastrous events but as processes. The outcome most feared was not death by starvation but destitution, total deprivation of assets.[16] In his later work he calls for a political contract established at a local level rather than intervention by the international humanitarian community.[17]

Keen argues that there are both winners and losers in famines, and more care needs to be taken over the distribution of relief to prevent appropriation by the powerful. Keen has analyzed the way famines are not prevented and, indeed, are often actually promoted by those who stand to gain—either from the famines themselves or from the relief operations. These winners can include the governments of countries where famines occur, local economic interests or warring factions, *and* international agencies or donor governments.[18]

Extending the analysis to international political economy, Duffield argues that what we have now is an entirely novel post–cold war situation—a situation of more or less permanent complex emergency.[19] Famine is rearticulated with counterinsurgency and conflict. Those who initially saw themselves as specialists responding to economic oppression and underdevelopment have instead adopted a political position and are engaging in human rights advocacy.[20]

POLITICAL ECONOMIES OF FAMINE

One of the things long known by those who have experienced famines is that not everybody suffers: there are winners as well as losers. This leads to silence about famine that can carry on down the generations, as this quotation shows: "They got the big house and maybe 100 acres around it. That is one of the reasons that nobody talks about the famine. Because there's nobody as greedy as a landowner or a property owner. . . . he wants more."[21] It is not just landowners who benefit. Again in Ireland, a study of eyewitness accounts in oral history concludes:

> The reason why relief food was often of such poor quality is in many accounts attributed to the diversion of supplies by local committees or powerful individuals or their agents, who are said to have sold it to friends and relations or to have used it to feed their own livestock. . . . The useless nature of [relief works], together with the circumstances of labour upon them helps to explain the general dislike of them which exists; as does the frequent opinion that the landlords and their sycophants "got the fat of the money" and used the schemes to benefit their own holdings. . . . "Grabbers" . . . took up the farms of evicted people. . . . The bitter memory of such "grabbing," whether by shopkeepers, agents, or strong farmers, was lasting; like other bitter memories it is often the cause of reticence among people today.[22]

David Keen's work looks at the benefits of famine *as part of* the ordinary social process, rather than as exceptional.[23] This follows earlier work by Amrita Rangasami that suggested that famine could be seen as a combination of exploitative processes that produce beneficiaries as well as victims.[24] According to Keen it is necessary to change our view of what famine is: "As long as we continue to identify famine simply with starving to death, the idea that famine may confer economic benefits is hard to credit."[25] If famine is not viewed simply as deprivation that leads to death by starvation, but as part of a wider process during which the whole way of life as well as the livelihood of certain groups of people are threatened, it can be seen that other groups might benefit from it. Failures of famine relief can be seen as part of the same process. Although inadequate relief measures make famine worse, Keen argues that such failures can also be a policy success for powerful local groups and can accord with the strategic interests of international donors.

Keen looks at the struggle over resources—a struggle for domination—that produced famine among the Dinka people in Sudan in the 1980s. His approach is Foucauldian in inspiration: it looks at the hidden functions that policy practices serve and at how agendas are shaped.[26] It does this by examining the concrete specifics of the exercise of power. The famine among the Dinka of southern Sudan can be seen as a combination of exploitative processes, in all of which the role of force is crucial. The first process was a loss of assets brought about largely by direct militia raids on the Dinka. Both the Sudanese government and local groups who were active in the militia benefited from this, Keen argues. The government gained in its strategy against the Sudan People's Liberation Army, in its attempt to gain access to oil reserves on Dinka land, in its general need for land for mechanized agriculture, and in its policies against Islamization. The local militia groups gained property seized, grazing, and people captured—either for their labor as slaves, the ransom money they might raise, or for sexual exploitation in the case of women.

The second process was the increase in prices. This was to the benefit of traders and merchants, who held stocks of grain until prices rose sufficiently for them to make a profit. A third process leading to famine was the restriction of the Dinka's normal survival strategies: their options were limited, in the main by the activities of the militia. Famine foods—wild foods or the milk and meat of their animals—were not available to them. They could not walk to other areas for fear of attack. Finally, the fourth process Keen describes was the inadequacy of international relief. Relief was a threat to groups benefiting from the famine, but donors and agencies went along with the vested interests of beneficiary groups. Aid was distributed by the army and a lot of it went for private gain. It was directed by the government to areas they wanted it to go, not to areas of greatest need: the latter were said to be inaccessible.

Action by international donors, including the EC, USAID, and the UN, was unhelpful, according to Keen, not only because donors followed the wishes of the Sudanese government, but also because they did not monitor the results of their work and did not address the underlying conflict. The definition of famine they used, "the widespread equation of famine with mortality," allowed "the presentation of a belated response as an early one."[27] Relief was too little too late, and the donors were too willing to listen to the views of the government, which Keen argues was one of the beneficiaries of the famine, as to what form relief should take: "Limited definitions of 'what was to be known' (including who was to be consulted) helped to underpin a narrow definition of what was to be done."[28] This only changed when media attention made it risky for the donors not to act; otherwise they followed their own strategic and political interests, which included respect for Sudanese sovereignty.

Keen argues that the implications for policy are that the wide impact of relief should be recognized. It is not just a question of providing food to those in need. To be effective, the violence and conflict that produce the famine process should be tackled.[29] There should be an attempt to understand the strategies and needs of the oppressors who benefit from the famine and to support the strategies of the victims. Sometimes an effective policy may be to provide large quantities of relief to all areas even though a lot of it may go to the exploiters, as this may reduce the pressure on the victims. Most significantly, the humanitarian sphere is not separate. In the Sudan, there was little monitoring of the relief effort and no attempt to tackle the conflict itself, which in Keen's analysis had *produced* the famine. It was the Dinka's lack of political or military power rather than any failure of entitlements or any overall shortage of food that led to their predicament. They had been a relatively well-off group before the famine.

Mark Duffield looks at how these processes of famine and aid can reinforce the power of already powerful groups by institutionalizing emergency situations. What had been seen as a disaster or a humanitarian emergency is now seen as institutionalized in the political economy of entire regions of the world. Duffield argues that "what has been neglected is that famines can result from the conscious exercise of power in pursuit of gain or advantage."[30] He goes on to suggest that a new analysis is needed for the new forms of political economy that are now in place in areas of "permanent emergency" such as the Horn of Africa: "Within this framework, famine can be regarded as an outcome of a process of impoverishment resulting from the transfer of assets from the weak to the politically strong."[31] This has serious implications, Duffield argues, for the international humanitarian system.

The situation in the Horn of Africa is a "regional parallel economy" that operates alongside the formal economy. This parallel economy is based on asset transfer from the weak to the strong; it is contested and controlled by different sectarian interests, some within the state. However, Duffield argues that this is only part of the structure of permanent emergency: "the disaster relief response of the international community also has a role. . . . aspects of this intervention also connect with the parallel economy."[32] Increasingly, disaster relief is channeled not through governments but through NGOs acting as contractual agents for international (state or UN) donors. Often in the form of consortia of a number of agencies, they operate in particular areas or around particular functions.[33] Despite this, much disaster relief has become increasingly important as a means of state support. This arises from the way relief is organized: government finance has benefited from artificially low official exchange rates; food aid has been diverted, for example, to military use; governments have by a variety of stratagems prevented food aid from reaching certain areas; profitable grain speculation has taken place.

Relief operations are usually unable to tackle the processes of resource depletion that give rise to famine. It is very difficult to attract support for any program that would do this, because such a program would be redistributing assets to the weak and as such would arouse local opposition from those whose interests are threatened. This opposition often cites the dependency that aid is said to produce. Further problems arise if the relief operation goes against sovereignty, as did relief work in Eritrea in the 1980s. Duffield concludes that

international emergency intervention, rather than eradicating the disaster situation, appears in many respects to strengthen it. By its nature . . .

[it] opens new avenues for the politically strong in terms of state financial support, legitimation, access to strategic resources and speculative profit. Unwittingly, it has become an integral part of an established political economy which, pathologically, is geared to the spread of absolute poverty and human degradation.[34]

The political economy of intervention is racist in character, due to the way developmentalism ignores the production of relations of power or reads them in terms of preexisting ethnic or racial groups.[35] Duffield argues that developmentalism is a mirror image of "New Barbarism"—the view of the post–cold war world as a new world (dis)order. This relationship in the external or international realm is paralleled by that in the internal or domestic realm between multiculturalism and new racism. Duffield claims that these two also mirror each other. Both pairs of apparent opposites—developmentalism/ New Barbarism and multiculturalism/new racism—have a large area of shared terrain. Both lack a concern with power, and both see ethnic identities as natural and rooted in history. Both share a functional approach that leads, in the case of developmentalism, to aid technocracy.

Duffield claims that what we are witnessing in these structures of permanent emergency is a withdrawal of the West, not increasing involvement, and the emergence of new political and economic forms, not a breakdown of stability. The new aid paradigm is not designed to solve the problems of areas such as Africa so much as to contain them. What is at stake is whether the inequalities and polarization between regions of the world (which are growing, not becoming smaller) and the instabilities to which they give rise can be managed effectively. Increased barriers to migrants and asylum seekers and the trend toward providing for refugees and war-affected populations in their own countries is compelling evidence of this movement toward containment.[36]

In what Duffield calls "post-modern conflict," what we are seeing is the emergence of novel political forms. Rather than an image of failed states, we have a series of "innovative and long-term adaptations to globalisation."[37] This includes the development of forms of political authority that are no longer based on territorial integrity or a bureaucratic system or even on consent. These include warlordism and the privatization of security. Alongside these are forms of economic activity that are outside the formal economy and yet often as significant or more so in value. The narcotics economy is an example. Despite the fact that it is "contrary to images of scarcity and breakdown" associated with civil war, "protracted instability is symptomatic of new and expanding forms of political economy."[38]

In this work we have moved a very long way indeed from the image of famine as caused by drought or crop failure. Keen's study of the Sudan emphasizes "the interaction between local processes of famine and the actions and discourses of donors,"[39] and he concludes: "The real roots of famine may lie less in a lack of purchasing power in the market . . . than in a lack of lobbying power within national (and international) institutions. Sen has emphasized how poverty can lead to famine. . . . it may be equally, or more, important to investigate how powerlessness leads to famine, as people's access to the means of force and political representation collapses."[40] Keen's study looks at the concrete details of the exercise of power and how certain practices are established as self-evident, although it tends to concentrate on identifying the functions of processes for *already powerful* groups, rather than exploring the production of sites of power or how their production might be contested. Duffield follows this in showing how the plethora of institutional arrangements built on less than accountable organizations have focused and concentrated power, making disaster a permanent way of profit for powerful interests and moving the process of decision and power even further from the victims.

FAMINE CRIMES

Alex de Waal argues that political arrangements are the most significant. Although his first writings were conceived as a challenge to Sen, de Waal's later work can be seen as an attempt to extend Sen's arguments to their political conclusion. De Waal argues that the eradication of famine is not a question of international humanitarianism but of a political contract that has to be framed locally. An anti-famine political contract involves "a political commitment by government, recognition of famine as a political scandal by the people, and lines of accountability from government to people that enable this commitment to be enforced."[41] This locates the solution to famines squarely in the political arena. The central question is what kind of political system would serve to prevent famine?[42] In this context a humanitarianism that claims to be separate from and not a part of politics is no help.[43]

De Waal's notion of a famine contract is not at all the same as the social contract advocated by Locke or Rousseau.[44] Rather, it arises from a popular movement that successfully claims a new right and forces an unwilling government to comply. He draws parallels with the civil rights movement in the United States or the pro-democracy movements in Eastern Europe. Following the success of the primary movement, the gains are defended by the secondary activism of lawyers and journalists.

The situation in Tigray in Ethiopia in 1984/85 is an example of the type of political contract de Waal is talking about.[45] We saw in chapter 4 how the Ethiopian government used the famine for their own political ends. In the rebel-held areas the famine was politicized in a radically different way, as part of a general sociopolitical mobilization.[46] The TPLF strategy conquered the famine, and de Waal finds it ironic that there was no attempt to repeat the practices of REST, whereas by contrast the new model that arose through the Band Aid operation in the government-held areas became the model for interventions elsewhere.[47] There was no publicity for what was going on, and the relief organizations, which were in fact very tightly linked with the liberation fronts, chose to adopt an ostensible humanitarian neutrality, or rather they were constrained to do so in order to continue to attract donations.[48]

On both sides of the conflict, the authorities involved in the distribution of relief supplies pretended to a neutral humanitarianism while explicitly using food aid to further their military and political objectives. Donor governments colluded in this so that their own political aims and their support for their chosen factions in the dispute could be maintained. Aid agencies continued to work and to claim that their work was charitable and not political. If they had not, their own continuance as organizations would have been threatened. According to de Waal's analysis, Western publics contributed for a series of dubious reasons, partly guilt, partly compassion, while continuing on the whole to remain safely remote from any actual political involvement.

Technical solutions to famines are harmful, but the problem is not a lack of political will, a missing link to bridge the gap between expertise and its implementation.[49] The growth of "the humanitarian international" has weakened the forms of political accountability that would have helped prevent famine. The humanitarian international is an international elite of professionals who staff aid agencies and who work as academics, journalists, consultants, conflict resolution specialists, and human rights workers. They share a common culture, can easily move between the different institutions, and "with each big relief operation, [become] more powerful and more privileged."[50] The new humanitarianism has been freed from its earlier limitations with disastrous consequences. The debates that followed the end of the cold war produced "new legal and ethical principles that justified unprecedented actions by international institutions" and made it more difficult to achieve an anti-famine political contract.[51] An example is Somalia, where the UN/U.S.–led intervention force was set in motion at just the point where local political movements that aimed at preventing and resolving famine were making progress, aided by a form of partnership between the Somalia Red Crescent Society and the International Committee of the Red Cross that had developed on the ground and, later, by the brief work of Mohamed Sahnoun as UN Secretary General's Special Representative in Somalia.[52]

"Actually existing humanitarianism," despite its adoption of abstract codes of conduct, suffers from three tendencies. First, it is regressive: on the whole aid empowers central authorities, particularly governments, and thus has a conservative, regressive effect—as part of the authority structure themselves, aid agencies are opaque and unaccountable, presenting "a sense of mystery and inscrutability."[53] Second, pressures on aid agencies as organizations and, increasingly, as government subcontractors mean that their own institutional interests will prevail over their stated aims. Their lack of a clear position and their need for a high media profile militate against any progressive political engagement. Finally, agencies adopt what has been called a "humanitarian code language," which involves, de Waal claims, systematic distortion of the realities on the ground. Agencies lie about where their resources go and deceive themselves about how far they are from meeting their own codes of conduct: "the duplicity of the humanitarian language makes frank evaluation impossible."[54] These three tendencies make it very difficult for humanitarian organizations, since "the aid process is almost always opposed to the very principles to which the humanitarian international aspires: rights, empowerment of the poor, democracy and accountability."[55]

The most important addition to the "humanitarian arsenal" is humanitarian intervention. De Waal argues that the hope of humanitarian intervention has not been fulfilled, although this hope brought together both international lawyers, who saw in it the possibility of the enforcement of human rights and the laws of war, and humanitarians, who hoped for "the triumph of compassion over political obstacles such as sovereignty."[56] What has happened instead is the rise of a new concept of "humanitarian impunity"—a privileged status for UN forces and humanitarian agencies: "the automatic legal privileging of *all* actions by *all* humanitarian agencies."[57] De Waal gives several examples:

> The UN resolutions adopted in connection with the flight of the Kurds and the Yugoslav and Somali conflicts all refer to the protection of aid convoys—a new doctrine in humanitarian action—while not one mentions the victims. The civilian population is regarded solely as the recipient of aid, which is lavishly provided with the best of intentions, even if it never reaches its intended target. Preoccupation with logistics eclipses concern for human beings, as if soap or milk powder could prevent bombs from falling on hospitals, or generosity could offer protection against murder and expulsion.[58]

Increasingly, military force was employed not to protect civilians but to protect aid convoys. It was the rights of humanitarians to carry out their operations, not the rights of victims, that were protected. The case of Somalia was "an extraordinary experiment in philanthropic imperialism." This military intervention was an example of

> the starkest manifestation of the power of the humanitarian international. In the abstract, there is a strong *prima facie* case for external intervention in a country without any form of political contract, in order to provide basic protection and assistance. The realities are very different. . . . intervention is the antithesis of politically progressive local accountability which is the essence of protection against famine.[59]

Throughout his work, de Waal is calling for attention to the realities on the ground: the practical problems of negotiations between conflicting interests in conflict situations, the impossibility of clear-cut codes of practice or directly applying abstract rules, and a recognition of the complexities of organizations claiming humanitarian motivation.

In this sense de Waal's argument is very close to that put forward in this book. However, despite his own warnings about the problems of "abstract" solutions, his suggestion of "an anti-famine political contract" tends also to be rather abstract, particularly in the way that it is linked to liberal democratic politics. To some extent it is that same liberal politics with its notion of a social contract that, woven as it is into the fabric of modernity, reflects and sustains much of the reliance on abstraction, whether in the form of abstract technical knowledge or abstract moral principle, of which de Waal is so critical.

TECHNOLOGIZATION

A series of critical approaches to war and hunger has been developed from the work of Duffield, Keen, and de Waal or independently. These approaches set out to overcome the limitations of earlier perspectives on famine and relief aid. The linkages between famine and conflict are explored, the limitations of existing modes of humanitarian intervention exposed, and features of conflict that promote hunger investigated. The analysis that focuses on so-called complex political emergencies is one of these approaches. It is one that was particularly well funded in the United Kingdom in the late 1990s, and a number of large research projects were started.[60] Other work includes Mary Anderson's injunction to "do no harm,"[61] which incorporates an interest in methods and procedures for conflict resolution, and the elaboration of ethical and humanitarian principles to guide agencies to "do the right thing."[62] The turn to local solutions advocated by de Waal is another.

In each case there is a risk that a retechnologization will take place, in other words, that the political implications of the critical approach will be forgotten in favor of a return to calculability. Also, there is a risk that the critical approach will do no more than overturn or reverse the previous orthodoxy.

Retechnologization takes place when we find the articulation of another series of general principles or rules that, it is claimed, can be applied to particular cases. For example, Mary Anderson accepts the ambiguous potential of aid in conflict situations, but despite this and her assertion that the framework tool she provides for analyzing the impact of aid on conflict "does not prescribe actions," it does nonetheless technologize. It identifies categories of information aid workers should find useful, organizes that information, points out relationships among the categories and "allows one to anticipate likely outcomes of programming decisions."[63] Her task is to "identify clear patterns in the ways that external aid worsens conflict" in order to "identify programming alternatives to avoid these negative impacts" and "predict what will happen in any given setting and choose programming approaches that are least likely to do harm and most likely to do good."[64] Her report concludes with a series of "steps which aid workers can follow to anticipate outcomes and make better choices among programming options."[65] Clearly this is an attempt to address the need to act with responsibility and to make decisions, however limited by circumstances, that will help to bring about desired aims. It acknowledges the need to engage with the particular— but it does not accept the corollary: that general rules about how to act cannot be prescribed. It still attempts to set out a program or, in other words, a technology—this time a technology of responsible action or what we might call prescribed responsibility. This approach is in line with modernity's preferences, but "a reliance on codes and frameworks as guides for action prevents the development of a politics of responsibility potentially better attuned to the context of crisis."[66]

David Campbell argues that the search for new codes in the face of humanitarian crises evident in Anderson's work and in the various codes so far established or debated—the Development Assistance Committee Guidelines, for example[67]—embodies the particular assumptions and logics of modernity. It is paralleled by a concern for normative frameworks in academic debate. Both are "in pursuit of moral criteria to establish normative principles that would separate the 'good' from the 'bad.'"[68] Both rely on a notion of humanism that is distinctly modern, and one that (it has been argued) is insufficiently human or sets humanitarianism too low. It assumes that the attainment of the distinct individuality characteristic of liberalism is enough to qualify as being human, whereas other writers contest this and contend that being human always already entails responsibility for the other man.[69] But Campbell is arguing not for a new principle, but for a historicized and politicized humanitarianism to replace the depoliticized, dehumanized neutrality currently advocated. Modernity's view of the individual human subject is of an individual who is by nature free until subjected to the arbitrary and controlling exercise of power. Power itself is localized in central, usually state, authority. In contrast, a Foucauldian view sees power as productive of subjects, not as merely controlling. Power does not exist as something to be possessed but as a power relation, and this power relation cannot take effect without resistance, otherwise it would not be a question of power. In this view, freedom only arises and subjects are only produced as such through relations of power. If freedom and autonomy are not seen as something absolute, but as always situated *within* relations of power, then our conception of human autonomy changes. Our aim then becomes, according to Campbell, "minimising domination in society, while realising that a state devoid of relations of power is impossible."[70] This is enabled by a rearticulation of human solidarity based not on the liberal notion of ourselves as preexisting subjects with inherent rights, but on our common and necessary subjection to practices of power and governmentality. It does not produce a new set of technical or normative principles, since what action should be taken in particular circumstances is "irretrievably political and immune to epistemological equations."[71]

The current search for codes and principles to direct humanitarianism in the face of concerns about its effects is one aspect of technologization that critical approaches encounter. We also find technologization when a series of propositions or policy recommendations that rely on quantification are produced, although in each case something different is involved. New objects of analysis are produced alongside the disciplines that gather knowledge about them. For the complex emergency approach, for example, we find that we need to measure not nutritional status but violence:

> What is urgently required is for aid donors to give greater attention to protecting the human rights and economic strategies of the most vulnerable groups. . . . [One] key starting point in any attempt to improve the effectiveness of international aid [includes] . . . changing what is counted and measured—moving away from a concentration on measuring nutritional status and towards assessing levels and types of violence.[72]

This can be seen as an attempt to recenter famine theory as a *structure* on conflict analysis, trying to erase the excess (the violence of the extralegal in Sen's approach, as discussed in chapter 3) by recentering around it. One center is substituted for another.[73] But "the force of *différance* prevents any system . . . from encompassing its other or its excess"[74] To attempt to form another system, one that can be closed and can produce technical answers (solutions that operate according to a rule that can be applied by experts), risks repeating the previous error. It leads to a denial of the need for or the possibility of political or ethical choice; since the answers are provided by an analysis that claims to be closed and complete (scientific), there is no opening for a decision or a judgment. If complex emergency theory calls for a rejection of the analysis of food supply or entitlements in favor of a study of levels and types of conflict, it may provide an alternative theoretical system, but it still endorses the possibility of closure. This endorsement sidelines the political and the ethical and defers to experts. The alternative is to accept the impossibility of closure, "the limit of any system of meaning."[75] The impossibility of knowing positively, once accepted, opens the possibility of the ethical relationship: "the excess to the system cannot be known positively; hence there is no beyond to . . . the undecidable. We must try, if we are to remain faithful to the ethical relationship, to heed its otherness to any system of conventional definition."[76]

REVERSAL OR UNDECIDABILITY?

The related risk that critical approaches to aid carry, in addition to that of retechnologization, is the risk of concluding that aid should be seen not as a *remedy* for famine but as its *cause*. Duffield and other writers have argued that famine relief and humanitarian aid strengthens the disaster situation and produces a structure of permanent emergency.[77] Forms of international action—through NGOs, food aid, development projects—have institutionalized famine as one of several forms of disaster and emergency. This approach has been objectified in institutional arrangements. These are now an integral part of a social system in which forms of oppression that produce and reproduce inequality, injustice, and disregard of human rights are perpetuated. The conclusion is that not only does international emergency intervention and aid *not solve the problem* of famine; aid, through the mechanisms of power and control that it enables to operate, *produces* famine.

This is a situation of inversion: where aid is no longer the *remedy*, aid is the *cause*. However, any simple opposition of remedy and cause breaks down—one is always haunted by the other. In modern logocentric thought, analysis proceeds through the production of a series of dichotomies: man/woman, memory/forgetting, inside/outside, and so on. These oppositions work only because one of the pair is always contaminated by a trace of the other. The concept of "inside," for example, has absolutely no meaning without that of "outside." Thus the distinctions through which this specific mode of thought operates are prone to collapse.[78] The example of the supplement is useful here. A supplement (to a book, for example) is at one and the same time *necessary* and *unnecessary*, because if the book is not complete, the supplement is not a supplement but part of the book. Viewed in this way, famine relief is the supplement.

The new approach to famine and complex emergency crucially does not admit to its own conclusion about relief. Despite arguing that aid causes, or renders possible, famine and human rights abuses, it is nevertheless *almost immediately* suggested that the solutions could be found if aid donors approached the situation in a different way.[79] This move is characteristic of logocentric analysis: the possibility of the negative is recognized—aid does indeed cause famine—but then in a move that is almost simultaneous, this possibility is discounted or rendered accidental—the problem with aid can be overcome through educating donors.

Following through the deconstructive analysis that I am attempting here, we could perhaps argue that, on the contrary, famine relief as supplement is *undecidable*: whether it solves or exacerbates the famine is undecidable—and hence *political*. We have here an example of the "double contradictory imperative."[80] On the one hand, famine relief must be given; food cannot be withheld from the starving. On the other hand, famine relief must be withheld; it is the relief aid that is causing the famine.[81] This leads to an aporia, which takes the form of a contradiction. But "ethics, politics and responsibility, *if there are any*, will only ever have begun with the experience and experiment of the aporia."[82] In other words, it is only through the logic of the aporia, *where a decision has to be made*, that we will arrive at something that can be called "political." Without this, what we are doing is following a program, claiming a priority for knowledge, and an epistemological certainty: "when a path is clear and given, when a certain knowledge opens up the way in advance, the decision is already made, it might as well be said that there is none to make: irresponsibly, and in good conscience, one simply applies or implements a programme."[83] It may not be possible to escape the program, but if this is what is happening, then moral or political responsibility does not come into it: "the condition of possibility of this thing called responsibility is a certain *experience and experiment of the possibility of the impossible: the testing of the aporia* from which one may invent the only *possible invention, the impossible invention.*"[84] It is through the experience of this contradiction or aporia, to which no answer can be found, that ethical responsibility becomes possible. By accepting the question of famine relief as undecidable, in the sense that an answer cannot be found through *knowledge,* the way is opened to the process of *ethico-political decision.*

Thus, while the Sen or Malthusian approaches to famines present relief as unproblematically the *solution,* and some of the work we have been discussing is taken to imply that relief is (more or less unproblematically) the *problem,* a Derridean deconstructive approach supposes that relief is the *undecidable*: it is not a question of formulating a more adequate theory of famine or a more sophisticated technology of relief, it is a question of politics and decision.[85]

There is nothing mysterious or difficult about what is being argued here. Many aid practitioners recognize that their job consists of tackling a series of dilemmas. There is no way that this aspect of the work can be avoided, and no way that these dilemmas can be resolved by some overall, all-embracing framework of rules or practice guidelines. Although I am not suggesting that we manage without them entirely, such frameworks only take us so far: they do not provide answers to specific cases. There are inevitably points where the rules or frameworks cannot be unproblematically applied. Reality does not match the categories we prepare for it, however carefully, with whatever expertise those categories are constructed. In practice, reality always exceeds expectations. The trick is to acknowledge that the dilemmas practitioners face are inescapable, and, more than that, these dilemmas are a reflection of the importance of the activity in which they are engaged. Were everything capable of being set down in advance, the crucial moment of ethico-political decision would be absent and the job of the aid practitioner or the commander of a military intervention or the member of a peacekeeping force would be that of an automatic application of a program. Very little human activity is like that—most is highly political or highly ethical or both. Involvement in situations of crisis and conflict is intensely so.

The existence of impossible dilemmas *does not* mean that we do nothing. Indeed, it is only in these situations that we can act responsibly. It brings us back to Derrida's comment:

> That justice exceeds law and calculation, that the unpresentable exceeds the determinable cannot and should not serve as an alibi for staying out of juridico-political battles, within an institution or a state or between institutions or states and others. . . . Not only *must* we . . . negotiate the relation between the calculable and the incalculable . . . but we *must* take it as far as possible, beyond the place we find ourselves and beyond the already identifiable zones of morality or politics or law, beyond the distinction between national and international, public and private, and so on.[86]

David Campbell emphasizes this point—that it is the presence of the undecidable that leads to politics rather than technology: "Were everything to be within the purview of the decidable, and devoid of the undecidable, then—as Derrida constantly reminds us—there would be no ethics, politics, or responsibility, only a programme, technology, and its irresponsible application."[87] The terrain of the undecidable is the "impossible" terrain. But this *does not* mean that taking responsibility limits one to "impossible, impractical and inapplicable decisions."[88] One must rather "assume a responsibility that announces itself as contradictory because it inscribes us from the very beginning of the game into a kind of necessary double obligation, a *double bind*."[89] For example, it is impossible at one and the same time to both give and withhold relief, but this is what we must take responsibility for. What this might imply is a responsibility for finding a way to contain in each decision the principle with the specificity of its application. In other words, in applying any principle, such as the need to give aid, divergences between the principle and "the concrete conditions of [its] implementation, the determined limits of [its] representation, [and] the abuses of or inequalities in [its] application as a result of certain interests, monopolies, or existing hegemonies" need to be denounced.[90]

In the case of famine relief, these divergences might arise through aid being offered that was inappropriate to the particular situation, through the misuse of aid by powerful groups within the relief administration, or through the appropriation of aid for military purposes. Resolving this in any one of a number of possible impossible ways "is what politics is all about."[91]

CONCLUSION

If the separations assumed by both theories of entitlement failure and some theories of complex emergencies and conflict-famines are accepted, the question becomes one of what duties or obligations there are on states to intervene to prevent human rights abuses and suffering. Much of the literature on food aid and famine takes this approach, as do debates on humanitarianism more generally. But we do not have to start from here—if we contest the dichotomies on which this thought is based and which sustain a view of the political as separate, we can perhaps move toward an approach based on an analysis of the relationships of *connection* between people. We then move from the abstract, logical, analytical approach implied by the question: "Should we *intervene* to stop exploitation and domination?" to the more practical, specific question: "*How* can we best act to promote good relations?"

This formulation draws on Carol Gilligan's work, which examines the different "moral" voices of men and women.[92] The former question—in the masculine mode—takes the manner of action for granted, presuming it to be a matter of fact; the latter assumes the necessity for action and considers what form it should take. The former sees a conflict between life and property (state sovereignty) that can be resolved by logical deduction, the latter the fracture of a human relationship that must be mended with its own thread. Rather than looking at the problem as one of understanding the logic of justification, what the "different voice" does is pose it as a question of the nature of choice: "There's really no way around it because there's no way you can do both at once, so you've got to decide, but you'll never know," is how Gilligan quotes the account given by Amy, an eleven-year-old girl in her study.[93] This is very close to Derrida's notion of the undecidable.

Famines can be seen not so much as the outcome of processes with winners and losers, though they are that, but as processes where relationships between people have produced unacceptable results and transgressed limits of humanity. The web of these relationships is more complex and extensive than simple separations into winners and losers, developed and underdeveloped, rich and poor can account for, and living with the inevitable antagonism—undecidability—at the heart of the social relation is arguably what we must learn to do.

In this context, famine theory becomes irrelevant. We do not need to ask "what caused the famine?" if famine is not seen as a natural or economic event or disaster.

It cannot be assumed, as is commonly done, that famine (any more than conflict) is an ill that the entire international community will fight against. This is a position reinforced by ideologies of famine as disaster. It is reinforced by ignoring that, as Rangasami reminds us, we all benefit in one way or another from famine. It is reinforced by positions that see the rule of law as unproblematically nonviolent. The work of Keen and Duffield has shown that an analysis of complex emergencies in the Horn of Africa can reveal numerous beneficiaries of famines and has made the link between poverty and powerlessness and between exploitation and violence, acknowledging the violence inherent in "peaceful" state and international structures of dominance and oppression. Although Keen pointed out that international donors also have much to gain from famine, the more comfortable assumption has been that the complexities or political difficulties of the situation have occasionally meant that donor governments have inadvertently prolonged or worsened the famine situation. I would argue that we need to look dispassionately at the way donor governments profit from famine. In order to do this, we need to differentiate between the governments and NGOs in donor countries and the motivation of people in those countries who, perhaps recognizing or remembering the ghosts of famines past, may wish to alleviate the suffering of fellow human beings elsewhere in the world. Occasionally, the latter can provoke useful action by donor governments. More frequently, this motivation is appropriated by those development professionals and NGOs who claim the expertise to translate these desires into practice. Their claim to neutrality and humanitarianism must be continually questioned. Their decisions are just that and their expertise is no more than a *claim* to knowledge. We need to inquire on whose behalf the agencies are acting, rather than assume that their own account can be accepted uncritically. Such assumptions can lead to episodes like that in Ethiopia where "famine assistance, provided primarily by Western governments and non-governmental organizations, reinforced the policies and programs that produced the 1984–1985 famine."[94] Such examples are not exceptional; indeed, they may be widespread. However, they are not confined to cases where famine is linked with military conflict. There are many instances where states under the rule of law have caused, condoned, or turned a blind eye to famines in their jurisdiction, as we have seen in the examples of China, Bengal, and Britain. Nor is the discussion confined to the extremes of famine. The implication of the argument I have put forward is that it applies equally to decisions about development and the alleviation of poverty more broadly.

The answer is *not* to stop providing famine relief, development assistance, and humanitarian aid. It is crucial to stress again that although I have claimed that famine relief can be regarded as *undecidable,* this does not mean that a decision cannot or should not be made. It merely implies that such a decision is just that: a political or ethical decision. It cannot be left to experts or the international community. It is not a technological or managerial matter that can be resolved by better theories or techniques. Whether any particular decision is just or not will remain unknown. But although justice itself is impossible, we have a duty to act with responsibility in addressing what Derrida calls the double contradictory imperative. This process—an interminable process of decision making and questioning—*is* politics. The problem exceeds "the order of theoretical determination, of knowledge, certainty, judgement, and of statements in the form of 'this is that.'"[95] Or, as Amy said: "You've got to decide, but you'll never know."[96]

Conclusion

Hunger and thirst are mindful as well as embodied states, and they come trailing their own metaphorical meanings and symbolic associations.
— NANCY SCHEPER-HUGHES, *DEATH WITHOUT WEEPING*

Aspects of hunger in the physical, embodied sense of a desire for food have been explored in this study of famine. Discursive practices constitute famine in modernity in particular ways and these technologize and depoliticize questions of famine relief. Practices of food aid, as disciplinary practices, impose a techno-disciplinary framework that naturalizes certain political relationships. Some forms of response to famines challenge this technologization, but these are retechnologized in developmentalism, humanitarianism, and other ways.

Nancy Scheper-Hughes, in her book *Death without Weeping*, makes a similar argument following a study of the medicalization of hunger in Brazil. There, people who are starving are given medical treatment (dietary supplements, tranquilizers, and so on) for a nervous complaint, *nervos* (what Scheper-Hughes calls "the madness of hunger"), instead of the food they need. Many die as a result, but the political consequences to the government of admitting to a problem of hunger and starvation among the population are averted. The people themselves do not quarrel with the description of their suffering as *nervos*, and Scheper-Hughes asks why. Hunger has been depoliticized and tamed by medicalization: "Through the idiom of *nervos*, the terror and violence of hunger are socialised and domesticated, their social origins concealed."[1] There are two routes for the sufferers. One contains the possibility of protest, of criticism. The other, which is the path they have taken, is to silence the pain, "surrendering more and more . . . to the technical domain of medicine, where [the symptoms] will be transformed into a 'disease' to be treated with an injection, a nerve pill, a soporific. Once safely medicated, however, the scream of protest is silenced, and the desperate message in the bottle is lost."[2] Scheper-Hughes's suggestion is that we should repoliticize medicine; she concludes by asking "what medicine might become if, beyond the humanitarian goals that it espouses, it could see in the suffering that enters the clinic an expression of the tragic experience of the world." Her response is: "We might have the basis for a liberation medicine, a new medicine, like a new theology, fashioned out of hope."[3]

I want to consider this response. Ironically, is it not precisely this *hope*, this desire, that got us into the predicament in the first place? Scheper-Hughes has pointed out the parallel between bodily hunger and starvation, an embodied state, and the hunger for knowledge or redemption associated with modernity and Western metaphysics. The hunger for certainty or completeness that drives modernity is an impossible desire: "Man as such is 'nature sick unto death,' derailed."[4] It is through this social fantasy that the symptom appears as some disturbing intrusion, something that we can overcome, and liberation appears possible.[5] Derrida argues that justice is impossible, we can only ever have justice to come. I argue with Derrida that in accepting this *as a promise, not as a project,* an alternative, one that does not technologize, might be found.

The hunger for certainty that drives the discursive and social practices surrounding famine relief and food aid is a peculiarly modern condition, one that produces a specific modern response to famine. Modernity's hunger is based on the view of certainty to be found in Plato. There, it is universal laws in their abstraction that are real and the world of change that is illusory. Plato equates *belief* with the changing, indefinite objects of everyday life, which may appear either beautiful or ugly, depending on one's point of view. *Knowledge,* on the other hand, is limited to the unchanging reality of absolutes, Beauty, and so on. It is philosophers who have access to truth: "those who are not philosophers are lost in multiplicity and change."[6] In modernity, the natural and social scientists have replaced Plato's philosophers. It is they who claim to have access to, and be the guarantors of, certainty and truth.

According to Friedrich Nietzsche, in this search for certainty modern Western philosophy has engaged in a process of dehistoricization and disembodiment. This entails depoliticization and technologization. Philosophers believe in what *is*, that is, in what is fixed or immutable.[7] However, they cannot find anything of the sort in the world, and they locate the reason for their failure in the deception of the senses. The escape from this illusion of history and becoming is an escape into the security of philosophy, that is, the security of disembodied, dehistoricized ideas in the mind.[8] The body is disregarded. This is a mistake:

> "Reason" is the cause of our falsification of the evidence of the senses. In so far as the senses show becoming, passing away, change, they do not lie. . . . Being is an empty fiction. The "apparent" world is the only one: the "real" world has only been *lyingly added.*[9]

Nietzsche thus inverts the Platonic view that it is change, mutation, and becoming that leads us astray.[10] On the contrary, it is our search, our hunger, for "unity, identity, duration, substance, cause, materiality, being" that has entangled us in error.

The perpetuation of the error can be located in language or in reason as the metaphysics of language: "I fear we are not getting rid of God because we still believe in grammar."[11] Western metaphysics, embodied in language, produces identity or essence through processes of exclusion: a constitutive outside is necessary, and its exclusion has to be immediately forgotten to produce the illusion of being. Derrida's work on metaphysics leads to the argument that justice is impossible and striving for justice is striving for something that we can never say, for certain, exists: we can have only justice *à venir,* justice to come, in the future, the *avenir.*

The process of technologization can be seen as one that works by concealing the futility of the search for certainty or sovereign subjectivity. There is a place for the political only if there can be no appeal to a higher authority whose claims are already thoroughly embedded, recognized, and legitimated. The political involves a process of negotiation or struggle between claims. Michel Foucault points out that knowledge is part of that struggle, not something outside it. Depoliticization, as we see it in the case of famines and of humanitarianism, arises when scientific absolutism's claim to be that higher authority succeeds. This has important political consequences since it is in a sense only by accepting the impossibility of solving the problem of famine in general that we can act to avert it in particular instances.

Modernity's desire or hunger for philosophical certainty, the sovereign subject, and the bounded society translates into processes that depoliticize and technologize. Physical hunger is treated as a social emergency, a humanitarian or economic crisis; this reflects the (all-too-human) hunger for emancipation, a better world, a solution to social ills in some utopian totality. Approaches to famine in the academic literature and in practices of intervention and aid generally involve this depoliticization and technologization. Political decisions are on the whole replaced by what David Campbell calls "a programme, technology and its irresponsible application."[12]

But far from being a problem that could be solved if only the technical procedures were improved, famine is a product of power relations. It is not a question of finding better early warning systems, more participatory development projects, or faster methods of delivering relief. Nor is it a question of seeking the deeper, more structural causes of famines, nor its complexities. Famine is a product of violence. Even where war is not implicated directly, the state enforces laws of property that can lead to some people's starvation. Aid processes and interventions to which technical concepts of famine give rise are practices that reproduce particular political and international power relations.[13]

One of the supports of a technologized approach is its claim to gender neutrality. It relies on the objectified, universal subject of legal-rationality. It seeks timeless, total, disembodied answers. Theory or general laws are where truth resides, not the practical, the particular, or the embodied. It operates through dichotomies such as subjective/objective, where opposites are hierarchically ordered and the quantifiable, the objective, the hard facts valorized.[14] The separations that are necessary to produce abstract theory are reflected in those that produce the masculine and the feminine and place them in a similar hierarchy. One place we see this is in the analysis of responses to famine and humanitarian crises, where a reaction of compassion, sympathy, and guilt to images of suffering is labeled emotional and hence of less value. What is needed, this way of thinking claims, is an appreciation of the root causes, the higher truth, before solutions can be found. Emotional responses are unhelpful.

The abstract, disembodied, degendered, calculating, nonemotive—and hence depoliticized—analysis is a technical approach that works only by deferring ethico-political questions. In studying famine, we have an issue that continually resists and challenges the process of depoliticization. Famine cannot help but be an emotive subject, and one that is embodied. The images of famine victims that we see or hear about may in a real sense be ghosts by the time we see them, but as specters they draw our attention to what has been and *must be* excluded to produce "the comfort of theories."[15]

As we saw in chapter 3, violence is implicated in both the process of law enforcement and in the founding moment of the law as a legal system. Both are, of course, associated with the state, which, by definition, has the authorized use of violence. The notion of undecidability leads to the conclusion that the moment of decision, unlike the application of a rule or the following of a code of law, is not calculable. It is precisely this incalculability that leads to the idea of the impossibility of justice and the need for ethico-political decision. The decision itself is a terrifying nontime or nonplace, where there is no subject and where we are facing the traumatic real. As was argued in chapter 5, this moment of decisioning has much in common with the "moment of concluding" in Lacan. The latter is the moment that constitutes the social order, but only through a precipitate gesture for which there is no guarantee. We have to make a move for which there are no secure grounds. This moment is, nevertheless, something that we must face: the fact that it is undecidable is not an excuse for inaction. It is in the very process of negotiation and contestation around the undecidable that politics takes place and that the social order and subjectivity is constituted. The temptation is to avoid this uncertainty, to move promptly to a reinstitution of certainty. Our method of control is technologization. The real is well and truly hidden and the social ideologically constituted as something within our theoretical grasp.

However, this production of an essence that we can grasp puts an end to the possibility of ethical decision. The ethical only returns as a search for ethical certainty, a moral code, accessible to reason. We see this in the search for moral criteria—ethical certainty—for intervention on humanitarian grounds. What is sought is a basis in knowledge for action, a technology of intervention. The search for moral criteria is not what we should be pursuing either. On the contrary, we must continue to negotiate the relation between the calculable and the incalculable in each particular case in which action is called for.

This includes negotiating boundaries such as the public/private and domestic/international. These distinctions are interesting. Jean Bethke Elshtain has argued that the distinction between public and private needs to be maintained.[16] This goes against much feminist debate, which contends that the private is political. If it is not maintained, Elshtain argues, then the private realm, which for her is the ethical realm, becomes calculable, in the same way that the public realm already is. Turning now to the domestic/international distinction, we can make a similar argument. If the public but *domestic* realm is the realm of the calculable where morality in terms of a fixed, codified ethic within a bounded community—the state—is possible, then the international community is in a sense unbounded and lacks a fixed morality. It remains an arena of decisioning and politics as well as ethics. Changing this and creating a codified international ethics by making the principles of humanitarianism explicit in international law could be highly dangerous.

This was taking place in the 1990s. Nonintervention and sovereignty were being renegotiated in the name of humanitarianism and "new norms were emerging about when and how the international community could justifiably intervene."[17] Boundaries were being drawn founded on claims to know—a new regime of truth—about what counts as ethnic conflict, human suffering, and so on. This meant that a technology of humanitarianism was being set up *to* replace the politics of decisioning and the responsibility that such a politics entails. Such a technology would provide grounds for government action justified by abstract, objective criteria.

Once an area is technologized in this way, the decisioning process is effectively embodied in definitions of the field and its subjects or objects of concern. Like a legal document, academic publications begin with definitions that set out what things are. If famine *is* a shortage of food, it is almost impossible to argue that food aid should *not* be sent to famine areas. Those who have the institutional or professional power that goes with what counts as a regime of truth in the modern world—techno-science—have the power to make definitions and thus to dictate what should be done. Part of the power of this technical authoritarianism rests on its incorporation and appropriation of the norm of openness and transparency. Its claim that rational debate is permitted, even welcomed, is perhaps its most ideologically powerful move. If humanitarianism is technologized, intervention is no longer a question of responsibility and political decisioning but the application of a new system of international law to a case. Any challenge would have to come from charismatic figures like Bob Geldof who can constitute (briefly) an opposing regime of truth.

The way we react to the problem of famine is analogous to the way we react to the problem of humanitarian crises in general. In both cases, by seeking a totalizing solution we avoid any ability to deal with the political reality of decisioning and the complexities of (impossible) possible solutions to actual difficulties. The practical political aim of this book is neither to understand famine nor to provide a solution. These two logocentric approaches both abstract and depoliticize.[18] In reacting to famine the way we do—as academics theorizing about famine and intervention; as development professionals, NGOs, and governments offering food aid to famine regions; as individuals responding to famine relief appeals; and as the international community providing humanitarian intervention—the form of our reaction is in part what constitutes us as subjects. It also constitutes an international community and the relationships within it. In a large part our reaction is a particularly modern one: we depoliticize and technologize famines, discounting political and ethical responsibility in favor of a search for abstract causes and criteria for aid. The aim of this book is simply to call for a repoliticization. This is not a once and for all process, but a continuing engagement.

It is useful to recall that there are no technical solutions: the search may respond to and maintain modernity's way of life, but it is futile. As Richard Ashley has put it, "there are no timeless, universal, already prepared answers. There is only the reality of actions working upon actions across all those varied localities where people struggle amidst difficulties, dangers and ambiguities to somehow make life go on."[19] The search for technical answers is itself political and supports the powerful, not the suffering. It is the buttress for forms of governance that reduce life to calculability.

Notes

INTRODUCTION

1. Michael Buerk, voice-over to Mohamed Amin's film report of the Ethiopian famine, *Nine O'Clock News*, BBC1, 23 October 1984.

2. My argument in this respect is similar to Zygmunt Bauman's in *Modernity and the Holocaust* (Ithaca, N.Y.: Cornell University Press, 1991).

3. Giorgio Agamben, *Homo Sacer: Sovereign Power and Bare Life*, trans. Daniel Heller-Roazen (Stanford, Calif.: Stanford University Press, 1998). Agamben develops Michel Foucault's work on governmentality and biopolitics; see, for example, Michel Foucault, *The History of Sexuality*, vol. 1, *An Introduction*, trans. Robert Hurley (Harmondsworth, England: Penguin Books, 1990).

4. Michel Foucault, "Truth and Power," in *Power/Knowledge: Selected Interviews and Other Writings 1972–1977 by Michel Foucault*, ed. Colin Gordon (Brighton, England: Harvester Press, 1980).

5. A number of writers have drawn attention to the predominance of and the problems with technical solutions to famines; their work is discussed in greater detail in chapter 6. See, for example, Alex de Waal, *Famine Crimes: Politics and the Disaster Relief Industry in Africa* (Oxford: African Rights and the International African Institute in association with James Currey, 1997), 1–2; Mark Duffield, "The Symphony of the Damned: Racial Discourse, Complex Political Emergencies, and Humanitarian Aid," *Disasters* 20, no. 3 (1996): 173–93. Others have discussed technologization in relation to security practices (Michael Dillon, *The Politics of Security* [London: Routledge, 1996]) and humanitarianism (David Campbell, "Why Fight:

Humanitarianism, Principles, and Post-Structuralism," *Millennium: Journal of International Studies* 27, no. 3 [1998]: 497–521.) For a recent discussion in relation to famine relief, see Barbara Hendrie, "Knowledge and Power: A Critique of an International Relief Operation," *Disasters* 21, no. 1 (1997): 57–76. For an earlier analysis of technocratic approaches to disasters, Hendrie refers to Kenneth Hewitt, *Interpretations of Calamity* (Winchester, England: Allen and Unwin, 1983).

6. For a discussion of the distinction between politics and the political, see Jenny Edkins, *Poststructuralism and International Relations: Bringing the Political Back In* (Boulder, Colo.: Lynne Rienner, 1999), chapter 1.

7. Mary B. Anderson, *Do No Harm: How Aid Can Support Peace—Or War* (Boulder, Colo.: Lynne Rienner, 1999), published earlier as "Do No Harm: Supporting Local Capacities for Peace through Aid" (Cambridge, Mass.: Collaborative for Development Action, Local Capacities for Peace Project, 1996).

8. De Waal, *Famine Crimes*, xvi.

9. Ibid.

10. Nicholas Xenos, *Scarcity and Modernity* (London: Routledge, 1989).

11. De Waal, *Famine Crimes*, xvi.

12. Mark Duffield, "NGOs, Disaster Relief, and Asset Transfer in the Horn: Political Survival in a Permanent Emergency," *Development and Change* 24 (1993): 131–57.

13. For a discussion of how this works in practice, see, for example, David Keen, *The Benefits of Famine: A Political Economy of Famine and Relief in Southwestern Sudan, 1983–1989* (Princeton: Princeton University Press, 1994); and Barbara Hendrie, "Knowledge and Power: A Critique of an International Relief Operation," *Disasters* 21, no. 1 (1997): 57–76. These writers are discussed further in chapter 6.

14. A number of writers have analyzed modernity's hunger for truth, including, for example, Michel Foucault, Jacques Derrida, Jacques Lacan, and Slavoj Žižek. I use their work here to explore responses to and responsibility for famine. I have given a detailed introduction to this body of thought in Jenny Edkins, *Poststructuralism and International Relations*.

15. David Campbell, "Why Fight," 521. See also David Campbell, *National Deconstruction: Violence, Identity, and Justice in Bosnia* (Minneapolis: University of Minnesota Press, 1998).

16. Michel Foucault, "Intellectuals and Power: A Conversation between Michel Foucault and Gilles Deleuze," in *Language, Counter-Memory, Practice: Selected Essays and Interviews*, ed. Donald F. Bouchard (Ithaca, N.Y.: Cornell University Press, 1977), 208.

17. Agamben traces the separation of bare life and politically qualified

life as a distinction drawn between the private or domestic sphere *(oikos)* and the public sphere *(polis)*.

1. PICTURES OF HUNGER

1. Michel Foucault, *The Order of Things.*

2. Giorgio Agamben, *Homo Sacer: Sovereign Power and Bare Life,* trans. Daniel Heller-Roazen (Stanford: Stanford University Press, 1998).

3. Lead-in to the report on the *Nine O'Clock News,* BBC1, 23 October 1984. The film was shot by Mohamed Amin of VisiNews.

4. Michael Buerk, *Nine O'Clock News,* BBC1, 23 October 1984.

5. John Simpson of the BBC, quoted in Mary Kay Magistad, "The Ethiopian Bandwagon: The Relationship between News Media Coverage and British Foreign Policy toward the 1984–85 Ethiopian Famine," master's thesis, Sussex University, 1985, 86.

6. Greg Philo, "From Buerk to Band Aid: The Media and the 1984 Ethiopian Famine," in *Getting the Message: News, Truth, and Power,* ed. Glasgow University Media Group (London: Routledge, 1993), 121.

7. Alex de Waal, *Evil Days: Thirty Years of War and Famine in Ethiopia,* An Africa Watch Report (New York: Human Rights Watch, 1991), 178.

8. Fintan O'Toole, "Hungry Eyes" (prod. Mary Price, research Ellis Hill), BBC Radio 4, 1 November 1995.

9. Extract from letter from Nicholas Cummins, JP, to the Duke of Wellington, 17 December 1846, quoted in R. Dudley Edwards and T. Desmond Williams, eds., *The Great Famine: Studies in Irish History 1845–1852* (Dublin: Browne and Nolan for the Irish Committee of Historical Sciences, 1956), 275. The letter was published in *The Times* on Christmas Eve, 24 December 1846.

10. Margaret Kelleher, *The Feminisation of Famine: Expressions of the Inexpressible?* (Cork: Cork University Press, 1997), 2.

11. Megan Vaughan's account of famine in Malawi is interesting in this context (*The Story of an African Famine: Genter and Famine in Twentieth-Century Malawi* [Cambridge: Cambridge University Press, 1987]).

12. Kelleher, *The Feminisation of Famine,* 228.

13. Extract from letter from Nicholas Cummins quoted in Kelleher, *The Feminisation of Famine,* 25.

14. David Arnold, *Famine: Social Crisis and Historical Change,* New Perspectives on the Past (Oxford: Basil Blackwell, 1988), ix.

15. See, for example, Peter Garnsey, *Famine and Food Supply in the Graeco-Roman World* (Cambridge: Cambridge University Press, 1988).

16. For accounts of the conflict from the EPLF and TPLF side, see, for example, Lionel Cliffe and Basil Davidson, eds., *The Long Struggle of Eritrea for Independence and Constructive Peace* (Nottingham, England: Spokesman, 1988); Dan Connell, *Against All Odds: A Chronicle of the Eritrean Revolution* (Trenton, N.J.: Red Sea Press, 1993); James Firebrace and Stuart Holland, *Never Kneel Down: Drought, Development, and Liberation in Eritrea* (Nottingham, England: Spokesman for War on Want, 1984); and Amrit Wilson, *The Challenge Road: Women and the Eritrean Revolution* (London: Earthscan, 1991).

17. See Mark Duffield and John Prendergast, *Without Troops and Tanks: The Emergency Relief Desk and the Cross Border Operation into Eritrea and Tigray* (Lawrenceville, N.J.: Red Sea Press, 1994) for a detailed examination of the Emergency Relief Desk, a consortium working in Eritrea.

18. *The Forbidden Land* (Alter-Ciné, 1989), videotape. See also Trish Silkin and Barbara Hendrie, "Research in the War Zones of Eritrea and Tigray," *Disasters* 21, no. 2 (1997): 166–76.

19. See Peter Cutler's work for a discussion of responses on the government side ("The Development of the 1983–1985 Famine in Northern Ethiopia," Ph.D. diss., London University School of Hygiene and Tropical Medicine, 1988).

20. Jason W. Clay and Bonnie K. Holcomb, *Politics and the Ethiopian Famine 1984–1985,* Cultural Survival Report 20 (Cambridge, Mass.: Cultural Survival, 1986), 193.

21. See, for example, Ian Potts and Michael Keating, *Humanitas II: Humanitarian Intervention* (Zeist, Netherlands: Television Trust for the Environment, 1992), videotape.

22. The symposium "Famine in Ethiopia: Learning from the Past to Prepare for the Future" was organized by the Ethiopian Relief and Rehabilitation Commission and the Economic Commission for Africa and the Inter-Africa Group in honor of the ten-year commemoration of the 1984/85 famine in Ethiopia. It was held in Addis Ababa from 15 to 18 March 1995. The symposium brought together a wide range of UN and government officials, donors, NGOs, and human rights organizations and researchers. Its statement was issued as "The Addis Ababa Statement on Famine in Ethiopia: Learning from the Past to Prepare for the Future," Ethiopian Relief and Rehabilitation Commission, Economic Commission for Africa, and Inter-Africa Group, in *Famine in Ethiopia: Learning from the Past to Prepare for the Future* (Addis Ababa, 18 March 1995), typescript.

23. See the paper given by Solomon Inquai at the symposium; interview with Vanessa Sayers, InterAfrica Group, Addis Ababa, April 1995.

24. This is represented as the view of recipient countries by researchers

elsewhere, such as Mark Duffield and John Prendergast in *Without Troops and Tanks.*

25. Ethiopian Relief and Rehabilitation Commission, "Addis Ababa Statement."

26. There remains inevitable disagreement about the causes of the famine or famines in Ethiopia. For example, de Waal argues strongly that while drought and the government's agricultural policies were contributory factors, "the principle cause of the famine was the counter insurgency campaign of the Ethiopian army and air force in Tigray and north Wollo during 1980–85" (De Waal, *Famine Crimes,* 115). He documents a series of inventions and distortions by government sources that claimed a series of failures of rainfall and accuses the RRC of "fabricating an explanation of a crisis" (114). Christopher Clapham, on the contrary, maintains that "drought was a major precipitant of the 1984 famine, which was also at its most intense in areas, notably Wollo, which were not directly affected by war; there were equally deep-seated ecological sources of famine. Insofar as government action caused the famine, it was as much through misguided agrarian policies as through war" (personal communication, 7 April 1999). See also Christopher Clapham, *Africa and the International System: The Politics of State Survival* (Cambridge: Cambridge University Press, 1996). Clapham points out that the 1995 Ethiopian government, like the 1985 one, had its own official mythology of the famine to maintain, in this case linked to the "struggle," especially in Tigray, and hence to war as a source of famine. The 1995 governments in Ethiopia and Eritrea comprised people previously involved in the TPLF and EPLF; a number of Western theorists of the 1980s and 1990s shared a similar link to that side in the war arising from the NGO solidarity with the insurgents when they were "partners in a common enterprise," that of delivering aid in "liberated areas" during the war (Clapham, *Africa and the International System,* 229). Clapham supports his position by describing the involvement of NGOs in antigovernment propaganda in the form of fabricated claims that the government side was diverting aid to the Soviet Union (ibid.). For another discussion of this issue, see Trish Silkin and Barbara Hendrie, "Research in the War Zones of Eritrea and Tigray."

27. Paul Donovan, "A Decade of Drought," *The Guardian,* 6 December 1994, Guardian Education, 9–11.

28. Donovan, "A Decade of Drought," 10.

29. "Life after Live Aid," dir. John Macguire, prod. Andrew Coggins (broadcast on BBC2, 28 July 1995).

30. Why 1995 should have become the year of commemoration is interesting. As with the Ethiopian famine, beginnings and endings are controversial. In Ireland's case, although "Black '47" is remembered as the most

catastrophic of the famine years, 1845 was the first year the potato blight appeared. Cormac Ó Gráda remarks on this in "Why Ireland Starved," *Times Literary Supplement*, 10 March 1995, 8.

31. Examples include John Killen, *The Famine Decade: Contemporary Accounts 1845–52* (Belfast: Blackstaff Press, 1991); Noel Kissane, *The Irish Famine: A Documentary History* (Dublin: National Library of Ireland, 1995); Helen Litton, *The Irish Famine: An Illustrated History* (Dublin: Wolfhound Press, 1994); Patrick O'Sullivan, ed. *The Meaning of the Famine* (New York: Leicester University Press, 1996); Cathal Póirtéir, *The Great Irish Famine*, Thomas Davis Lecture Series (Cork: Mercier Press in association with RTE, 1995); and Cathal Póirtéir, ed., *Famine Echoes* (Dublin: Gill and Macmillan, 1995), published to accompany the RTE radio series of the same name. Terry Eagleton, *Heathcliffe and the Great Hunger* (London: Verso, 1995), although containing only a brief essay on understandings of the famine (1–26), seems to have jumped on the bandwagon. Other recent works include P. M. Austin Bourke, *The Visitation of God? The Potato and the Great Irish Famine* (Dublin: Lilliput Press, 1993); Donal Kerr, *A Nation of Beggars? Priests, People, and Politics in Famine Ireland 1846–52* (Oxford: Clarendon Press, 1994); Christine Kinealy, *This Great Calamity: The Irish Famine, 1845–52* (Dublin: Gill and Macmillan, 1994). Before this, standard works included R. Dudley Edwards and T. Desmond Williams, *The Great Famine: Studies in Irish History 1845–1852* (Dublin: Browne and Nolan, for the Irish Committee of Historical Sciences, 1956), commissioned for the 100th anniversary; and Cecil Woodham-Smith, *The Great Hunger* (London: Hamish Hamilton, 1962).

32. John Percival, *The Great Famine: Ireland's Potato Famine 1845–51* (London: BBC Books, 1995). The series, entitled *The Great Famine* and first broadcast in 1995, was produced by BBC Northern Ireland, executive producer Maureen Gallagher, producer John Percival, director Peter Lawrence. There were radio programs, too. As well as the RTE program referred to above, there was one on Radio 4: Fintan O'Toole, "Hungry Eyes" (prod. Mary Price, research Ellis Hill), BBC Radio 4, 1 November 1995. Web sites were active, and famine memorials were constructed.

33. See Stephen J. Campbell, *The Great Irish Famine: Words and Images from the Famine Museum, Strokestown Park, County Roscommon* (Strokestown, Ireland: Famine Museum, 1994).

34. Niall O'Ciosáin, "Hungry Grass," *Circa* (1995): 24–27.

35. Woman of Doire na Mainsear, Anagaire, County Donegal, quoted in Roger J. McHugh, "The Famine in Irish Oral Tradition," in *The Great Famine*, ed. R. Dudley Edwards and T. Desmond Williams, 391–436 (Dublin: Browne and Nolan, 1956).

36. Account from County Donegal, Ireland, in McHugh, "Famine in Irish Oral Tradition," 430.

37. Kelleher, *The Feminisation of Famine*, 5, 113–14.

38. Ibid., 154, note 15.

39. Ibid., 228.

40. Christine Kinealy, *A Death-Dealing Famine: The Great Hunger in Ireland* (London: Pluto Press, 1997), 1–15. This divide is the subject of an article by Brendan Bradshaw, "Nationalism and Historical Scholarship in Modern Ireland," *Irish Historical Studies* 26, no. 104 (1989): 329–51.

41. Kinealy, *Death-Dealing Famine*, 2.

42. Ibid., 5.

43. As examples, Kinealy quotes Peter Mathias and Roy Foster (*Death-Dealing Famine*, 5).

44. Ibid., 9. The role of relief practices is discussed further in chapter 4.

45. Kinealy, *Death-Dealing Famine*, 3.

46. Quoted in ibid., 4.

47. Ibid., 13–14.

48. James Donnelly, "The Construction of the Memory of the Famine in Ireland and the Irish Diaspora 1850–1900," paper presented at Cambridge University, 1996, cited in Kinealy, *Death-Dealing Famine*, 13.

2. THE EMERGENCE OF FAMINE IN MODERNITY

1. Michel Foucault, *The Order of Things: An Archaeology of the Human Sciences* (London: Routledge, 1970).

2. Ibid., 236.

3. Ibid., 237.

4. Ibid., 235.

5. Ibid., 54–55.

6. Michel Foucault, *Power/Knowledge: Selected Interviews and Other Writings 1972–1977 by Michel Foucault,* trans. Colin Gordon (Brighton, England: Harvester Press, 1980), 131.

7. Michel Foucault, *The History of Sexuality,* vol. 2, *The Use of Pleasure,* trans. Robert Hurley (Harmondsworth, England: Penguin Books, 1992), 11–12. For a further discussion of Foucault's work, see my *Poststructuralism and International Relations: Bringing the Political Back In* (Boulder, Colo.: Lynne Rienner, 1999); see also Hubert L. Dreyfus and Paul Rabinow, *Michel Foucault: Beyond Stucturalism and Hermeneutics* (Hemel Hempstead, England: Harvester Press, 1982). The second edition (Chicago: University of Chicago Press, 1983) has Foucault's complete original "Afterword (1983)," 229–52, which appears in an edited version as "On the Genealogy of Ethics:

An Overview of Work in Progress," in *The Foucault Reader: An Introduction to Foucault's Thought,* 340–72, ed. Paul Rabinow (New York: Random House, 1984).

8. Foucault, *The Order of Things,* 252.

9. Ibid., 252–53.

10. Ibid., 251.

11. Stephen Devereux, *Theories of Famine* (Hemel Hempstead, England: Harvester Wheatsheaf, 1993), 9.

12. De Waal argues the contrary. Alex de Waal, "A Reassessment of Entitlement Theory in the Light of Recent Famines in Africa," *Development and Change* 21, no. 3 (1990): 470.

13. Michel Foucault, "Intellectuals and Power: A Conversation between Michel Foucault and Gilles Deleuze," in *Language, Counter-Memory, Practice: Selected Essays and Interviews,* ed. Donald F. Bouchard (Ithaca, N.Y.: Cornell University Press, 1977), 208.

14. *Concise Oxford Dictionary* (1982), quoted in Devereux, *Theories of Famine,* 10.

15. M. Lowneberg et al., 1974, quoted in ibid., 11.

16. W. Paddock and P. Paddock, 1967, quoted in ibid., 12.

17. Peter Cutler, 1985, quoted in ibid., 15.

18. Peter Walker, 1989, quoted in ibid., 16.

19. Alex de Waal, "The Perception of Poverty and Famines," *International Journal of Moral and Social Studies* 2, no. 3 (1987): 257.

20. See also David Arnold, *Famine: Social Crisis and Historical Change,* New Perspectives on the Past (Oxford: Basil Blackwell, 1988), 12–13.

21. Nizela Idriss, Alhi-bel, Koundjar, Chad, quoted in Nigel Cross and Rhiannon Barker, eds., *At the Desert's Edge: Oral Histories from the Sahel* (London: Panos, SOS Sahel, 1994), 156–57.

22. Cross and Barker, *At the Desert's Edge,* 120.

23. E. Margaret Crawford, "William Wilde's Table of Irish Famines 900–1850," in *Famine: The Irish Experience, 900–1900: Subsistence Crises and Famines in Ireland,* ed. E. Margaret Crawford (Edinburgh: John Donald Publishers, 1989), 7.

24. Arnold, *Famine,* 16.

25. E. Margaret Crawford, "William Wilde's Table of Irish Famines 900–1850." Present-day accounts from the Sahel and elsewhere do the same; for example, see Cross and Barker, *At the Desert's Edge.*

26. Joel Mokyr, *Why Ireland Starved: A Quantitative and Analytical History of the Irish Economy, 1800–1850* (London: George Allen and Unwin, 1983), 7 (citations omitted). Mokyr's analysis is wide ranging, detailed, and challenging.

27. Foucault, *The Order of Things,* 265.

28. Ibid., 275.

29. Robin D. S. Yates, "War, Food Shortages, and Relief Measures in Early China," in *Hunger in History: Food Shortage, Poverty, and Deprivation,* ed. Lucile F. Newman (Oxford: Blackwell, 1990), 149.

30. "Prayer for Times of Famine," *Book of Common Prayer* of the Church of England, 1562.

31. Audrey I. Richards, *Land, Labour, and Diet in Northern Rhodesia: An Economic Study of the Bemba Tribe* (London: Oxford University Press for the International Institute of African Languages and Cultures, 1939), ix–x.

32. Ibid., 7.

33. Ibid., 398.

34. Ibid., 400.

35. Piero Camporesi, *Bread of Dreams: Food and Fantasy in Early Modern Europe,* trans. David Gentilcore (Chicago: University of Chicago Press, 1989), 17.

36. Ibid.

37. Ibid., 17–18.

38. Ibid., 125.

39. Ibid., 127.

40. Ibid., 127–28.

41. Nancy Scheper-Hughes, "The Madness of Hunger: Sickness, Delirium, and Human Needs," *Culture, Medicine, and Psychiatry* 12, no. 4 (1988): 429–58.

42. Nancy Scheper-Hughes, *Death without Weeping: The Violence of Everyday Life in Brazil* (Berkeley: University of California Press, 1992), 199.

43. Ibid., 174.

44. Ibid., 199.

45. Ibid., 174.

46. Ibid., 172.

47. Ibid., 171.

48. Ibid., 202–3.

49. Ibid., 196.

50. "Nature" is of course itself a constructed category. For a discussion see William Chaloupka and R. McGreggor Cawley, "The Great Wild Hope: Nature, Environmentalism, and the Open Secret," in *In the Nature of Things: Language, Politics, and the Environment,* ed. Jane Bennett and William Chaloupka (Minneapolis: University of Minnesota Press, 1993), 3–23.

51. *Book of Common Prayer.*

52. Peter Garnsey, "Responses to Food Crisis in the Ancient Mediterranean World," in *Hunger in History: Food Shortage, Poverty, and Deprivation,* ed. Lucile F. Newman (Oxford: Blackwell, 1990), 141.

53. Ibid., 141–42.

54. Ibid., 143.

55. Yates, "War in Early China," 165.

56. Ibid., 167.

57. Foucault, *The Order of Things,* 312.

58. Ibid., 313.

59. Thomas Malthus, *An Essay on the Principle of Population,* World's Classics (Oxford: Oxford University Press, 1993), 61. Also reprinted in the Cambridge text, T. R. Malthus, *An Essay on the Principle of Population,* trans. Patricia James, Cambridge Texts in the History of Political Thought (Cambridge: Cambridge University Press, 1992), 42–43.

60. This has been discussed in the British context in Britain (Mitchell Dean, *The Constitution of Poverty: Toward a Theory of Liberal Governance* [London: Routledge, 1991]), but resonates with the treatment of famine on the global scale. See also Schram's work on 1990s welfare discourse in the United States (Sanford F. Schram, *Words of Welfare: The Poverty of Social Science and the Social Science of Poverty* [Minneapolis: University of Minnesota Press, 1995]).

61. Malthus, *Principle of Population,* Cambridge edition. The introduction by David Winch to this edition provides a useful analysis of the influence and context of Malthus's work.

62. Malthus, *Principle of Population,* Oxford edition, 13.

63. Garrett Hardin, "Lifeboat Ethics: The Case against Helping the Poor," *Psychology Today* 8 (1974): 38–43, 123–26.

64. Interview with Tony Hall, ex-Oxfam Information Officer and journalist, Addis Ababa, April 1995.

65. Debora MacKenzie, "The People Problem: Will Tomorrow's Children Starve?" *New Scientist,* 3 September 1994, 24–34. Pessimists include neo-Malthusians such as Lester Brown of the Worldwatch Institute in Washington and Paul Ehrlich; optimists, according to MacKenzie, include agricultural research scientists.

66. Martin Walker, "Overcrowding Points to Global Famine," *The Guardian,* 15 August 1994, 18. The report reviewed is Lester Brown, *Full House* (Worldwatch Institute, 1994).

67. Lester R. Brown, *State of the World 1996: A Worldwatch Institute Report on Progress towards a Sustainable Society* (London: Earthscan Publications, 1996).

68. Amartya Sen, "Population: Delusion and Reality," *New York Review of Books* 15, no. 15 (1994): 62–71.

69. See the special issue edited by Raymond F. Hopkins and Donald J. Puchala, "The Global Political Economy of Food," and their paper in it, "Perspectives on the International Relations of Food," *International Or-*

ganisation 36 (1978): 581–616. This work will be discussed more fully in chapter 4.

70. Donella H. Meadows et al., *The Limits to Growth: A Report for the Club of Rome's Project on the Predicament of Mankind* (London: Pan Books, 1974).

71. See, for example, Hunger Project, *Ending Hunger: An Idea Whose Time Has Come* (New York: Praeger Special Studies, 1985).

72. Michael Gross and Mary Beth Averill, "Evolution and Patriarchal Myths of Scarcity and Competition," in *Discovering Reality,* ed. Sandra Harding and Merrill B. Hintikka (Dordrecht, Netherlands: D. Reidel, 1983), 80. Gross and Averill argue that the perception of nature that sees life as a competitive struggle in a world of scarcity is a gendered view deriving largely from the male experience. Theories of famine that search for a cause and a technological solution are gendered.

73. Malthusianism is accepted by many environmentalists. This is discussed again in chapter 4 in relation to food for work programs addressed to environmental rehabilitation.

74. Nicholas Xenos, *Scarcity and Modernity* (London: Routledge, 1989).

75. Ibid., 2–3.

76. Ibid., 35.

77. Michel Foucault, *The Order of Things,* 257; Foucault does not entirely escape Malthusian notions of prehistory here. The debates around these issues of the transition were discussed in the previous chapter.

78. Ibid., 251.

79. Ibid., 257.

80. Marshall Sahlins argues that, contrary to traditional wisdom, hunter-gatherers were "the original affluent society" because "to assert that hunters are affluent is to deny then that the human condition is an ordained tragedy, with man the prisoner at hard labour of a perpetual disparity between his unlimited wants and his insufficient means. For there are two possible courses to affluence. Wants may be 'easily satisfied' either by producing much or desiring little" (*Stone Age Economics* [London: Tavistock, 1974], 1–2). He adds, "the hunter, one is tempted to say, is 'uneconomic man'" (13).

81. For another approach to scarcity and market economics, see Karl Polanyi, *The Great Transformation: The Political and Economic Origins of Our Time* (Boston: Beacon Press, 1944); Pieter Tijmes and Reginald Luijf, "The Sustainability of Our Common Future: An Inquiry into the Foundations of an Ideology," *Technology in Society* 17, no. 3 (1995): 327–36; and Louis Dumont, *From Mandeville to Marx: The Genesis and Triumph of Economic Ideology* (Chicago: University of Chicago Press, 1977). Polanyi argues that "as gradually the laws governing a market economy were apprehended,

these laws were put under the authority of Nature herself. . . . economic society was founded on the grim realities of Nature; if man disobeyed the laws which ruled that society, the fell executioner would strangle the offspring of the improvident. The laws of competitive society were put under the sanction of the jungle. The true significance of the tormenting problem of poverty now stood revealed: economic society was subjected to laws which were not human laws. . . . a dichotomy appeared which marked the birth of nineteenth century consciousness" (Polanyi, *Great Transformation*, 125–26).

82. Ester Boserup, *The Conditions of Agricultural Growth: Economics of Agrarian Change under Population Pressure* (London: Earthscan, 1993).

83. Nicole Ball, "Understanding the Causes of African Famine," *Journal of Modern African Studies* 14, no. 3 (1976): 517–22.

84. Nicole Ball, "The Myth of the Natural Disaster," *Ecologist* 5, no. 10 (1975): 368–71.

85. Mark Nathan Cohen, "Prehistoric Patterns of Hunger," in *Hunger in History: Food Shortage, Poverty, and Deprivation*, ed. Lucile F. Newman (Oxford: Blackwell, 1990), 57. See also his *The Food Crisis in Prehistory: Overpopulation and the Origins of Agriculture* (New Haven: Yale University Press, 1977).

86. Cohen, "Prehistoric Patterns of Hunger," 59.

87. Ibid., 58.

88. Ibid.

89. Ibid., 59.

90. Ibid., 72. Ethnographic evidence from contemporary hunter-gatherer societies backs up these arguments. Paleographic evidence shows that with the introduction of farming, rates of disease observable on bones increase, and remains indicate that farmers were usually less well nourished than their hunter-gatherer predecessors.

91. Ibid., 73.

92. Ibid., 76.

93. For a discussion of recent approaches to this topic, see David R. Harris, "An Evolutionary Continuum of People-Plant Interaction," in *Foraging and Farming: The Evolution of Plant Exploitation*, ed. David R. Harris and Gordon C. Hillman (London: Unwin Hyman, 1989), 11–26; and Cohen, *The Food Crisis in Prehistory*, 1–14, for a broader review.

94. David Rindos, *The Origins of Agriculture: An Evolutionary Perspective* (New York: Academic Press, 1984), 99; David Rindos, "Darwinism and Its Role in the Explanation of Domestication," in *Foraging and Farming: The Evolution of Plant Exploitation*, ed. David R. Harris and Gordon C. Hillman (London: Unwin Hyman, 1989), 27–41. Although Rindos's argument points to the complex linkages between human social behavior, popu-

lation, and food, it nevertheless contains Malthusian assumptions about population pressure (Rindos, "Darwinism and Domestication," 32).

95. The Marxist response to this might be that unstable systems worked well for a few—the exploiters—and that this explained their continuance.

96. Rindos, "Darwinism and Domestication," 36.

97. Ibid.

98. The latter, of course, sees the transition to agriculture as an adaptation that reduces the physiological stress on humans that occurred in previous modes of subsistence. Cultural change and the adoption of a settled way of life is seen as leading to a reduction in mortality and an improved stability of food supply—a reduction of periods of scarcity.

99. Rindos, "Darwinism and Domestication," 38.

100. Robley Matthews et al., "Global Climate and the Origins of Agriculture," in *Hunger in History: Food Shortage, Poverty, and Deprivation*, ed. Lucile F. Newman (Oxford: Blackwell, 1990), 41.

101. Cohen, *The Food Crisis in Prehistory*, 286.

102. Giorgio Agamben, *Homo Sacer: Sovereign Power and Bare Life*, trans. Daniel Heller-Roazen (Stanford: Stanford University Press, 1998).

103. Foucault, *History of Sexuality*, vol. 1, 3.

104. Barbara Hendrie, "Knowledge and Power: A Critique of an International Relief Operation," *Disasters* 21, no. 1 (1997): 57–76.

105. Agamben, *Homo Sacer*, 8.

106. Ibid., 9.

107. Ibid., 133.

108. Alex de Waal, *Famine That Kills: Dafur, Sudan, 1984–1985* (Oxford: Clarendon Press, 1989).

109. Woman in Korodegaga, Ethiopia, quoted in Patrick Webb and Joachim von Braun, *Famine and Food Security in Ethiopia: Lessons for Africa*, (Chichester: John Wiley for the International Food Policy Research Institute, 1994).

110. Account from the Rosses, County Donegal (Roger J. McHugh, "The Famine in Irish Oral Tradition," in *The Great Famine*, ed. R. Dudley Edwards and T. Desmond Williams [Dublin: Browne and Nolan, 1956], 434–35).

111. This is demonstrated in the attitudes of relief workers at the refugee camps in the Sudan described by Barbara Hendrie (Barbara Hendrie, "Knowledge and Power").

112. Margaret Kelleher, *The Feminisation of Famine: Expressions of the Inexpressible?* (Cork: Cork University Press, 1997), 29.

113. Ibid., 19.

114. Ibid., 229.

115. Ibid., 39. For a further discussion of how modernity's processes of

gendering produce women life-givers and men life-takers, see Jean Bethke Elshtain, *Women and War*, 2d ed. (Chicago: University of Chicago Press, 1995).

116. Foucault, *The Order of Things*, xv.

117. Ibid., xxiv.

3. AVAILABILITY AND ENTITLEMENT

1. Amartya Sen, *Poverty and Famines: An Essay on Entitlements and Deprivation* (Oxford: Clarendon Press, 1981; and Amartya Sen, "The Food Problem: Theory and Policy," *Third World Quarterly* 4, no. 3 (1982): 447–59. I outline Sen's approach in chapter 6.

2. Sen, *Poverty and Famines*, 4.

3. Ibid., 43.

4. For a full discussion of the policy implications of entitlements approaches see Jean Drèze and Amartya Sen, *Hunger and Public Action* (Oxford: Oxford University Press 1993).

5. Despite this, entitlement theory has by no means replaced the emphasis on food shortages that characterize food availability approaches.

6. Sen, *Poverty and Famines*, 1.

7. Ibid.

8. Ibid., 3.

9. Ibid.

10. Ibid., 45. I discuss the implications of Sen's exclusions in the second part of the chapter.

11. Sen, *Poverty and Famines*, 6.

12. Ibid., 75.

13. Ibid.

14. Sen, "The Food Problem," 450.

15. Ibid., 83.

16. Meghnad Desai, "Story-Telling and Formalism in Economics: The Instance of Famine," *International Social Science Journal* 113 (1987): 387–400.

17. For example, Nicole Ball, "African Famine"; Keith Griffin, *World Hunger and the World Economy* (London: Macmillan, 1987); Frances Moore Lappé and Joseph Collins, *World Hunger: Twelve Myths*, rev. ed. (London: Earthscan, 1988). See also Manushi Collective, "Drought: 'God-Sent' or 'Man-Made' Disaster?" in *Third World—Second Sex*, vol. 2, *Women's Struggles and National Liberation: Third World Women Speak Out*, ed. Miranda Davies (London: Zed Books, 1983).

18. Ball, "African Famine," 517–18.

19. Lionel Cliffe, "Capitalism or Feudalism: the Famine in Ethiopia," *Review of African Political Economy* 1 (1974); Lars Bondestam, "People and Capitalism in the North-Eastern Lowlands of Ethiopia," *Journal of Modern African Studies* 12, no. 3 (1974); Randall Baker, "The Need for Long Term Strategies in Areas of Pastoral Nomadism," in *Drought in Africa,* ed. David Dalby and R. J. Harrison Church (London: University of London, Centre for African Studies, 1973); Claude Meillassoux, "Development or Exploitation: Is the Sahel Famine Good Business?" *Review of African Political Economy* 1 (August–November 1974).

20. Sen, *Poverty and Famines,* 57. The acronym is clever.

21. See, for example, Devereux, *Theories of Famine*; David Coates, "Unit 2: The Production of Hunger," in *Block 1: Food for Thought,* ed. James Anderson, D103 Society and Social Science: A Foundation Course. (Milton Keynes: Open University, 1991).

22. For examples of work on vulnerability, see Patrick Webb and Joachim von Braun, *Famine and Food Security in Ethiopia: Lessons for Africa* (Chichester: John Wiley for the International Food Policy Research Institute, 1994); Michael J. Watts and Hans G. Bohle, "The Space of Vulnerability: The Causal Structure of Hunger and Famine," *Progress in Human Geography* 17, no. 1 (1993): 43–67; Mesfin Wolde Miriam, *Rural Vulnerability to Famine in Ethiopia 1958–1977* (London: Intermediate Technology Publications, 1987).

23. Susanna Davies, "Are Coping Strategies a Cop-Out?," *IDS Bulletin* 24, no. 4 (1993): 60–72.

24. Meghnad Desai, "Story-Telling and Formalism in Economics: The Instance of Famine," *International Social Science Journal* 113 (1987), 392.

25. Jean Drèze and Amartya Sen, *Hunger and Public Action.*

26. Devereux, *Theories of Famine*. Books like that of Stephen Devereux, which provide a survey of theories of famine, often fall into this camp.

27. H. W. Singer, "Book Review: *Poverty and Famines* by Amartya Sen," *International Affairs* 58, no. 2 (1982): 335–36.

28. For example the Bowbrick-Sen dispute (G. Allen, "Famines—the Bowbrick-Sen Dispute and Some Related Issues," *Food Policy* 11, no. 3 [1986]: 259–63; P. Bowbrick, "The Causes of Famine—A Refutation of Sen Theory," *Food Policy* 11, no. 2 [1986]: 105–24; P. Bowbrick, "Rejoinder: An Untenable Hypothesis on the Causes of Famine," *Food Policy* 12, no. 1 [1987]: 5–9; Amartya Sen, "The Causes of Famine—A Reply," *Food Policy* 11, no. 2 [1986]: 125–32; Amartya Sen, "Rejoinder: An Untenable Hypothesis on the Causes of Famine—Reply," *Food Policy* 12, no. 1 [1987]: 10–14); and the Sen-Nolan dispute (Amartya Sen, "The Causation and Prevention of

Famines—A Reply," *Journal of Peasant Studies* 21, no. 1 [1993]: 29–40; Peter Nolan, "The Causation and Prevention of Famines: A Critique of A. K. Sen," *Journal of Peasant Studies* 21, no. 1 [1993]: 1–28).

29. Amrita Rangasami, "Failure of Exchange Entitlements Theory of Famine," *Economic and Political Weekly* 20, nos. 41, 42 (1985): 1747–52, 1797–801. For an interesting study of the origins of the famine codes of India, see David Hall-Matthews, "Historical Roots of Famine Relief Paradigms: Ideas on Dependency and Free Trade in India in the 1870s," *Disasters* 20, no. 3 (1996): 216–30.

30. Rangasami, "Failure," 1798.

31. Ibid., 1799.

32. Ibid., 1748.

33. Ibid.

34. Ibid., 1749.

35. Ibid.

36. Ibid., 1750. Accounts of famines as complex emergencies still do this.

37. Sen, *Poverty and Famines*, 162.

38. Ben Fine, "Entitlement Failure?" *Development and Change* 28, no. 4 (1997): 617–47.

39. Sen, *Poverty and Famines*, 164.

40. Charles Gore, "Entitlement Relations and 'Unruly' Social Practices: A Comment on the Work of Amartya Sen," *Journal of Development Studies* 29, no. 3 (1993): 429–60. He also draws attention to the work of Bernard Schaffer and H. Wen-hsien ("Distribution and the Theory of Access," *Development and Change* 6, no. 2 [1975]: 13–36) on access rules that in practice determine entitlements to state-provided services or benefits.

41. Gore, "Entitlement Relations and 'Unruly' Social Practices," 447.

42. Gore bases his approach to this literature on the review by E. P. Thompson, "The Moral Economy Reviewed," in *Customs in Common*, ed. E. P. Thompson (London: Merlin Press, 1991), chapter 5. Other works that Gore cites include: David Arnold, "Looting, Grain Riots, and Government Policy in South India 1918," *Past and Present* 84 (1979): 111–45; David Arnold, *Famine: Social Crisis and Historical Change*, New Perspectives on the Past (Oxford: Basil Blackwell, 1988); Sally Falf Moore, *Law as Process: An Anthropological Approach* (London: Routledge and Kegan Paul, 1983); J. C. Scott, *Weapons of the Weak: Everyday Forms of Peasant Resistance* (New Haven: Yale University Press, 1985); L. A. Tilly, "Food Entitlement, Famine, and Conflict," in *Hunger and History: The Impact of Changing Food Production and Consumption Patterns on Society*, ed. R. I. Rotberg and T. K. Rabb (Cambridge: Cambridge University Press, 1985). He draws attention to work on famine that stresses the importance of the notion of the moral economy, though he points to the danger of treating traditional

"moral economy" and modern "market relations" as separate, with the for-
mer seen as giving way to the latter (Jeremy Swift, "Why Are Rural People
Vulnerable to Famine?" *IDS Bulletin* 20, no. 2 [1989]: 8–15; Michael Watts,
Silent Violence: Food Famine and Peasantry in Northern Nigeria [Berkeley:
University of California Press, 1983]).

43. Gore, "Entitlement Relatons and 'Unruly' Social Practices," 447–51.

44. Fine, "Entitlement Failure?" 629–30.

45. Ibid., 637–38. Gore and Fine's conclusions are similar to the conclusion reached in this chapter, albeit arrived at by different routes. Both stress
social relations; Gore points to the need for continual renegotiation of power
relations and Fine to the power embedded in existing social structures.

46. See, for example, E. Clay, "Famine, Food Insecurity, Poverty, and
Public Action," *Development Policy Review* 9 (1991): 307–12; de Waal,
"Reassessment of Entitlement Theory in the Light of Recent Famines in Africa," *Development and Change* 21, no. 3 (1990): 474–78; C. G. Locke and
F. Z. Ahmadi-Esfahani, "Famine Analysis: A Study of Entitlement in Sudan,
1984–1985," *Economic Development and Cultural Change* 41, no. 2 (1993):
363–76; S. R. Osmani, "Comments on Alex de Waal's 'Reassessment of En-
titlement Theory in the Light of Recent Famines in Africa,'" *Development
and Change* 22 (1991): 587–96; and Michael J. Watts and Hans G. Bohle,
"The Space of Vulnerability: The Causal Structure of Hunger and Famine,"
Progress in Human Geography 17, no. 1 (1993): 43–67, all discussed in Patrick Webb and Joachim von Braun, *Famine and Food Security in Ethiopia:
Lessons for Africa* (Chichester: John Wiley for the International Food Policy
Research Institute, 1994).

47. Jeremy Swift, "Understanding and Preventing Famine and Famine
Mortality," *IDS Bulletin* 24, no. 4 (1993): 1.

48. De Waal, *Famine That Kills: Dafur, Sudan, 1984–85* (Oxford: Clarendon Press, 1989).

49. De Waal, "Reassessment," 483.

50. Ibid., 473.

51. Ibid., 475.

52. For a rebuttal of de Waal's argument and for a discussion of Sen's argument that not selling assets to buy food can be accounted for within entitlement theory by the concept of intertemporal entitlements—the choice is
between starving now or starving later—see Osmani, "Comments on Alex
de Waal." See also de Waal's response, "Logic and Application: A Reply to
S. R. Osmani," *Development and Change* 22 (1991): 597–608.

53. De Waal, "Reassessment," 483.

54. De Waal, "Reply," 605.

55. De Waal, *Famine That Kills,* 28

56. The analysis here has focused on de Waal's work in *Famine That*

Kills. His later work is concerned with the role of conflict and the complexities of humanitarian aid and is discussed in chapter 6.

57. Raymond F. Hopkins and Donald J. Puchala, "Perspectives on the International Relations of Food," *International Organisation* 36 (1978): 581–616.

58. Barbara Hendrie, "Knowledge and Power: A Critique of an International Relief Operation," *Disasters* 21, no. 1 (1997): 63.

59. Ibid.

60. Ibid., 64.

61. Mitchell Dean, "A Genealogy of the Government of Poverty," *Economy and Society* 21, no. 3 (1992): 215–51.

62. Kirsten Hastrup, "Hunger and the Hardness of Facts," *Man*, n.s., 28, no. 4 (1993): 727–39.

63. Scientific, rationalist thought is itself argued by many writers to be a gendered approach to knowledge. See, for example, Evelyn Fox Keller, *Reflections on Gender and Science* (New Haven: Yale, 1985).

64. De Waal, "Reassessment."

65. Jacques Derrida, "Force of Law: The 'Mystical Foundation of Authority,'" in *Deconstruction and the Possibility of Justice*, ed. David Gray Carlson, Drucilla Cornell, and Michel Rosenfeld (New York: Routledge, 1992): 3–67.

66. Sen, *Poverty and Famines*.

67. In his examination of the speech act theory of J. L. Austin, Derrida uses an approach of the type I draw on here. He questions the way Austin uses processes of exclusion to produce the "essence" of the matter under discussion—the "performative" speech act—by placing the "risk" outside, as the excluded failure—the failed performative. Jacques Derrida, "Signature Event Context," in *Limited Inc*, ed. Jacques Derrida (Evanston, Ill.: Northwestern University Press, 1988): 1–23.

68. For Derrida's discussions of logocentrism, see, for example, Jacques Derrida, *Of Grammatology*, trans. Gayatri Chakravorty Spivak (Baltimore: Johns Hopkins University Press, 1976); and *Writing and Difference*, trans. Alan Bass (London: Routledge, 1978). See also my *Poststructuralism and International Relations: Bringing the Political Back In* (Boulder, Colo.: Lynne Rienner, 1999).

69. For the process of differentiation, see, for example, Jacques Derrida, *Positions*, trans. Alan Bass (London: Athlone Press, 1987): 8–9, 28–29.

70. Henry Staten, *Wittgenstein and Derrida* (Oxford: Basil Blackwell, 1984).

71. Derrida, "Signature Event Context," 17.

72. Ibid.

73. Ibid., 15.

74. Sen, *Poverty and Famines*, 45.

75. Ibid., 1.

76. Ibid., 40.

77. Alex de Waal, "Reassessment."

78. Sen, *Poverty and Famines*, 50, note 11.

79. Begoña Aretxaga, "Striking with Hunger: Cultural Meanings of Political Violence in Northern Ireland," in *The Violence Within: Cultural and Political Opposition in Divided Nations*, ed. Kay B. Warren (Boulder, Colo.: Westview Press 1993): 217–53.

80. Ibid., 223. Aretxaga does not make a distinction here between pacifist hunger strikes and those that are part of an armed conflict. She makes a link with famines, noting that "the 1981 fast had deep historical resonances; many people in Ireland, although disagreeing with the hunger strikers, thought the English were again starving Irish people" as in the Great Hunger—the "potato famine" of the 1840s (ibid., 250). See also Allen Feldman, *Formations of Violence: The Narrative of the Body and Political Terror in Northern Ireland* (Chicago: University of Chicago Press, 1991), chapter 6, 218–69.

81. Sen, *Poverty and Famines*, 1.

82. Ibid., 40.

83. Bernard Shaw, *Man and Superman* (Harmondsworth: Penguin, 1946), 196, quoted in Sen, *Poverty and Famines*, 40.

84. Ibid.

85. Ibid.

86. This distinction is necessary to uphold "a concept of law which allows the invalidity of law to be distinguished from its immorality" (Herbert Hart, quoted by Sen, *Poverty and Famines*, 49).

87. Ibid.

88. Ibid., 166. Sen seems to recognize the problem with his own argument (or, as Derrida might say, deconstruction happens). I interpret the phrase he uses here, "legality with a vengeance," as meaning legality gone beyond itself, legality that has gotten out of hand. In Lacanian terms, the phrase evokes that which is in legality more than legality itself (for a discussion of how naming produces this surplus, see Slavoj Žižek, *The Sublime Object of Ideology* (London: Verso, 1989), 97. I am arguing that law is *always already* like this—out of hand—in the sense that it always already involves a founding and an enforcing violence. Derrida's point is that law is not, as might be expected, a nonviolent, consensual, ordering mechanism. On the contrary, it always embodies violence. Thus it should be no surprise that "starvation deaths can reflect legality" (Sen, *Poverty and Famines*, 166) because legality is always "legality with a vengeance" (ibid.).

89. Derrida, "Force of Law," 5–6.

90. Ibid., 13.

91. Ibid., 40. This brings us back to the notion of "limit"; as Derrida says, "Here the discourse comes up against its limit: in itself, in its performative power itself. It is what . . . I call the mystical. Here a silence is walled up in the violent structure of the founding act. Walled up, walled in because silence is not exterior to language" (13–14).

92. Ibid., 36.

93. Ibid.

94. Ibid., 35. Here, fascinatingly, Derrida makes the link between this undecidable moment of foundation and the mystical, or what Lacan might call the "Real." Another similarity, of course, is that Lacan sees time as acting retroactively in a way similar to Derrida: "What is realised in my history is not the past definite of what was, since it is no more, or even the present perfect of what has been in what I am, but the future anterior of what I shall have been for what I am in the process of becoming" (Jacques Lacan, *Écrits: A Selection*, trans. Alan Sheridan [London: Tavistock, 1977], 86).

95. Derrida, "Force of Law," 35.

96. For a discussion of the relation of the subject and the symbolic order in Lacanian terms, see, for example, Žižek, *The Sublime Object*. The Lacanian approach that Žižek presents argues that what we call "social reality" is only constituted by excluding the real. The real is that which cannot be symbolized or spoken of; it is in moments of terror and violence that we confront the real.

97. Nancy Scheper-Hughes, "The Madness of Hunger: Sickness, Delirium, and Human Needs," *Culture, Medicine, and Psychiatry* 12, no. 4 (1988): 429–58.

98. Kirsten Hastrup, "Hunger and the Hardness of Facts"; Barbara Hendrie, "Knowledge and Power," 63–64.

99. I am using the term "technologized" to mean calculable and quantifiable, part of a system of "techniques" or a program of rules that, it is claimed, can be applied unproblematically in different practical cases. What we call "reality" is broken down and studied by specialists in narrow areas using "scientific" methods. This produces a claim to expert knowledge that directs action, without allowing any room for responsibility. See the discussion in chapter 1.

100. Derrida, "Force of Law," 16. For Derrida, justice is incalculable.

101. Ibid.

102. Ibid., 23.

103. Ibid., 24.

104. Ibid.

105. Ibid., 24–25.

106. Drucilla Cornell, *The Philosophy of the Limit* (London: Routledge 1992), 155.

107. Ibid., 157.

108. Sen, *Poverty and Famines*, 1.

109. Ibid., 8.

110. Examples of firsthand accounts of famines can be found in Paul Richard Bohr, *Famine in China and the Missionary: Timothy Richard as Relief Administrator and Advocate of National Reform, 1876–1884* (Cambridge: Harvard University, East Asian Research Center, 1972); Peter Garnsey, *Famine and Food Supply in the Graeco-Roman World* (Cambridge: Cambridge University Press, 1988); Roger J. McHugh, "The Famine in Irish Oral Tradition," in *The Great Famine*, eds. R. Dudley Edwards and T. Desmond Williams (Dublin: Browne and Nolan, 1956), 391–436; Nancy Scheper-Hughes, *Death without Weeping: the Violence of Everyday Life in Brazil* (Berkeley: University of California Press, 1992); and Patrick Webb and Joachim von Braun, *Famine and Food Security in Ethiopia: Lessons for Africa* (Chichester, England: John Wiley for the International Food Policy Research Institute, 1994); and accounts of war and famine in Alex de Waal, *Evil Days: Thirty Years of War and Famine in Ethiopia*, Africa Watch Report (New York: Human Rights Watch, 1991); Jason W. Clay, and Bonnie K. Holcomb, *Politics and the Ethiopian Famine 1984–1985*, Cultural Survival Report 20 (Cambridge, Mass.: Cultural Survival, 1986); and Jason W. Clay, Sandra Steingraber, and Peter Niggli, *The Spoils of Famine: Ethiopian Famine Policy and Peasant Agriculture* (Cambridge, Mass.: Cultural Survival, 1988).

111. In famines in China, exchanging children between families has been reported. See Jasper Becker, *Hungry Ghosts: China's Secret Famine* (London: John Murray, 1996) for an extended discussion of cannibalism during the famines of the 1960s.

112. Other horrors of famines stretch the imagination in this area. Are we to regard people as searching for "ownerships" to add to what Sen might term their "entitlement bundles" when they consider options such as prostitution, conversion to other religions, selling their children into slavery, and the like?

113. Setting aside food supply leaves Sen with a problem when he attempts to define famines. He has to end up by saying that we can recognize one when we see one. Sen, *Poverty and Famines*, 39–40.

114. David McLellan, ed., *Karl Marx: Selected Writings* (Oxford: Oxford University Press, 1977), 436.

115. Food is a very particular type of commodity. Gore points out that the socially accepted moral rules that regulate food and provisioning change at times when people suffer from hunger and famine. They are historically specific, ranging, for example, from norms of reciprocity and sharing among peasant communities, in one case, to a morality of distress, where the normal

obligations to children and dependents are replaced by the primacy of the survival of particular groups, such as parents, in another. They are also the subject of negotiation and struggle (Gore, "Entitlement Relations and 'Unruly' Social Practices," 445–50). See also Sahlins's discussion of food as a gift (*Stone Age Economics* [London: Tavistock, 1974], 215–19). Ben Fine's work on food is interesting here, too ("Entitlement Failure?" *Development and Change* 28, no. 4 [1997]: 617–47).

116. Sen, *Poverty and Famines*, 2, note 3.

117. Basil Ashton et al., "Famine in China, 1958–1961," *Population and Development Review* 10, no. 4 (1984): 613–45. See also Becker, *Hungry Ghosts*.

118. For accounts of the Great Hunger see, for example, R. Dudley Edwards and T. Desmond Williams, eds., *The Great Famine: Studies in Irish History 1845–1852* (Dublin: Browne and Nolan for the Irish Committee of Historical Sciences, 1956); and other references given in chapter 1.

119. Sen, *Poverty and Famines*, 52–85.

120. Michel Foucault, *Power/Knowledge: Selected Interviews and Other Writings 1972–1977 by Michel Foucault*, trans. Colin Gordon (Brighton, England: Harvester Press, 1980), 133.

121. Sen, *Poverty and Famines*, 39.

122. Malthus, *An Essay on the Principle of Population*, trans. Patricia James (Cambridge: Cambridge University Press, 1992), 61.

123. Sen, *Poverty and Famines*, 162.

124. See, for example, Michel Foucault, *The Order of Things: An Archaeology of the Human Sciences* (London: Tavistock, 1970), 256–58. See also Pieter Tijmes and Reginald Luijf, "The Sustainability of Our Common Future: An Inquiry into the Foundations of an Ideology," *Technology in Society* 17, no. 3 (1995): 327–36. For a discussion that sees Sen's work as challenging the reliance of classical economics on scarcity, see Meghnad Desai, "Story-Telling and Formalism in Economics: The Instance of Famine," *International Social Science Journal* 113 (1987): 387–400.

125. Michel Foucault, *Power/Knowledge*, 134–38. For an interesting parallel discussion of too rapid universalization and too rapid historicization, see Žižek's reflections on the ideological: Žižek, *The Sublime Object*, 49–50. From the Marxist point of view, Žižek argues, the ideological move is to make that which is particular and historical appear universal—so famines appear as a consequence of the failure of the economic system. This is overrapid universalization. In Lacanian terms, the very opposite—overrapid historicization—is also ideological. In this, famines are seen as nothing more than particular breakdowns that appear in specific places at distinct historical conjunctures.

126. Foucault, *Power/Knowledge,* 136.

127. Keen follows this argument, taking his lead from Foucault in his *Benefits of Famine.*

128. Foucault, *Power/Knowledge,* 136.

129. This is Žižek's phrase. See Slavoj Žižek, *The Indivisible Remainder: An Essay on Schelling and Related Matters* (London: Verso, 1996): 214–15 and 234, note 26, for another discussion of universalism and historicism.

4. PRACTICES OF AID

1. The argument about sovereignty and intervention is another example of the struggle to set the agenda and define the terms of the aid process. Famine relief is being renarrated as "humanitarian intervention."

2. David Keen, *The Benefits of Famine: A Political Economy of Famine and Relief in Southwestern Sudan, 1983–1989* (Princeton: Princeton University Press, 1994). Keen's work is discussed in chapter 6; it draws on Clay and Schaffer, *Room for Manoeuvre.* A similar argument about the Ethiopian case has been made in Jason W. Clay and Bonnie K. Holcomb, *Politics and the Ethiopian Famine 1984–1985,* Cultural Survival Report 20 (Cambridge, Mass.: Cultural Survival, 1986). See also Jason W. Clay, Sandra Steingraber, and Peter Niggli, *The Spoils of Famine: Ethiopian Famine Policy and Peasant Agriculture* (Cambridge, Mass.: Cultural Survival, 1988); and Peter Cutler, "The Development of the 1983–1985 Famine in Northern Ethiopia" (Ph.D. diss., London University School of Hygiene and Tropical Medicine, 1988).

3. Michel Foucault, *Discipline and Punish: The Birth of the Prison,* trans. Alan Sheridan (London: Allen Lane, 1977; reprint, Harmondsworth, England: Penguin, 1991). Aspects of Foucault's work have been used by a number of other writers in relation to accounts of social policy, specifically welfare provision and poverty. See, for example, Mitchell Dean, *The Constitution of Poverty: Toward a Theory of Liberal Governance* (London: Routledge, 1991); Mitchell Dean, "A Genealogy of the Government of Poverty," *Economy and Society* 21, no. 3 (1992): 215–51; Nancy Fraser, *Unruly Practices: Power, Discourse, and Gender in Contemporary Social Theory* (Cambridge, England: Polity, 1989); Nancy Fraser and Linda Gordon, "A Genealogy of Dependency: Tracing a Keyword of the U.S. Welfare State," *Signs* 19, no. 2 (1994): 309–36; Sanford F. Schram, *Words of Welfare: The Poverty of Social Science and the Social Science of Poverty* (Minneapolis: University of Minnesota Press, 1995). A Foucauldian approach to policy in agriculture and development is also used by Clay and Schaffer; see Edward J. Clay and

B. B. Schaffer, eds., *Room for Manoeuvre: An Exploration of Public Policy in Agriculture and Rural Development* (Cambridge, Mass.: Cultural Survival, 1984). This looks at how the policy discourse operates.

4. Mark Duffield, "Eritrea and Tigray: Changing Organisational Issues in Cross-Border Relief Assistance 1983–1992," in *Meeting Needs: NGO Coordination in Practice,* ed. Jon Bennett (London: Earthscan, 1995), 61.

5. An example of similar work using a Foucauldian approach is Barbara Hendrie's study of the organization of a refugee camp in the Sudan in the 1980s ("Knowledge and Power: A Critique of an International Relief Operation," *Disasters* 21, no. 1 [1997]: 57–76).

6. Michel Foucault, *The Archaeology of Knowledge,* trans. A. M. Sheridan Smith (London: Routledge, 1989), 49.

7. Michel Foucault, "Politics and the Study of Discourse," in *The Foucault Effect: Studies in Governmentality,* ed. Graham Burchell, Colin Gordon, and Peter Miller (London: Harvester Wheatsheaf, 1991), 59–60.

8. Ibid., 62–63.

9. Ibid., 63.

10. Michel Foucault, "Truth and Power," in *Power/Knowledge: Selected Interviews and Other Writings 1972–1977 by Michel Foucault,* ed. Colin Gordon (Brighton, England: Harvester, 1980), 131.

11. This includes work that looks at food aid as part of foreign policy. See, for example, Vernon W. Ruttan, *Why Food Aid?* (Baltimore: Johns Hopkins University Press, 1993); and Enrica Augelli and Craig Murphy, *America's Quest for Supremacy and the Third World: A Gramscian Analysis* (London: Pinter, 1988); for work on the "international food regime"—the global food regime—see Raymond F. Hopkins and Donald J. Puchala, editors of the special issue "The Global Political Economy of Food," which includes their own paper, "Perspectives on the International Relations of Food" (*International Organisation* 36 [1978]: 581–616); or the "international hunger regime" as analyzed by Peter Uvin in *The International Organisation of Hunger,* (London: Kegan Paul, 1994)); and for work that debates the moral issues, see Uvin, *International Organisation of Hunger*; Ruttan, *Why Food Aid?*; and Edward J. Clay and Olav Stokke, eds., *Food Aid Reconsidered: Assessing the Impact on Third World Countries* (London: Cass in collaboration with the European Association of Development Research and Training Institutes, 1991). A review of work on foreign aid in general appears in Sven Holdar, "The Study of Foreign Aid: Unbroken Ground in Geography," *Progress in Human Geography* 17, no. 4 (1993): 453–70; and a Gramscian analysis in Augelli and Murphy, *America's Quest for Supremacy.*

12. Ruttan, *Why Food Aid?*

13. Theodore W. Schultz, "Value of U.S. Farm Surpluses to Under-

developed Countries," *Journal of Farm Economics* 42, no. 5 (1960): 1019–30.

14. Singer attacks the distinction between duty and charity and argues that if by giving money to famine relief or population control, rather than spending it on trivia, the affluent can prevent starvation, they "ought to give the money away, and it is wrong not to do so" (Peter Singer, "Famine, Affluence, and Morality," *Philosophy and Public Affairs* 1, no. 3 [1972]: 229–43). Hardin coined the phrase "lifeboat ethics" to describe what he called "the case against helping the poor." His argument was based on the limited capacity of the earth and the risk of overpopulation: the neo-Malthusian view. See Garrett Hardin, "Lifeboat Ethics: The Case against Helping the Poor," *Psychology Today* 8 (1974): 38–43, 123–26. For a general discussion of the debate about ethics and hunger or famine, see William Aiken and Hugh LaFollette, eds., *World Hunger and Morality*, 2d ed. (Upper Saddle River, N.J.: Prentice Hall, 1996). For earlier collections see William Aiken and Hugh LaFollette, eds., *World Hunger and Moral Obligation* (Englewood Cliffs, N.J.: Prentice-Hall, 1977); and Charles R. Beitz et al., eds. *International Ethics: A Philosophy and Public Affairs Reader* (Princeton: Princeton University Press, 1985). Whether nations can have duties beyond those to their own citizens is a question raised by Stanley Hoffman, *Duties beyond Borders: On the Limits and Possibilities of Ethical International Politics* (Syracuse: Syracuse University Press, 1981). Onora O'Neill argues that there are no ethically neutral descriptions that can be appealed to for facts about famine. She goes on to develop a Kantian-based theory of obligation; the implications of this approach are that a transformation in the international economic order is required by justice. A just global order would be one designed to meet human needs, including material needs. The present global order clearly does not do this: the material needs of a vast number of people are not met. In this context terms such as aid, loans, or gifts are inappropriate. See Onora O'Neill, *Faces of Hunger: An Essay on Poverty, Justice, and Development*, Studies in Applied Philosophy, vol. 3 (London: Allen & Unwin, 1986).

15. See, for example, Frances Moore Lappé and Joseph Collins, *World Hunger: Twelve Myths*, rev. ed. (London: Earthscan, 1988); Susan George, *How the Other Half Dies: The Real Reasons for World Hunger* (Harmondsworth, England: Penguin, 1976); Nicole Ball, "The Myth of the Natural Disaster," *Ecologist* 5, no. 10 (1975): 368–71.

16. Hopkins and Puchala, *Global Political Economy of Food*.

17. They use a standard definition of a regime as "a set of rules, norms, or institutional expectations that govern a social system," similar to others used in the international relations literature; see Stephen Krasner, ed., *International*

Regimes (Ithaca, N.Y.: Cornell University Press, 1983). It is interesting to compare this approach with Sen's work on entitlements: both stress the importance of legitimation and social practices as opposed to exclusive concern with food production and supply.

18. Hopkins and Puchala, *Global Political Economy of Food,* 601–2.

19. Ibid., 615.

20. See section 4 of Ruttan, *Why Food Aid.*

21. Ibid., 131.

22. Raymond F. Hopkins, "Reform in the International Food Aid Regime: The Role of Consensual Knowledge," *International Organisation* 46, no. 1 (1992): 236.

23. Ibid., 240.

24. Uvin, *International Organisation of Hunger,* 79.

25. Those who dispute this, the radical critics who instead would argue that the West causes the problems of the third world, are marginalized. For Hopkins, their approach is not based on acceptance of the same scientific epistemology as the food epistemic community he studies.

26. Hopkins, "Reform," 225.

27. Ibid., 240.

28. Patrick Webb and Joachim von Braun, *Famine and Food Security in Ethiopia: Lessons for Africa* (Chichester: John Wiley for the International Food Policy Research Institute, 1994).

29. Gayle E. Smith, "Emerging from Crisis: From Relief to Development," *Humanitarian Monitor,* February 1995, 28–29.

30. Of course, in the context of the cross-border operation during the war, relief was seen by the NGO consortia as legitimate because of its neutrality and humanitarian purpose in a way that development aid was not. For a discussion of these points see Mark Duffield and John Prendergast, *Without Troops and Tanks: The Emergency Relief Desk and the Cross Border Operation into Eritrea and Tigray* (Lawrenceville, N.J.: Red Sea Press, 1994), 112–13.

31. As in the workshop held at IDS in March 1994 and funded by the Overseas Development Administration (ODA). See Simon Maxwell and Margaret Buchanan-Smith, eds., "Linking Relief and Development," a special issue of the *IDS Bulletin* 25: no. 4 (Brighton, England: Institute of Development Studies, 1994).

32. Margaret Buchanan-Smith and Simon Maxwell, "Linking Relief and Development: an Introduction and Overview," *IDS Bulletin* 25, no. 4 (1994): 2.

33. I explore why and the implications of this support in the next chapter.

34. Pat Holden, "ODA's Approach to Linking Relief and Development," *IDS Bulletin* 25, no. 4 (1994): 105–6.

35. Duffield, "Eritrea and Tigray." Duffield sees the need to come to terms with a situation of permanent emergency and argues that an accommodation has already taken place. Relief activity has come to play an unexpected role in North-South relations. The accommodation "has produced an unprecedented integration of so-called neutral humanitarian assistance with the dynamics of violence" (42).

36. Smith, "Emerging from Crisis."

37. ERRA, "Towards the Rational Use of Emergency Food Aid in Eritrea: Challenges and Opportunities" (Eritrean Relief and Rehabilitation Agency, 1994).

38. For a general discussion of food for work programs, see Webb and von Braun, *Famine and Food Security*, 106–14; Jean Drèze and Amartya Sen, *Hunger and Public Action* (Oxford: Oxford University Press, 1993), 113–18.

39. ERRA, "Emergency Food Aid," 6.

40. Ibid., 7.

41. Ibid., 5.

42. For a discussion of "dependency" in relation to welfare discourse, see Fraser and Gordon, "Genealogy of Dependency."

43. Smith, "Emerging from Crisis," 29.

44. Ibid.

45. Alex de Waal, *Evil Days: Thirty Years of War and Famine in Ethiopia*, An Africa Watch Report (New York: Human Rights Watch, 1991), 154.

46. See, for example, Duffield and Prendergast, *Without Troops*.

47. Peter Gill, *A Year in the Death of Africa: Politics, Bureaucracy, and the Famine* (London: Paladin, 1986), 137.

48. Ibid., 138.

49. Barbara Hendrie, "Cross-Border Relief Operations in Eritrea and Tigray," *Disasters* 13, no. 4 (1989): 351–60.

50. Ibid.

51. Hussein M. Adam, "Formation and Recognition of New States: Somaliland in Contrast to Eritrea," *Review of African Political Economy* 21, no. 59 (1994): 21–38.

52. John Sorenson, "Discourses on Eritrean Nationalism and Identity," *Journal of Modern African Studies* 29, no. 2 (1991): 308.

53. Jason W. Clay and Bonnie K. Holcomb, *Politics and the Ethiopian Famine 1984–1985*, Cultural Survival Report 20 (Cambridge, Mass.: Cultural Survival, 1986), 3.

54. See, for example, Jenny Hammond and Nell Druce, *Sweeter than Honey: Ethiopian Women and Revolution: Testimonies of Tigrayan Women* (Trenton, N.J.: Red Sea Press, 1990), 127–29, where the TPLF is described organizing a resettlement program.

55. Clay and Holcomb, *Politics and the Ethiopian Famine,* 3. On the question of independent research in the rebel-held areas, see Trish Silkin and Barbara Hendrie, "Research in the War Zones of Eritrea and Tigray," *Disasters* 21, no. 2 (1997): 166–76.

56. Clay and Holcomb, *Politics and the Ethiopian Famine,* 4.

57. See ibid. and Jason W. Clay, Sandra Steingraber, and Peter Niggli, *The Spoils of Famine: Ethiopian Famine Policy and Peasant Agriculture* (Cambridge, Mass.: Cultural Survival, 1988).

58. Clay and Holcomb, *Politics and the Ethiopian Famine,* 91, 192.

59. Ibid., 86.

60. Ibid., 26.

61. Ibid., 29.

62. John Sorenson, *Imagining Ethiopia: Struggles for History and Identity in the Horn of Africa* (New Brunswick, N.J.: Rutgers University Press, 1993), 101. Sorensen gives an extensive discussion of discourses of the Ethiopian famine and relief efforts in his book, which looks at the discursive construction of Ethiopia, Eritrea, and the Horn of Africa using an analysis that draws particularly on Noam Chomsky.

63. Such assessments and comparisons are difficult. The EPLF systems were clearly also highly organized.

64. ERRA, "Final Crop Assessment and Food Aid Needs" (Eritrean Relief and Rehabilitation Agency, 1995).

65. Christine Kinealy, *This Great Calamity: The Irish Famine, 1845–52* (Dublin: Gill and Macmillan, 1994), 351.

66. Ibid., 353.

67. Ibid., 355–56.

68. Ibid., 356.

69. Ibid., 354.

70. Ibid., 358.

71. Report to the Relief Commissioners, quoted in Kinealy, *This Great Calamity,* 139.

72. Lord Palmerston, quoted in ibid., 219.

73. Ibid., 359.

74. Zygmunt Bauman, *Modernity and the Holocaust* (Ithaca, N.Y.: Cornell University Press, 1991), 91.

75. Ibid., 95.

76. The research involved a series of interviews with officials from the ERRA, the Ministry of Agriculture, and the Ministry of Local Government in Asmara and provincial offices; representatives of Western NGOs, including the Lutheran World Federation, Norwegian Church Aid, Oxfam Belgique, and Oxfam UK; a representative of USAID; officers from the UN World Food Programme Eritrea, UNICEF, and the UNHCR; officials from local NGOs

such as REST and the Inter Africa Group; other local organizations, including the Eritrean Constitutional Commission, the Ethiopian Commission for Refugees and Returnees, National Union of Eritrean Women, and the University of Asmara; and community representatives. During my visit to Eritrea and Ethiopia, I traveled with a consultant for Oxfam-Belgique on an assessment and monitoring visit to food for work sites in four provinces of Eritrea. This monitoring exercise was undertaken in conjunction with ERRA. My interpretations, which of course are my own, are based on participant observation of meetings, interviews, and site visits. For a summary of the itinerary and further details of the field trip and interviews carried out in Asmara and Addis Ababa, see Jenny Edkins, "Technologising the International: Pictures of Hunger, Concepts of Famine, Practices of Aid" (Ph.D. diss., University of Wales Aberystwyth, 1997), appendices A and B, 347–53.

77. ERRA, "Emergency Food Aid," 8.

78. Details of budgets, work and payment norms, etc. are taken from *Ministry of Agriculture FFW Plans and Ration Norms for 1995*, reproduced as appendix 9 in Norah Gibson, Yohannes Teggay, and Ashghedom Tewolde, "Draft Report of the Evaluation of Food Aid Operations of the Eritrean Relief and Rehabilitation Agency, January 31–February 25, 1995" (Oxfam Belge/Dutch Interchurch Aid, 1995).

79. Thomas P. O'Neill, "The Organisation and Administration of Relief, 1845–1852," in *The Great Famine: Studies in Irish History 1845–1852*, ed. R. Dudley Edwards and T. Desmond Williams (Dublin: Browne and Nolan for the Irish Committee of Historical Sciences, 1956), 230.

80. Foucault, *Discipline and Punish*, 242.

81. Webb, *Famine and Food Security*, 111.

82. Foucault, *Discipline and Punish*, 243.

83. Sites visited were Tessanie and surrounding villages, Gash-Setit; Agordat, Barka; Degasse and Ghedynazay, Engerne District, Mansura subprovince, Barka; Keren, Senhit; Mei Awalit, Halhal, Bogos sub-province, Senhit; Afabet, Sahel Province; Nacfa, Sahel Province; Gz'Gza, Sahel.

84. Mechanized microdam construction was also taking place in other areas.

85. Webb, *Famine and Food Security*.

86. Ibid., 112–13.

87. Melissa Leach and James Fairhead, "Natural Resource Management: The Reproduction and Use of Environmental Misinformation in Guinea's Forest-Savanna Transition Zone," *IDS Bulletin* 25, no. 2 (1994): 81–87.

88. Webb, *Famine and Food Security*, 107.

89. Simon Maxwell and Alemayehu Lirenso, "Linking Relief and Development: An Ethiopian Case Study," *IDS Bulletin* 25, no. 4 (1994): 65.

90. Drèze and Sen, *Hunger and Public Action*, 115.

91. Gibson, "Food Aid Operations," 5.

92. Slavoj Žižek, *The Sublime Object of Ideology* (London: Verso, 1989).

93. Gibson, "Food Aid Operations," 9.

94. Webb, *Famine and Food Security,* 108.

95. Drèze and Sen, *Hunger and Public Action,* 114.

96. Maxwell and Lirenso, "Linking."

97. Ibid., 74. There have been problems in Eritrea, too, and the Eritrean government took a strong line in October 1995, when it expelled two UN World Food Program and two USAID officials for "creating obstacles to the smooth flow of U.S. aid to Eritrea" (Associated Press [eritrea-l@relay.doit.wisc.edu, 21 October 1995]) and "interfering in the affairs" of Eritrea (Reuters [eritrea-l@relay.doit.wisc.edu, 21 October 1995]).

98. This paragraph is based on discussions and conversations during my visit to Eritrea and Ethiopia in March/April 1995.

99. Hopkins, "Reform."

100. Allan Hoben, "Paradigms and Politics: The Cultural Construction of Environmental Policy in Ethiopia," *World Development* 23, no. 6 (1995): 1007–21.

101. Foucault, *Discipline and Punish,* 268.

102. Ibid., 271.

103. Ibid., 252.

104. Ibid., 275.

105. Ibid., 276.

106. Fintan O'Toole argues that this was how famine was seen in the Ireland of the 1840s. Fintan O'Toole, "Hungry Eyes," prod. Mary Price, research Ellis Hill (BBC Radio 4, 1 November 1995).

107. Letter from Sir Charles Trevelyan, September 1846, quoted in O'Neill, "Relief," 255.

108. Foucault, *Discipline and Punish,* 300.

5. RESPONSE AND RESPONSIBILITY

1. Michael Buerk, BBC *Six O'Clock News,* 23 October 1984. There has been some discussion of the background in earlier chapters and there are overviews of the famines of the 1980s and aid responses in Alex De Waal, *Evil Days: Thirty Years of War and Famine in Ethiopia,* Africa Watch Report (New York: Human Rights Watch, 1991); Jason W. Clay and Bonnie K. Holcomb, *Politics and the Ethiopian Famine 1984–1985,* Cultural Survival Report 20 (Cambridge, Mass.: Cultural Survival, 1986); Jason W. Clay, Sandra Steingraber, and Peter Niggli, *The Spoils of Famine: Ethiopian Famine Policy and Peasant Agriculture* (Cambridge, Mass.: Cultural Survival, 1988);

Peter Cutler, "The Development of the 1983–1985 Famine in Northern Ethiopia" (Ph.D. diss., London University School of Hygiene and Tropical Medicine, 1988); Dawit Wolde Giorgis, *Red Tears: War, Famine, and Revolution in Ethiopia* (Trenton, N.J.: Red Sea Press, 1989); Peter Gill, *A Year in the Death of Africa: Politics, Bureaucracy, and the Famine* (London: Paladin, 1986); Patrick Webb and Joachim von Braun, *Famine and Food Security in Ethiopia: Lessons for Africa* (Chichester, England: John Wiley for the International Food Policy Research Institute, 1994).

2. Mark Duffield, "Complex Emergencies and the Crisis of Developmentalism," *IDS Bulletin* 25, no. 4 (1994): 37–45; John Harriss, ed., *The Politics of Humanitarian Intervention* (London: Pinter in association with Save the Children Fund and the Centre for Global Governance, 1995); and Oliver Ramsbotham and Tom Woodhouse, *Humanitarian Intervention in Contemporary Conflict: A Reconceptualisation* (Cambridge: Polity, 1996).

3. I am not trying to argue that we can account for everything at the level of the individual or person. Žižek distinguishes between what he calls the realist Lacan of the 1950s, whose notion of the social order was Durkheimian: the always already preexisting horizon of the social world, which provides the support or validation of subjectivity; and the fictionalist Lacan, who sees the social as deriving from the experience of individuals, not preexisting, but with a paradoxical twist that argues that this does not imply a reduction of the social to the amalgamation of individual experience (Slavoj Žižek, *The Indivisible Remainder: An Essay on Schelling and Related Matters* [London: Verso, 1996], 137–38).

4. For a statement and critique of developmentalism, see Mark Duffield, "The Symphony of the Damned: Racial Discourse, Complex Political Emergencies, and Humanitarian Aid," *Disasters* 20, no. 3 (1996): 173–93.

5. Ian Craib, "Some Comments on the Sociology of the Emotions," *Sociology* 29, no. 1 (1995): 151–58.

6. Kirsten Hastrup, "Hunger and the Hardness of Facts," *Man*, n.s. 28, no. 4 (1993): 727–39.

7. The attack on Band Aid–Live Aid events "posited some motivations—compassion, solidarity, judgement—as nobler than others—charity, guilt, emotion" (Henrietta Lidchi, "All in the Choosing Eye: Charity, Representation, and Developing World" [Ph.D. diss., Open University, 1993], 127).

8. See, for example, Nicholas J. Wheeler, "Making Sense of Humanitarian Outrage," *Irish Studies in International Affairs* 7 (1996): 31–40.

9. Zygmunt Bauman argues that the technologization of violence was an important feature of the Holocaust and that rather than being seen as an exception it should be seen as part of modernity. The Holocaust "showed what the rationalising, designing, controlling dreams and efforts of modern civilisation are able to accomplish if not mitigated, curbed or counteracted"

(*Modernity and the Holocaust* [Ithaca, N.Y.: Cornell University Press, 1991], 93).

10. For a discussion of this point and others, see Ken Booth, "Human Wrongs and International Relations," *International Affairs* 71, no. 1 (1995): 103–26.

11. See David Campbell, *Politics without Principle: Sovereignty, Ethics, and the Narratives of the Gulf War,* Critical Perspectives on World Politics (Boulder, Colo.: Lynne Rienner, 1993); and his "The Politics of Radical Interdependence: A Rejoinder to Daniel Warner," *Millennium* 25, no. 1 (1996): 129–41. See also his *National Deconstruction: Violence, Identity, and Justice in Bosnia* (Minneapolis: University of Minnesota Press, 1998).

12. I am referring here, for example, to François Debrix, "Deploying Vision, Simulating Action: The United Nations and Its Visualisation Strategies in a New World Order," *Alternatives* 21 (1996): 67–92; and Cynthia Weber, *Simulating Sovereignty: Intervention, the State, and Symbolic Exchange,* Cambridge Studies in International Relations, vol. 37 (Cambridge: Cambridge University Press, 1995).

13. Judith Butler, *Gender Trouble: Feminism and the Subversion of Identity* (New York: Routledge, 1990). For a discussion of the distinction between performativity and Žižek's Lacanian approach, see Judith Butler, "Arguing with the Real," in her *Bodies That Matter: On the Discursive Limits of "Sex"* (London: Routledge, 1993), 187–222; and Slavoj Žižek, "Beyond Discourse Analysis," in *New Reflections on the Revolutions of Our Time,* ed. Ernesto Laclau (London: Verso, 1990), 249–60.

14. Jacques Derrida, *The Other Heading: Reflections on Today's Europe,* trans. Pascale-Anne Brault and Michael B. Naas (Bloomington: Indiana University Press, 1992). I explore the question of the double contradictory imperative and the Derridean approach more thoroughly in the next chapter.

15. For a discussion of the drive to ontological fullness, see Jenny Edkins and Véronique Pin-Fat, "The Subject of the Political," in *Sovereignty and Subjectivity,* ed. Jenny Edkins, Nalini Persram, and Véronique Pin-Fat (Boulder, Colo.: Lynne Rienner, 1999), 1–18; the question of the hunger for certainty is discussed further in the conclusion of the present book.

16. Richard Ashley, "The Achievements of Post-Structuralism," in *International Theory: Positivism and Beyond,* ed. Steve Smith, Ken Booth, and Marysia Zalewski (Cambridge: Cambridge University Press, 1996), 240–53.

17. For an account from the point of view of the journalists who handled the stories, see Paul Harrison and Robin Palmer, *News out of Africa: Biafra to Band Aid* (London: Hilary Shipman, 1986). See also Peter Gill, *A Year in the Death of Africa: Politics, Bureaucracy, and the Famine* (London: Paladin, 1986). A valuable summary of news media coverage is provided in Mary

Kay Magistad, "The Ethiopian Bandwagon: The Relationship between News Media Coverage and British Foreign Policy toward the 1984–85 Ethiopian Famine" (master's thesis, Sussex University, 1985). See also Peter Cutler, "The Development of the 1983–1985 Famine in Northern Ethiopia" (Ph.D. diss., London University School of Hygiene and Tropical Medicine, 1988) for an account of the impact of the increased attention in terms of activities in Ethiopia; and John Sorenson, *Imagining Ethiopia: Struggles for History and Identity in the Horn of Africa* (New Brunswick, N.J.: Rutgers University Press, 1993), chapter 4.

18. See, for example, Eoin Devereux's discussion of telethon television in Ireland, "Good Causes, God's Poor, and Telethon Television," *Media, Culture, and Society* 18 (1996): 47–68; Greg Philo, "From Buerk to Band Aid: The Media and the 1984 Ethiopian Famine," in *Getting the Message: News, Truth, and Power*, ed. Glasgow University Media Group (London: Routledge, 1993); and, of course, Bob Geldof, *Is That it?* (Harmondsworth, England: Penguin, 1986). Also see Dawit, *Red Tears*, 188–220. For a discussion of media coverage in general, see Martin Shaw, *Civil Society and Media in Global Crises: Representing Distant Violence* (London: Pinter, 1996).

19. As I discussed in the previous chapter, assistance was given through different channels to both sides in the conflict.

20. Dawit, *Red Tears*, 189.

21. Ibid., 217.

22. For a summary of the press and television coverage in the various stages of response, see Nikki van der Gaag and Cathy Nash, "Images of Africa: The UK Report (Sponsored by Oxfam and the EEC)," (FAO/FFHC Rome, 1987), 33–42.

23. As, for example, in the World in Action program on 12 November 1984. Philo, "From Buerk to Band Aid," 120.

24. For highly critical work, see Anne Simpson, "Charity Begins at Home," *Ten-8* 19 (1985): 21–26; Adrian Hart, "Consuming Compassion: The Live Aid Phenomenon," *Links* 28 (1987): 15–17; and Robert Allen, "Bob's Not Your Uncle," *Capital and Class* 30 (winter 1986): 31–37. See Keith Tester, *Media, Culture, and Morality* (London: Routledge, 1994) for a more general discussion.

25. The images in the media coverage presented a particular problem for the NGOs, whose own policy of posing fundamental questions of justice and equality was challenged. Clearly the images shown had produced an enormous response, but did that justify them? See van der Gaag and Nash, "Images of Africa," 76. This question and the subsequent campaign in the agencies for guidelines for positive images is discussed in detail by Lidchi, "All in the Choosing Eye." Lidchi characterizes the debate as one between educationalists and fund-raisers; she argues that the positive images of the

194 · NOTES TO CHAPTER 5

influential educationalists are just as manipulative and no more a reflection of reality.

26. Adrian Hart, "Images of the Third World," in *Looking beyond the Frame: Racism, Representation, and Resistance,* ed. Michelle Reeves and Jenny Hammond, Links, no. 34 (Oxford: Third World First, 1989), 12–17; Michelle Reeves, "The Politics of Charity," also in *Looking beyond the Frame,* 7–11.

27. Robert Allen, "Bob's Not Your Uncle," 37.

28. Stan Rijven, Greil Marcus, and Will Straw, *Rock for Ethiopia,* papers from the Third International Conference on Popular Music Studies, IASPM Working Paper 7, Montreal, July 1985.

29. Lidchi, "All in the Choosing Eye," 126–27. I have noted in chapter 4 that the so-called participatory approaches in the South are part of a de-politicization. The reaction in the North then could be seen as paralleling this, rather than contrasting with it.

30. Stuart Hall and Martin Jacques, "People Aid: A New Politics Sweeps the Land," *Marxism Today,* July 1986, 10–14. Dick Hebdige takes a similar stance; I return to his analysis later. See Dick Hebdige, *Hiding in the Light: On Images and Things* (London: Routledge, 1988).

31. Live Aid is notorious for the fact that one performer, Phil Collins, took part in both the London and Philadelphia concerts. A helicopter trans-ported him from Wembley to the tarmac next to the Concorde ("Live Aid 10th Anniversary," BBC2, 15 July 1995).

32. Hall and Jacques, "People Aid."

33. Philo, "From Buerk to Band Aid."

34. See also Dick Hebdige's account of the challenge it posed to the poli-tics of the New Right, *Hiding in the Light,* 216–23.

35. Allen, "Bob's Not Your Uncle." Geldof had been dubbed "Saint Bob."

36. Penelope Ploughman, "The American Print News Media 'Construc-tion' of Five Natural Disasters," *Disasters* 19, no. 4 (1995): 308–26.

37. Ploughman, "American Print," 319. Jonathan Benthall's discussion of the construction of disasters is of interest here also. See his *Disasters, Relief, and the Media* (London: I. B. Tauris, 1993).

38. Ibid., chapter 5. Benthall's account draws on Vladimir Propp, *Morph-ology of the Folktale,* trans. Laurence Scott, 2d ed., (Austin: University of Texas Press, 1968).

39. See, for example, Kalí Tal, *Worlds of Hurt: Reading the Literature of Trauma* (Cambridge: Cambridge University Press, 1996); David Healy, *Im-ages of Trauma: From Hysteria to Post-Traumatic Stress Disorder* (London: Faber & Faber, 1993); and Cathy Caruth, ed., *Trauma: Explorations in Memory* (Baltimore: Johns Hopkins University Press, 1995). For a critical

approach, see Paul Antze and Michael Lambek, eds., *Tense Past: Cultural Essays in Trauma and Memory* (New York: Routledge, 1996).

40. Kai Erikson, "Notes on Trauma and Community," in Caruth, *Trauma*.

41. Slavoj Žižek, *The Metastases of Enjoyment* (London: Verso, 1994), 210.

42. Ibid., 211.

43. Žižek's discussion here is specifically of the situation in Sarajevo, where "the true passive observers are the citizens of Sarajevo themselves," not those in the West who do not act (ibid.).

44. Ibid.

45. For a discussion that looks at the use of images of children specifically, see Erica Burman, "Innocents Abroad: Western Fantasies of Childhood and the Iconography of Emergencies," *Disasters* 18, no. 3 (1994): 238–53. See my figure 11 in this book for an image from the Mohamed Amin film.

46. Slavoj Žižek, *Enjoy Your Symptom: Jacques Lacan in Hollywood and Out* (New York: Routledge, 1992), 103.

47. Žižek, *Metastases of Enjoyment*, 76.

48. Steve Bell, "International Community," *The Guardian* (London), 3 August 1994, cartoon, reference no. 477.3.8.94.

49. Žižek, *Metastases of Enjoyment*, 74.

50. Žižek, *Indivisible Remainder*, 133.

51. Žižek, *Tarrying with the Negative: Kant, Hegel, and the Critique of Ideology*, Post-Contemporary Interventions (Durham, N.C.: Duke University Press, 1993), 237.

52. Žižek, *Indivisible Remainder*, 135. The act (or agency) and the social order (or structure) are not simply opposed, but are, as Žižek expresses it, "entwined in a constitutive way: the symbolic order, qua 'atemporal' trans-subjective structure which predetermines the subject's place *hinges on a temporal act (of precipitate recognition) not 'covered' by the big Other*" (143).

53. Ibid., 137.

54. Ibid., 142.

55. Ibid., 135.

56. Ibid.

57. Ibid., 135–36.

58. Ibid., 134–35. See also Slavoj Žižek, *Tarrying with the Negative*, 73–77, and for a different discussion of the same theme of presupposing the positing, Slavoj Žižek, *The Sublime Object of Ideology* (London: Verso, 1989), 224–31.

59. Žižek, *Indivisible Remainder*, 135. In other words, there isn't some preexisting social order (or series of subject positions) into which we are

interpellated. The position only comes into existence when it is *assumed* (taken up, taken for granted) by the subject.

60. Geldof, *Is That It?* 271.

61. It is also a gesture that incorporates ethico-political responsibility. After the trauma of the moment of traversing the fantasy, the subject and the social are reconstituted. Simon Critchley makes the link between trauma and the constitution of the subject as ethical in his reading of Levinas: "It is only because the subject is unconsciously constituted through the trauma of contact with the real that we might have the audacity to speak of goodness, transcendence, communication, etc. and moreover to speak of these terms in relation to the topology of our desire and not simply in terms of some reactionary and pious wish fulfilment. Without trauma, there would be no ethics, no Levinasian ethics of phenomenology and no Lacanian/Freudian ethics of psychoanalysis. Without such an ethics, there could be no politics that could refuse the domination of the category of totality and the hateful hegemony of the pleasure principle" (Simon Critchley, "Ethics? Subject as Trauma/ Philosophy as Melancholy" [paper presented at the Literature and Ethics Conference Department of English, University of Wales, Aberystwyth, July 1996], 32). *Because* the subject is constituted in the face of trauma—the Real of traumatic suffering, disaster, destruction, *because* the subject is constituted around a traumatic impossibility—in the face of its own limits, its own finitude, *then* it is possible to talk of the ethical subject and the ethical response to the other.

62. Hebdige, *Hiding in the Light,* 220.

63. Ibid., 221.

64. Ibid., 222.

65. An example of the retechnologizing process was the way the agencies, such as Save the Children and Christian Aid, set up studies of the imagery used in television broadcasts; criteria were drawn up and programs instituted to ensure that proper techniques of representation were used in future. For a study of this process, see Lidchi, "All in the Choosing Eye."

66. The Band Aid response is to increase demands on "world governments," to move the interpellation to the international community. The latter is ambiguous as, at the same time, the Band Aid movement expects individuals to accept interpellation as members of the world themselves (as persons).

67. Geldof, *Is That It?* 9–10. "Praise of the assembled people at the festival or at the political forum is always a critique of representation. The legitimising instance, in the city as in language—speech or writing and the arts, is the representer present in person: source of legitimacy and sacred origin." Jacques Derrida, *Of Grammatology,* trans. Gayatri Chakravorty Spivak (Baltimore: Johns Hopkins University Press, 1976), 296.

68. And, as we have already noted, the critics' view itself is ideological—the ideology of science produces its own enjoyment and fantasy. For an overview of approaches to ideology, see Slavoj Žižek, ed., *Mapping Ideology* (London: Verso, 1994), in particular his first chapter, "The Spectre of Ideology," 1–33.

69. Žižek, *Sublime Object*, 125.

70. Ibid., 127.

71. Ibid.

72. See Rangasami's comments in Fintan O'Toole, "Hungry Eyes," prod. Mary Price, research Ellis Hill (BBC Radio 4, 1 November 1995). See also Amitra Rangasami, "Failure of Exchange Entitlements Theory of Famine," *Economic and Political Weekly* 20, no. 41 (1985): 1747–52; no. 42 (1985): 1797–801.

73. Hebdige, *Hiding in the Light*, 222.

74. Roger Waters, Radio KAOS, "The Tide Is Turning (after Live Aid)," Roger Waters Music Ltd./Pink Floyd Music Publishers, 1987.

75. Žižek, *Tarrying with the Negative*, 237.

76. Slavoj Žižek, *For They Know Not What They Do: Enjoyment as a Political Factor* (London: Verso, 1991).

77. Open University, Programme D103 (1), "Using Television."

78. Josué de Castro, *The Geopolitics of Hunger* (New York: Monthly Review Press, 1952).

79. This was the title of a program examining the responses to the Ethiopian famine: Ilan Ziv, *Consuming Hunger (1) Getting the Story (2) Shaping the Image* (broadcast on BBC4, 18 and 19 February 1987, Tamouz Productions).

80. Alex de Waal, *Famine That Kills: Dafur, Sudan, 1984–1985* (Oxford: Clarendon Press, 1989).

81. Her argument is based on a Lacanian approach (Drucilla Cornell, *The Imaginary Domain: Abortion, Pornography, and Sexual Harassment* [London: Routledge, 1995]). Cornell's position is not anti-pornography. States with the highest levels of anti-pornography campaigns have the highest levels of violence, specifically violence against women (153).

82. Ibid., 149.

83. Ibid., 148.

84. See, for example Hart, "Consuming Compassion," and Ziv, *Consuming Hunger*.

85. Žižek, *Indivisible Remainder*, 190.

86. Ibid., 189; italics in original. We can draw out here the link between desire and ideology. The impossible is prohibited, thereby creating the *illusion* of attainability and hence desire. Illusion is basic to the ideological in Žižek, but in contrast to the traditional Marxist view of ideology as false consciousness—an illusion that prevents the realization of "real" interests—

here ideology is an illusion masking the *unattainability* of the object of desire. The gap between the official motivation of desire, without which desire cannot exist, and the function of desire in enabling us to live with a primordial lack is at the root of the power of, and the need for, the ideological.

87. Ibid., 231.

88. It is these obstacles perhaps that are threatened by the Live Aid approach—an approach that stresses *possibilities*, not *difficulties*. Maybe developmentalists see Live Aid's enjoyment as a threat to their desire. "But it's not that easy!" they cry.

89. Žižek, *Indivisible Remainder*, 190.

90. What Žižek does not do, so far at least, is to link this with modernity. He sees the constitutive lack as transhistorical.

91. *Live Aid 10th Anniversary*, 15 July 1995; *Life After Live Aid*, dir. John MacGuire, prod. Andrew Coggins (broadcast on BBC2, 28 July 1995).

92. See Ethiopian Relief and Rehabilitation Commission, Economic Commission for Africa, and InterAfrica Group, "The Addis Ababa Statement on Famine in Ethiopia: Learning from the Past to Prepare for the Future," in *Famine in Ethiopia: Learning from the Past to Prepare for the Future* (Addis Ababa, 18 March 1995, unpublished typescript).

93. Band Aid was wound up specifically to avoid it becoming yet another "institution."

94. Alex de Waal, personal communication, January 1997.

95. Jacques Derrida, "Force of Law: The 'Mystical Foundation of Authority,'" in *Deconstruction and the Possibility of Justice*, ed. David Gray Carlson, Drucilla Cornell, and Michel Rosenfeld (New York: Routledge, 1992), 3–67.

96. Žižek, *Tarrying with the Negative*, 237.

97. Žižek, *Indivisible Remainder*, 137; emphasis in original.

98. Ibid., 138; italics in original.

99. Ibid., 140.

100. Ibid., 142. This is what Žižek calls "going through the fantasy."

6. COMPLEX EMERGENCY AND (IM)POSSIBLE POLITICS

1. See, for example, Rakiya Omaar and Alex de Waal, "Humanitarianism Unbound? Current Dilemmas Facing Multi-Mandate Relief Operations in Political Emergencies," Discussion Paper no. 5 (African Rights, 1994); and Joanna Macrae and Anthony Zwi, eds., *War and Hunger: Rethinking International Responses to Complex Emergencies* (London: Zed Books in association with Save the Children Fund [UK], 1994).

2. Simon Maxwell and Margaret Buchanan-Smith, eds., "Linking Relief and Development," special issue of *IDS Bulletin* 25, no. 4 (1994).

3. Mark Duffield, "Complex Emergencies and the Crisis of Developmentalism," *IDS Bulletin* 25, no. 4 (1994): 37–45. This debate was discussed in chapter 4.

4. As discussed in chapter 4, in Ethiopia aid was appropriated by the government and allegedly used to enforce genocidal resettlement policies, while in Eritrea relief supplies sustained the eventually victorious rebel fronts in the liberation war. See Jason W. Clay, Sandra Steingraber, and Peter Niggli, *The Spoils of Famine: Ethiopian Famine Policy and Peasant Agriculture* (Cambridge, Mass.: Cultural Survival, 1988); Mark Duffield and John Prendergast, *Without Troops and Tanks: The Emergency Relief Desk and the Cross Border Operation into Eritrea and Tigray* (Lawrenceville, N.J.: Red Sea Press, 1994); and John Sorenson, *Imagining Ethiopia: Struggles for History and Identity in the Horn of Africa* (New Brunswick, N.J.: Rutgers University Press, 1993).

5. Richard McCall, "Confronting the New World Disorder," *DHA News,* May/June 1995, quoted in Alex de Waal, *Famine Crimes: Politics and the Disaster Relief Industry in Africa* (Oxford: African Rights and the International African Institute in association with James Currey, 1997), 203.

6. Duffield, "Complex Emergencies," 38.

7. Rakiya Omaar and Alex de Waal have proposed the alternative phrase "political emergencies," and Duffield had earlier used the term "permanent emergency." See Rakiya Omaar and Alex de Waal, "Humanitarianism Unbound?" 2; Mark Duffield, "NGOs, Disaster Relief, and Asset Transfer in the Horn: Political Survival in a Permanent Emergency," *Development and Change* 24 (1993): 131–57.

8. For discussion of the use of the term in the Sudan, see Ataul Karim et al., "OLS Operation Lifeline Sudan: A Review" (unpublished independent report with administrative support from the UN Department of Humanitarian Affairs, 1996), 43.

9. Joanna Macrae and Anthony Zwi, "Famine, Complex Emergencies, and International Policy in Africa: An Overview," in Macrae and Zwi, *War and Hunger,* 21.

10. Duffield, "Complex Emergencies," 38.

11. Ibid., 38.

12. Larry Minear and Thomas G. Weiss, *Mercy under Fire: War and the Global Humanitarian Community* (Boulder, Colo.: Westview Press, 1995), 17.

13. See, for example, Nicholas Stockton, "In Defence of Humanitarianism," *Disasters* 22, no. 4 (1998): 352–60; Joanna Macrae, "The Death of

Humanitarianism? An Anatomy of the Attack," *Disasters* 22, no. 4 (1998): 309–17.

14. De Waal's critique of Sen was considered in chapter 3. See Alex de Waal, *Famine That Kills: Dafur, Sudan, 1984–1985* (Oxford: Clarendon Press, 1989); Mark Duffield and John Prendergast, *Without Troops and Tanks: The Emergency Relief Desk and the Cross Border Operation into Eritrea and Tigray* (Lawrenceville, N.J.: Red Sea Press, 1994); and David Keen, *The Benefits of Famine: A Political Economy of Famine and Relief in Southwestern Sudan, 1983–1989* (Princeton: Princeton University Press, 1994).

15. William DeMars, "Mercy without Illusion: Humanitarian Action in Conflict," *Mershon International Studies Review* (supplement to *International Studies Quarterly*) 40, no. S1 (1996): 81–89. It should be noted that they draw heavily on the work of Amitra Rangasami.

16. De Waal, *Famine That Kills.*

17. Alex de Waal, *Famine Crimes: Politics and the Disaster Relief Industry in Africa* (Oxford: African Rights and the International African Institute in association with James Currey, 1997).

18. Keen, *Benefits of Famine.*

19. Duffield, "Complex Emergencies."

20. The work of African Rights is notable here (Omaar and de Waal, "Humanitarianism Unbound," for example).

21. "Jimmy," Strokestown; quoted in O'Toole, "Hungry Eyes."

22. Roger J. McHugh, "The Famine in Irish Oral Tradition," in *The Great Famine,* ed. R. Dudley Edwards and T. Desmond Williams (Dublin: Browne and Nolan, 1956), 409–29.

23. Keen, *Benefits of Famine.*

24. Rangasami's work was also discussed in chapter 3. Amitra Rangasami, "Failure of Exchange Entitlements Theory of Famine," *Economic and Political Weekly* 20, no. 41 (1985): 1747–52; no. 42 (1985): 1797–801.

25. Keen, *Benefits of Famine,* 6–7.

26. Ibid., 9–11. This approach is drawn from the work of E. J. Clay and B. B. Schaffer, eds., *Room for Manoeuvre: An Exploration of Public Policy in Agriculture and Rural Development* (Cambridge, Mass.: Cultural Survival, 1984).

27. Keen, *Benefits of Famine,* 198.

28. Ibid., 198.

29. To do this it is necessary to understand the political economy of violence. For example, "there may be considerable objective, as well as subjective, rationality in 'political' violence that is aimed at changing or maintaining the laws and procedures governing the distribution of resources in a society. . . . Economic threats and opportunities may be as important in explaining the continuation of war as the more openly declared political and

military objectives" (Mats Berdal and David Keen, "Violence and Economic Agendas in Civil Wars: Some Policy Implications," *Millennium: Journal of International Studies* 26, no. 3 [1997]: 795–818; 798). If this is not understood it can undermine peace processes, which tend to assume a certain irrationality about conflict.

30. Mark Duffield, "NGOs, Disaster Relief," 131.

31. Ibid., 134–135.

32. Ibid., 140.

33. The Eritrean International Agency for Cooperation, or Inter-agency Agricultural Consortium, formed in 1983, was an example of a consortium formed with a specific purpose, in this case to operate behind the lines in Eritrea (interview with Ian Robinson, 3 August 1994). EIAC was a splinter group from Euro-Action Accord, which up until then had been a consortium of twenty-six NGOs from Europe and Canada.

34. Duffield, "NGOs, Disaster Relief," 148.

35. Mark Duffield, "The Symphony of the Damned: Racial Discourse, Complex Political Emergencies, and Humanitarian Aid," *Disasters*, 20, no. 3 (1996): 173–93.

36. Mark Duffield, "Humanitarian Intervention in Africa: Adapting to Separate Development," *New Political Economy* 2, no. 2 (summer 1997): 336–66; Mark Duffield, "Containing Systemic Crisis: The Regionalisation of Welfare and Security Policy," in *World Orders in the Making: Humanitarian Intervention and Beyond*, ed. Jan Nederveen Pieterse (Basingstoke, England: Macmillan, 1998), 80–110; and Mark Duffield, "NGO Relief in War Zones: Towards an Analysis of the New Aid Paradigm," *Third World Quarterly* 18, no. 3 (1997): 527–42.

37. Mark Duffield, "Post-Modern Conflict: Warlords, Post-Adjustment States, and Private Protection," *Journal of Civil Wars* 1, no. 1 (April 1998): 65–102.

38. Ibid., 65.

39. Keen, *Benefits of Famine*, 236.

40. Ibid., 213.

41. De Waal, *Famine Crimes*, 2.

42. Ibid., 1.

43. Ibid., 6.

44. Ibid., 11.

45. Ibid., 112–32.

46. Ibid., 127–31.

47. Ibid., 132.

48. Ibid., 131.

49. Ibid., 1.

50. Ibid., 85.

51. Ibid., 158.

52. Ibid., 168–72. See Mohamed Sahnoun, *Somalia: The Missed Opportunities* (Washington, D.C.: U.S. Institute for Peace, 1994).

53. De Waal, *Famine Crimes,* 138.

54. Ibid., 144.

55. Ibid., 145.

56. Ibid., 155–56.

57. Ibid., 190.

58. Françoise Boucher-Saulnier, "Peacekeeping Operations above International Law," in F. Jean, ed., *Life, Death, and Aid: the Médecins sans Frontières Report on World Crisis Intervention* (London: Routledge, 1993), 128; quoted in de Waal, *Famine Crimes,* 190.

59. De Waal, *Famine Crimes,* 181.

60. See, for example Lionel Cliffe, "Complexity of Conflict: Coping with Crises of State Collapse," *Third World Quarterly* 20, no. 1 (1999): 9–11, and the rest of this special issue, including Jonathan Goodhand and David Hulme, "From Wars to Complex Political Emergencies: Understanding Conflict and Peace-Building in the New World Disorder," *Third World Quarterly* 20, no. 1 (1999): 13–26.

61. Mary B. Anderson, "Do No Harm: Supporting Local Capacities for Peace through Aid" (Collaborative for Development Action, Local Capacities for Peace Project, 1996). See also Mary B. Anderson, *Do No Harm: How Aid Can Support Peace—or War* (Boulder, Colo.: Lynne Rienner, 1999).

62. Hugo Slim, "Doing the Right Thing: Relief Agencies, Moral Dilemmas, and Moral Responsibility in Political Emergencies and War," *Disasters* 21, no. 3 (1997): 244–57; Nicholas Leader, "Proliferating Principles; or How to Sup with the Devil without Getting Eaten," *Disasters* 22, no. 4 (1998): 288–308.

63. Anderson, *Do No Harm: Peace—Or War,* 75.

64. Anderson "Do No Harm: Local Capacities," 5.

65. Ibid., 55.

66. David Campbell, "Why Fight: Humanitarianism, Principles, and Post-Structuralism," *Millennium: Journal of International Studies* 27, no. 3 (1998): 501.

67. Development Assistance Committee, "DAC Guidelines on Conflict, Peace and Development Co-Operation," (OECD, 1997).

68. Campbell, "Why Fight," 503.

69. Ibid., 505.

70. Ibid., 512.

71. Ibid., 521.

72. David Keen and Ken Wilson, "Engaging with Violence: A Reassessment of Relief in Wartime," in Macrae and Zwi, eds., *War and Hunger,* 220.

73. Derrida, *Writing and Difference*, trans. Alan Bass (London: Routledge, 1978), 278–79.

74. Cornell, *The Philosophy of the Limit* (London: Routledge, 1992), 2.

75. Ibid., 1.

76. Ibid.

77. Duffield, "Complex Emergencies."

78. Jacques Derrida, *Of Grammatology*, trans. Gayatri Chakravorty Spivak (Baltimore: Johns Hopkins, 1976); Derrida, *Writing and Difference*.

79. See, for example, Keen, *Benefits of Famine*, 235; Duffield, "Complex Emergencies," 43; Omaar and de Waal, "Humanitarianism Unbound," 2–3.

80. Jacques Derrida, *The Other Heading: Reflections on Today's Europe*, trans. Pascale-Anne Brault and Michael B. Naas (Bloomington: Indiana University Press, 1992), 79.

81. This draws on the discussion in Derrida, *The Other Heading*, 38–39.

82. Ibid., 41.

83. Ibid.

84. Ibid.; italics in original.

85. In this regard my approach is very close to that of Duffield and Keen, although not to that of some of the writers who have drawn on their work.

86. Derrida, "Force of Law: The 'Mystical Foundation of Authority,'" in *Deconstruction and the Possibility of Justice*, ed. David Gray Carlson, Drucilla Cornell, and Michel Rosenfeld (New York: Routledge, 1992), 28.

87. David Campbell, "The Deterritorialisation of Responsibility: Levinas, Derrida, and Ethics after the End of Philosophy," *Alternatives* 19, no. 4 (1994): 477. See also Simon Critchley, *The Ethics of Deconstruction: Derrida and Levinas* (Oxford: Blackwell, 1992), 199.

88. Derrida, *The Other Heading*, 45–46.

89. Ibid., 29.

90. Ibid., 52. For an example of a challenge to the way general guidelines are drawn from the analysis of a particular case, in this instance a case of internal war, see Trish Silkin and Barbara Hendrie, "Research in the War Zones of Eritrea and Tigray," *Disasters* 21, no. 2 (1997): 166–76. Silkin and Hendrie contest the need for neutrality and argue instead for a recognition of the specificity of each particular case.

91. Derrida, *The Other Heading*, 52.

92. Carol Gilligan, *In a Different Voice: Psychological Theory and Women's Development* (Cambridge: Harvard University Press, 1982; reprinted with a new preface, 1993).

93. Ibid., 32.

94. Clay, Steingraber, and Niggli, *The Spoils of Famine*, 3.

95. Derrida, *The Other Heading*, 81.

96. Gilligan, *In a Different Voice*, 32.

CONCLUSION

1. Nancy Scheper-Hughes, *Death without Weeping: The Violence of Everyday Life in Brazil* (Berkeley: University of California Press, 1992), 214.

2. Ibid.

3. Ibid., 215.

4. Slavoj Žižek, *The Sublime Object of Ideology* (London: Verso, 1989), 181.

5. Slavoj Žižek, *Looking Awry: An Introduction to Jacques Lacan through Popular Culture* (Cambridge: MIT Press, 1991), 140.

6. Plato, *Republic* (Harmondsworth, England: Penguin, 1955), 244.

7. Friedrich Nietzsche, *Twilight of the Idols,* trans. R. J. Hollingdale (Harmondsworth, England: Penguin, 1990).

8. This is the "comfort of theories" (Marysia Zalewski, "'All These Theories and Yet the Bodies Keep Piling Up': Theories, Theorists, Theorising," in *International Theory: Positivism and Beyond,* ed. Steve Smith, Ken Booth, and Marysia Zalewski [Cambridge: Cambridge University Press, 1996], 352). This is particularly important in relation to disaster, where technologization "serves to displace the disturbing implications" and render it "'knowable' and hence 'do-able'" (Barbara Hendrie, "Knowledge and Power: A Critique of an International Relief Operation," *Disasters* 21, no. 1 [1997]: 63–64).

9. Nietzsche, *Twilight of the Idols,* 46.

10. In addition, he removes the possibility of illusion, at least in the sense that Plato implies: "We have abolished the real world: what world is left? the apparent world perhaps? . . . But no! *with the real world we have also abolished the apparent world!*" (ibid., 51; italics in original).

11. Ibid., 48.

12. David Campbell, "The Deterritorialisation of Responsibility: Levinas, Derrida, and Ethics after the End of Philosophy," *Alternatives* 19, no. 4 (1994): 477.

13. This argument is made in chapter 4, where a Foucauldian approach is used to analyze practices of food aid.

14. Kirsten Hastrup, "Hunger and the Hardness of Facts," *Man,* n.s., 28, no. 4 (1993): 727–39.

15. Marysia Zalewski, "All These Theories."

16. Jean Bethke Elshtain, *Public Man, Private Woman: Women in Social and Political Thought,* 2d ed. (Princeton: Princeton University Press, 1993).

17. Laura W. Reed and Carl Kayson, eds., *Emerging Norms of Justified Intervention: A Collection of Essays from a Project of the American Academy of Arts and Sciences* (Cambridge, Mass.: American Academy of Arts and Sciences, Committee on International Security Studies, 1993), 5.

18. For an account of the distinction between these approaches within

logocentric thought, see Martin Hollis and Steve Smith, *Explaining and Understanding International Relations* (Oxford: Clarenden Paperbacks, 1990).

19. Richard Ashley, "The Achievements of Post-Structuralism," in *International Theory: Positivism and Beyond*, ed. Steve Smith, Ken Booth, and Marysia Zalewski (Cambridge: Cambridge University Press, 1996), 244.

Selected Bibliography

Adam, Hussein M. "Formation and Recognition of New States: Somaliland in Contrast to Eritrea." *Review of African Political Economy* 21, no. 59 (1994): 21–38.

Agamben, Giorgio. *Homo Sacer: Sovereign Power and Bare Life*. Trans. Daniel Heller-Roazen. Stanford: Stanford University Press, 1998.

Aiken, William, and Hugh LaFollette, eds. *World Hunger and Morality*. 2d ed. Englewood Cliffs, N.J.: Prentice Hall, 1977.

Allen, G. "Famines—The Bowbrick-Sen Dispute and Some Related Issues." *Food Policy* 11, no. 3 (1986): 259–63.

Allen, Robert. "Bob's Not Your Uncle." *Capital and Class* 30 (winter 1986): 31–37.

Amin, Mohamed. "A Vision of the Truth." *Refugees* (October 1989): 22–25.

Anderson, Mary B. *Do No Harm: How Aid Can Support Peace—Or War*. Boulder, Colo.: Lynne Rienner, 1999.

———. "Do No Harm: Supporting Local Capacities for Peace through Aid." Cambridge, Mass.: Collaborative for Development Action, Local Capacities for Peace Project, 1996.

Antze, Paul, and Michael Lambek, eds. *Tense Past: Cultural Essays in Trauma and Memory*. New York: Routledge, 1996.

Aretxaga, Begoña. "Striking with Hunger: Cultural Meanings of Political Violence in Northern Ireland." In *The Violence Within: Cultural and Political Opposition in Divided Nations*, ed. Kay B. Warren, 217–53. Boulder, Colo.: Westview Press, 1993.

Arnold, David. *Famine: Social Crisis and Historical Change*. New Perspectives on the Past. Oxford: Basil Blackwell, 1988.

———. "Looting, Grain Riots, and Government Policy in South India 1918." *Past and Present* 84 (1979): 111–45.

Ashley, Richard. "The Achievements of Post-Structuralism." In *International Theory: Positivism and Beyond,* ed. Steve Smith, Ken Booth, and Marysia Zalewski, 240–53. Cambridge: Cambridge University Press, 1996.

Ashton, Basil, et al. "Famine in China, 1958–1961." *Population and Development Review* 10, no. 4 (1984): 613–45.

Augelli, Enrica, and Craig Murphy. *America's Quest for Supremacy and the Third World: A Gramscian Analysis.* London: Pinter, 1988.

Baker, Randall. "The Need for Long Term Strategies in Areas of Pastoral Nomadism." In *Drought in Africa,* ed. David Dalby and R. J. Harrison Church. London: University of London, 1973.

Ball, Nicole. "African Famine." In *World Hunger and the World Economy,* Keith Griffin. London: Macmillan, 1987.

———. "The Myth of the Natural Disaster." *Ecologist* 5, no. 10 (1975): 368–71.

———. "Understanding the Causes of African Famine." *Journal of Modern African Studies* 14, no. 3 (1976): 517–22.

Bauman, Zygmunt. *Modernity and the Holocaust.* Ithaca, N.Y.: Cornell University Press, 1991.

Becker, Jasper. *Hungry Ghosts: China's Secret Famine.* London: John Murray, 1996.

Beitz, Charles R., et al., eds. *International Ethics: A Philosophy and Public Affairs Reader.* Princeton: Princeton University Press, 1985.

Bell, Steve. "International Community." *The Guardian* (London), 3 August 1994, cartoon, reference no. 477.3.8.94.

Benthall, Jonathan. *Disasters, Relief, and the Media.* London: I. B. Tauris, 1993.

Berdal, Mats, and David Keen. "Violence and Economic Agendas in Civil Wars: Some Policy Implications." *Millennium: Journal of International Studies* 26, no. 3 (1997): 795–818.

Bohr, Paul Richard. *Famine in China and the Missionary: Timothy Richard as Relief Administrator and Advocate of National Reform, 1876–1884.* Cambridge: Harvard University, East Asian Research Center, 1972.

Bondestam, Lars. "People and Capitalism in the North-Eastern Lowlands of Ethiopia." *Journal of Modern African Studies* 12, no. 3 (1974).

Booth, Ken. "Human Wrongs and International Relations." *International Affairs* 71, no. 1 (1995): 103–26.

Boserup, Ester. *The Conditions of Agricultural Growth: Economics of Agrarian Change under Population Pressure.* London: Earthscan, 1993.

Boucher-Saulnier, Françoise. "Peacekeeping Operations above International

Law." In *Life, Death, and Aid: The Médecins sans Frontières Report on World Crisis Intervention*, ed. F. Jean. London: Routledge, 1993.

Bourke, P. M. Austin. *The Visitation of God? The Potato and the Great Irish Famine*. Dublin: Lilliput Press, 1993.

Bowbrick, P. "The Causes of Famine—A Refutation of Sen Theory." *Food Policy* 11, no. 2 (1986): 105–24.

———. "Rejoinder: An Untenable Hypothesis on the Causes of Famine." *Food Policy* 12, no. 1 (1987): 5–9.

Bradshaw, Brendan. "Nationalism and Historical Scholarship in Modern Ireland," *Irish Historical Studies* 26, no. 104 (1989): 329–51.

Brown, Lester R. *State of the World 1996: A Worldwatch Institute Report on Progress towards a Sustainable Society*. London: Earthscan Publications, 1996.

———. *Full House*. Worldwatch Institute, 1994.

Buchanan-Smith, Margaret, and Simon Maxwell. "Linking Relief and Development: An Introduction and Overview." *IDS Bulletin* 25, no. 4 (1994): 2.

Burman, Erica. "Innocents Abroad: Western Fantasies of Childhood and the Iconography of Emergencies." *Disasters* 18, no. 3 (1994): 238–53.

Butler, Judith. *Bodies That Matter: On the Discursive Limits of "Sex."* London: Routledge, 1993.

———. *Gender Trouble: Feminism and the Subversion of Identity*. New York: Routledge, 1990.

Campbell, David. "The Deterritorialisation of Responsibility: Levinas, Derrida, and Ethics after the End of Philosophy." *Alternatives* 19, no. 4 (1994): 455–84.

———. *National Deconstruction: Violence, Identity, and Justice in Bosnia*. Minneapolis: University of Minnesota Press, 1998.

———. "The Politics of Radical Interdependence: A Rejoinder to Daniel Warner." *Millennium* 25, no. 1 (1996): 129–41.

———. *Politics without Principle: Sovereignty, Ethics, and the Narratives of the Gulf War*. Critical Perspectives on World Politics. Boulder, Colo.: Lynne Rienner, 1993.

———. "Why Fight: Humanitarianism, Principles, and Post-Structuralism." *Millennium: Journal of International Studies* 27, no. 3 (1998): 497–521.

Campbell, Stephen J. *The Great Irish Famine: Words and Images from the Famine Museum, Strokestown Park, County Roscommon*. Strokestown, Ireland: Famine Museum, 1994.

Camporesi, Piero. *Bread of Dreams: Food and Fantasy in Early Modern Europe*. Trans. David Gentilcore. Chicago: University of Chicago Press, 1989.

Caruth, Cathy, ed. *Trauma: Explorations in Memory*. Baltimore: Johns Hopkins University Press, 1995.

Chaloupka, William, and R. McGreggor Cawley. "The Great Wild Hope: Nature, Environmentalism, and the Open Secret." In *In the Nature of Things: Language, Politics, and the Environment,* ed. Jane Bennett and William Chaloupka, 3–23. Minneapolis: University of Minnesota Press, 1993.

Clapham, Christopher. *Africa and the International System: The Politics of State Survival.* Cambridge: Cambridge University Press, 1996.

Clay, E. "Famine, Food Insecurity, Poverty, and Public Action." *Development Policy Review* 9 (1991): 307–12.

Clay, Edward J., and B. B. Schaffer, eds. *Room for Manoeuvre: An Exploration of Public Policy in Agriculture and Rural Development.* Cambridge, Mass.: Cultural Survival, 1984.

Clay, Edward J., and Olav Stokke, eds. *Food Aid Reconsidered: Assessing the Impact on Third World Countries.* London: Cass in collaboration with the European Association of Development Research and Training Institutes, 1991.

Clay, Jason W., and Bonnie K. Holcomb, *Politics and the Ethiopian Famine 1984–1985.* Cultural Survival Report 20. Cambridge, Mass.: Cultural Survival, 1986.

Clay, Jason W., Sandra Steingraber, and Peter Niggli. *The Spoils of Famine: Ethiopian Famine Policy and Peasant Agriculture.* Cambridge, Mass.: Cultural Survival, 1988.

Cliffe, Lionel. "Complexity of Conflict: Coping with Crises of State Collapse." *Third World Quarterly* 20, no. 1 (1999): 9–11.

Cliffe, Lionel, and Basil Davidson, eds. *The Long Struggle of Eritrea for Independence and Constructive Peace.* Nottingham, England: Spokesman, 1988.

Cohen, Mark Nathan. *The Food Crisis in Prehistory: Overpopulation and the Origins of Agriculture.* New Haven: Yale University Press, 1977.

———. "Prehistoric Patterns of Hunger." In *Hunger in History: Food Shortage, Poverty, and Deprivation,* ed. Lucile F. Newman. Oxford: Blackwell, 1990.

Connell, Dan. *Against All Odds: A Chronicle of the Eritrean Revolution.* Trenton, N.J.: Red Sea Press, 1993.

Cornell, Drucilla. *The Imaginary Domain: Abortion, Pornography, and Sexual Harassment.* London: Routledge, 1995.

———. *The Philosophy of the Limit.* London: Routledge, 1992.

Craib, Ian. "Some Comments on the Sociology of the Emotions." *Sociology* 29, no. 1 (1995): 151–58.

Crawford, E. Margaret. "William Wilde's Table of Irish Famines 900–1850." In *Famine: The Irish Experience, 900–1900: Subsistence Crises and Fam-*

ines in Ireland, ed. E. Margaret Crawford, 1–30. Edinburgh: John Donald Publishers, 1989.

Critchley, Simon. *The Ethics of Deconstruction: Derrida and Levinas.* Oxford: Blackwell, 1992.

———. "Ethics? Subject as Trauma/Philosophy as Melancholy." Paper presented at the Literature and Ethics Conference, Department of English, University of Wales, Aberystwyth, July 1996.

Cross, Nigel, and Rhiannon Barker, eds. *At the Desert's Edge: Oral Histories from the Sahel.* London: Panos, SOS Sahel, 1994.

Cutler, Peter. "The Development of the 1983–1985 Famine in Northern Ethiopia." Ph.D. diss., London University School of Hygiene and Tropical Medicine, 1988.

Davies, Susanna. "Are Coping Strategies a Cop-Out?" *IDS Bulletin* 24, no. 4 (1993): 60–72.

Dawit Wolde Giorgis. *Red Tears: War, Famine, and Revolution in Ethiopia.* Trenton, N.J.: Red Sea Press, 1989.

Dean, Mitchell. *The Constitution of Poverty: Toward a Theory of Liberal Governance.* London: Routledge, 1991.

———. "A Genealogy of the Government of Poverty." *Economy and Society* 21, no. 3 (1992): 215–51.

Debrix, François. "Deploying Vision, Simulating Action: The United Nations and Its Visualisation Strategies in a New World Order." *Alternatives* 21 (1996): 67–92.

de Castro, Josué. *The Geopolitics of Hunger.* New York: Monthly Review Press, 1952.

DeMars, William. "Mercy without Illusion: Humanitarian Action in Conflict." *Mershon International Studies Review* (supplement to *International Studies Quarterly*) 40, no. S1 (1996): 81–89.

Derrida, Jacques. "Force of Law: The 'Mystical Foundation of Authority.'" In *Deconstruction and the Possibility of Justice*, ed. David Gray Carlson, Drucilla Cornell, and Michel Rosenfeld, 3–67. New York: Routledge, 1992.

———. *Of Grammatology.* Trans. Gayatri Chakravorty Spivak. Baltimore: Johns Hopkins University Press, 1976.

———. *The Other Heading: Reflections on Today's Europe.* Trans. Pascale-Anne Brault and Michael B. Naas. Bloomington: Indiana University Press, 1992.

———. *Positions.* Trans. Alan Bass. London: Athlone Press, 1987.

———. "Signature Event Context." In *Limited Inc*, ed. Jacques Derrida, 1–23. Evanston, Ill.: Northwestern University Press, 1988.

———. *Writing and Difference.* Trans. Alan Bass. London: Routledge, 1978.

Desai, Meghnad. "Story-Telling and Formalism in Economics: The Instance of Famine." *International Social Science Journal* 113 (1987): 387–400.

Development Assistance Committee. "DAC Guidelines on Conflict, Peace, and Development Co-Operation." OECD, 1997.

Devereux, Eoin. "Good Causes, God's Poor, and Telethon Television." *Media, Culture, and Society* 18 (1996): 47–68.

Devereux, Stephen. *Theories of Famine*. Hemel Hempstead, England: Harvester Wheatsheaf, 1993.

de Waal, Alex. *Evil Days: Thirty Years of War and Famine in Ethiopia*. Africa Watch Report. New York: Human Rights Watch, 1991.

———. *Famine Crimes: Politics and the Disaster Relief Industry in Africa*. Oxford: African Rights and the International African Institute in association with James Currey, 1997.

———. *Famine That Kills: Dafur, Sudan, 1984–1985*. Oxford: Clarendon Press, 1989.

———. "Logic and Application: A Reply to S. R. Osmani." *Development and Change* 22 (1991): 597–608.

———. "The Perception of Poverty and Famines." *International Journal of Moral and Social Studies* 2, no. 3 (1987): 251–62.

———. "A Reassessment of Entitlement Theory in the Light of Recent Famines in Africa." *Development and Change* 21, no. 3 (1990): 474–78.

Dillon, Michael. *The Politics of Security*. London: Routledge, 1996.

Donnelly, James. "The Construction of the Memory of the Famine in Ireland and the Irish Diaspora 1850–1900." Paper delivered at Cambridge University, March 1996.

Donovan, Paul. "A Decade of Drought." *The Guardian* (London), 6 December 1994, Guardian Education, 9–11.

Dreyfus, Hubert L., and Paul Rabinow. *Michel Foucault: Beyond Stuctural-ism and Hermeneutics*. Hemel Hempstead, England: Harvester Press, 1982; 2d ed., Chicago: University of Chicago Press, 1983, with a second afterword by Michel Foucault, 229–52.

Drèze, Jean, and Amartya Sen. *Hunger and Public Action*. Oxford: Oxford University Press, 1993.

Duffield, Mark. "Complex Emergencies and the Crisis of Developmental-ism." *IDS Bulletin* 25, no. 4 (1994): 37–45.

———. "Containing Systemic Crisis: The Regionalisation of Welfare and Security Policy." In *World Orders in the Making: Humanitarian Intervention and Beyond*, ed. Jan Nederveen Pieterse, 80–110. Basingstoke, England: Macmillan, 1998.

———. "Eritrea and Tigray: Changing Organisational Issues in Cross-Border Relief Assistance 1983–1992." In *Meeting Needs: NGO Coordination in Practice*, ed. Jon Bennett. London: Earthscan, 1995.

———. "Humanitarian Intervention in Africa: Adapting to Separate Development." *New Political Economy* 2, no. 2 (summer 1997): 336–66.

———. "NGO Relief in War Zones: Towards an Analysis of the New Aid Paradigm." *Third World Quarterly* 18, no. 3 (1997): 527–42.

———. "NGOs, Disaster Relief, and Asset Transfer in the Horn: Political Survival in a Permanent Emergency." *Development and Change* 24 (1993): 131–57.

———. "Post-Modern Conflict: Warlords, Post-Adjustment States, and Private Protection." *Journal of Civil Wars* 1, no. 1 (April 1998): 65–102.

———. "The Symphony of the Damned: Racial Discourse, Complex Political Emergencies, and Humanitarian Aid." *Disasters* 20, no. 3 (1996): 173–93.

Duffield, Mark, and John Prendergast. *Without Troops and Tanks: The Emergency Relief Desk and the Cross Border Operation into Eritrea and Tigray.* Lawrenceville, N.J.: Red Sea Press, 1994.

Dumont, Louis. *From Mandeville to Marx: The Genesis and Triumph of Economic Ideology.* Chicago: University of Chicago Press, 1977.

Eagleton, Terry. *Heathcliffe and the Great Hunger.* London: Verso, 1995.

Edkins, Jenny. *Poststructuralism and International Relations: Bringing the Political Back In.* Boulder, Colo.: Lynne Rienner, 1999.

———. "Technologising the International: Pictures of Hunger, Concepts of Famine, Practices of Aid." Ph.D. diss., University of Wales Aberystwyth, 1997.

Edkins, Jenny, and Véronique Pin-Fat. "The Subject of the Political." In *Sovereignty and Subjectivity,* ed. Jenny Edkins, Nalini Persram, and Véronique Pin-Fat, 1–18. Boulder, Colo.: Lynne Rienner, 1999.

Edwards, R. Dudley, and T. Desmond Williams, eds. *The Great Famine: Studies in Irish History 1845–1852.* Dublin: Browne and Nolan for the Irish Committee of Historical Sciences, 1956.

Ellmann, Maud. *The Hunger Artists: Starving, Writing, and Imprisonment.* London: Virago, 1993.

Elshtain, Jean Bethke. *Public Man, Private Woman: Women in Social and Political Thought.* 2d ed. Princeton: Princeton University Press, 1993.

———. *Women and War.* 2d ed. Chicago: University of Chicago Press, 1995.

Erikson, Kai. "Notes on Trauma and Community." In *Trauma: Explorations in Memory,* ed. Cathy Caruth. Baltimore: Johns Hopkins University Press, 1995.

ERRA. "Final Crop Assessment and Food Aid Needs." Eritrean Relief and Rehabilitation Agency, 1995.

———. "Towards the Rational Use of Emergency Food Aid in Eritrea: Challenges and Opportunities." Eritrean Relief and Rehabilitation Agency, 1994.

Ethiopian Relief and Rehabilitation Commission, Economic Commission for Africa, and InterAfrica Group. "The Addis Ababa Statement on Famine in Ethiopia: Learning from the Past to Prepare for the Future." In *Famine in Ethiopia: Learning from the Past to Prepare for the Future*. Addis Ababa, 18 March 1995, unpublished typescript.

Feldman, Allen. *Formations of Violence: The Narrative of the Body and Political Terror in Northern Ireland*. Chicago: University of Chicago Press, 1991.

Fine, Ben. "Entitlement Failure?" *Development and Change* 28, no. 4 (1997): 617–47.

Firebrace, James, and Stuart Holland. *Never Kneel Down: Drought, Development, and Liberation in Eritrea*. Nottingham, England: Spokesman for War on Want, 1984.

Foucault, Michel. *The Archaeology of Knowledge*. Trans. A. M. Sheridan Smith. London: Routledge, 1989.

———. *Discipline and Punish: The Birth of the Prison*. Trans. Alan Sheridan. London: Allen Lane, 1977; reprint, Harmondsworth, England: Penguin, 1991.

———. *The History of Sexuality*. Vol. 1, *An Introduction*. Trans. Robert Hurley. Harmondsworth, England: Penguin Books, 1990.

———. *The History of Sexuality*. Vol. 2, *The Use of Pleasure*. Trans. Robert Hurley. Harmondsworth, England: Penguin Books, 1992.

———. "Intellectuals and Power: A Conversation between Michel Foucault and Gilles Deleuze." In *Language, Counter-Memory, Practice: Selected Essays and Interviews*, ed. Donald F. Bouchard. Ithaca, N.Y.: Cornell University Press, 1977.

———. "On the Genealogy of Ethics: An Overview of Work in Progress." In *The Foucault Reader: An Introduction to Foucault's Thought*, 340–72, ed. Paul Rabinow. New York: Random House, 1984.

———. *The Order of Things: An Archaeology of the Human Sciences*. London: Tavistock, 1970.

———. "Politics and the Study of Discourse." In *The Foucault Effect: Studies in Governmentality*, ed. Graham Burchell, Colin Gordon, and Peter Miller. London: Harvester Wheatsheaf, 1991.

———. *Power/Knowledge: Selected Interviews and Other Writings 1972–1977 by Michel Foucault*. Trans. Colin Gordon. Brighton, England: Harvester Press, 1980.

———. "Truth and Power." In *Power/Knowledge: Selected Interviews and Other Writings 1972–1977 by Michel Foucault*, ed. Colin Gordon. Brighton, England: Harvester Press, 1980.

Fraser, Nancy. *Unruly Practices: Power, Discourse, and Gender in Contemporary Social Theory*. Cambridge, England: Polity, 1989.

Fraser, Nancy, and Linda Gordon. "A Genealogy of Dependency: Tracing a Keyword of the U.S. Welfare State." *Signs* 19, no. 2 (1994): 309–36.

Garnsey, Peter. "Responses to Food Crisis in the Ancient Mediterranean World," in *Hunger in History: Food Shortage, Poverty, and Deprivation,* ed. Lucile F. Newman (Oxford: Blackwell, 1990), 126–46.

———. *Famine and Food Supply in the Graeco-Roman World.* Cambridge: Cambridge University Press, 1988.

Geldof, Bob. *Is That It?* Harmondsworth, England: Penguin, 1986.

George, Susan. *How the Other Half Dies: The Real Reasons for World Hunger.* Harmondsworth, England: Penguin, 1976.

Gibson, Norah, Yohannes Teggay, and Ashghedom Tewolde. "Draft Report of the Evaluation of Food Aid Operations of the Eritrean Relief and Rehabilitation Agency, January 31–February 25, 1995." Oxfam Belge/ Dutch Interchurch Aid, 1995.

Gill, Peter. *A Year in the Death of Africa: Politics, Bureaucracy, and the Famine.* London: Paladin, 1986.

Gilligan, Carol. *In a Different Voice: Psychological Theory and Women's Development.* Cambridge: Harvard University Press, 1982; reprinted with a new preface, 1993.

Goodhand, Jonathan, and David Hulme. "From Wars to Complex Political Emergencies: Understanding Conflict and Peace-Building in the New World Disorder." *Third World Quarterly* 20, no. 1 (1999): 13–26.

Gore, Charles. "Entitlement Relations and 'Unruly' Social Practices: A Comment on the Work of Amartya Sen." *Journal of Development Studies* 29, no. 3 (1993): 429–60.

Gross, Michael, and Mary Beth Averill. "Evolution and Patriarchal Myths of Scarcity and Competition." In *Discovering Reality,* ed. Sandra Harding and Merrill B. Hintikka. Dordrecht, Netherlands: D. Reidel, 1983.

Hall, Stuart, and Martin Jacques. "People Aid: A New Politics Sweeps the Land." *Marxism Today,* July 1986, 10–14.

Hall-Matthews, David. "Historical Roots of Famine Relief Paradigms: Ideas on Dependency and Free Trade in India in the 1870s." *Disasters* 20, no. 3 (1996): 216–30.

Hammond, Jenny, and Nell Druce. *Sweeter than Honey: Ethiopian Women and Revolution: Testimonies of Tigrayan Women.* Trenton, N.J.: Red Sea Press, 1990.

Hardin, Garrett. "Lifeboat Ethics: The Case against Helping the Poor." *Psychology Today* 8 (1974): 38–43, 123–26.

Harris, David R. "An Evolutionary Continuum of People-Plant Interaction." In *Foraging and Farming: The Evolution of Plant Exploitation,* ed. David R. Harris and Gordon C. Hillman, 11–26. London: Unwin Hyman, 1989.

Harrison, Paul, and Robin Palmer. *News out of Africa: Biafra to Band Aid.* London: Hilary Shipman, 1986.

Harriss, John, ed. *The Politics of Humanitarian Intervention.* London: Pinter in association with Save the Children Fund and the Centre for Global Governance, 1995.

Hart, Adrian. "Consuming Compassion: The Live Aid Phenomenon." *Links* 28 (1987): 15–17.

———. "Images of the Third World." In *Looking beyond the Frame: Racism, Representation, and Resistance,* ed. Michelle Reeves and Jenny Hammond, 12–17. [*Links,* no. 34] Oxford: Third World First, 1989.

Hastrup, Kirsten. "Hunger and the Hardness of Facts." *Man,* n.s., 28, no. 4 (1993): 727–39.

Healy, David. *Images of Trauma: From Hysteria to Post-Traumatic Stress Disorder.* London: Faber & Faber, 1993.

Hebdige, Dick. *Hiding in the Light: On Images and Things.* London: Routledge, 1988.

Hendrie, Barbara. "Cross-Border Relief Operations in Eritrea and Tigray." *Disasters* 13, no. 4 (1989): 351–60.

———. "Knowledge and Power: A Critique of an International Relief Operation." *Disasters* 21, no. 1 (1997): 57–76.

Hewitt, Kenneth. *Interpretations of Calamity.* Winchester, England: Allen and Unwin, 1983.

Hoben, Allan. "Paradigms and Politics: The Cultural Construction of Environmental Policy in Ethiopia." *World Development* 23, no. 6 (1995): 1007–21.

Hoffman, Stanley. *Duties beyond Borders: On the Limits and Possibilities of Ethical International Politics.* Syracuse: Syracuse University Press, 1981.

Holdar, Sven. "The Study of Foreign Aid: Unbroken Ground in Geography." *Progress in Human Geography* 17, no. 4 (1993): 453–70.

Holden, Pat. "ODA's Approach to Linking Relief and Development." *IDS Bulletin* 25, no. 4 (1994): 105–6.

Hollis, Martin, and Steve Smith, *Explaining and Understanding International Relations.* Oxford: Clarendon Paperbacks, 1990.

Hopkins, Raymond F. "Reform in the International Food Aid Regime: The Role of Consensual Knowledge." *International Organisation* 46, no. 1 (1992): 236.

Hopkins, Raymond F., and Donald J. Puchala. "Perspectives on the International Relations of Food." *International Organisation* 36 (1978): 581–616.

Hopkins, Raymond F., and Donald J. Puchala, eds. "The Global Political Economy of Food." Special issue of *International Organisation* 36 (1978).

Hunger Project. *Ending Hunger: An Idea Whose Time Has Come.* New York: Praeger Special Studies, 1985.

Karim, Ataul, et al. "OLS Operation Lifeline Sudan: A Review." Unpublished independent report with administrative support from the UN Department of Humanitarian Affairs, 1996.

Keen, David. *The Benefits of Famine: A Political Economy of Famine and Relief in Southwestern Sudan, 1983–1989.* Princeton: Princeton University Press, 1994.

Keen, David, and Ken Wilson. "Engaging with Violence: A Reassessment of Relief in Wartime." In *War and Hunger: Rethinking International Responses to Complex Emergencies,* ed. Macrae and Zwi, 209–21. London: Zed Books in association with Save the Children Fund (UK), 1994.

Kelleher, Margaret. *The Feminisation of Famine: Expressions of the Inexpressible?* Cork: Cork University Press, 1997.

Keller, Evelyn Fox. *Reflections on Gender and Science.* New Haven: Yale, 1985.

Kerr, Donal. *A Nation of Beggars? Priests, People, and Politics in Famine Ireland 1846–52.* Oxford: Clarendon Press, 1994.

Killen, John. *The Famine Decade: Contemporary Accounts 1845–52.* Belfast: Blackstaff Press, 1991.

Kinealy, Christine. *A Death-Dealing Famine: The Great Hunger in Ireland.* London: Pluto Press, 1997.

———. *This Great Calamity: The Irish Famine, 1845–52.* Dublin: Gill and Macmillan, 1994.

Kissane, Noel. *The Irish Famine: A Documentary History.* Dublin: National Library of Ireland, 1995.

Krasner, Stephen, ed. *International Regimes.* Ithaca, N.Y.: Cornell University Press, 1983.

Lacan, Jacques. *Écrits: A Selection.* Trans. Alan Sheridan. London: Tavistock, 1977.

Lappé, Frances Moore, and Joseph Collins. *World Hunger: Twelve Myths.* Rev. ed. London: Earthscan, 1988.

Leach, Melissa, and James Fairhead. "Natural Resource Management: The Reproduction and Use of Environmental Misinformation in Guinea's Forest-Savanna Transition Zone." *IDS Bulletin* 25, no. 2 (1994): 81–87.

Leader, Nicholas. "Proliferating Principles; or How to Sup with the Devil without Getting Eaten." *Disasters* 22, no. 4 (1998): 288–308.

Lidchi, Henrietta. "All in the Choosing Eye: Charity, Representation, and Developing World." Ph.D. diss., Open University, 1993.

"Life after Live Aid." Dir. John Macguire, prod. Andrew Coggins. Broadcast on BBC2, 28 July 1995.

Litton, Helen. *The Irish Famine: An Illustrated History*. Dublin: Wolfhound Press, 1994.

Locke C. G., and F. Z. Ahmadi-Esfahani. "Famine Analysis: A Study of Entitlement in Sudan, 1984–1985." *Economic Development and Cultural Change* 41, no. 2 (1993): 363–76.

MacKenzie, Debora. "The People Problem: Will Tomorrow's Children Starve?" *New Scientist*, 3 September 1994, 24–34.

Macrae, Joanna. "The Death of Humanitarianism? An Anatomy of the Attack." *Disasters* 22, no. 4 (1998): 309–17.

Macrae, Joanna, and Anthony Zwi, eds. *War and Hunger: Rethinking International Responses to Complex Emergencies*. London: Zed Books in association with Save the Children Fund (UK), 1994.

Magistad, Mary Kay. "The Ethiopian Bandwagon: The Relationship between News Media Coverage and British Foreign Policy toward the 1984–85 Ethiopian Famine." Master's thesis, Sussex University, 1985.

Malthus, Thomas. *An Essay on the Principle of Population*. Trans. Patricia James. Cambridge Texts in the History of Political Thought. Cambridge: Cambridge University Press, 1992.

———. *An Essay on the Principle of Population*. World's Classics. Oxford: Oxford University Press, 1993.

Manushi Collective. "Drought: 'God-Sent' or 'Man-Made' Disaster?" In *Third World, Second Sex*, vol. 2, *Women's Struggles and National Liberation: Third World Women Speak Out,* ed. Miranda Davies. London: Zed Books, 1983.

Matthews, Robley, et al. "Global Climate and the Origins of Agriculture." In *Hunger in History: Food Shortage, Poverty, and Deprivation,* ed. Lucile F. Newman. Oxford: Blackwell, 1990.

Maxwell, Simon, and Alemayehu Lirenso. "Linking Relief and Development: An Ethiopian Case Study." *IDS Bulletin* 25, no. 4 (1994): 65.

Maxwell, Simon, and Margaret Buchanan-Smith, eds. "Linking Relief and Development." Special issue of *IDS Bulletin* 25, no. 4 (1994).

McHugh, Roger J. "The Famine in Irish Oral Tradition." In *The Great Famine,* ed. R. Dudley Edwards and T. Desmond Williams, 391–436. Dublin: Browne and Nolan, 1956.

McLellan, David, ed. *Karl Marx: Selected Writings*. Oxford: Oxford University Press, 1977.

Meadows, Donella H., et al. *The Limits to Growth: A Report for the Club of Rome's Project on the Predicament of Mankind*. London: Pan Books, 1974.

Meillassoux, Claude. "Development or Exploitation: Is the Sahel Famine Good Business?" *Review of African Political Economy* 1, August–November 1974.

Minear, Larry, and Thomas G. Weiss. *Mercy under Fire: War and the Global Humanitarian Community.* Boulder, Colo.: Westview Press, 1995.

Miriam, Mesfin Wolde. *Rural Vulnerability to Famine in Ethiopia 1958–1977.* London: Intermediate Technology Publications, 1987.

Mokyr, Joel. *Why Ireland Starved: A Quantitative and Analytical History of the Irish Economy, 1800–1850.* London: George Allen and Unwin, 1983.

Moore, Sally Falf. *Law as Process: An Anthropological Approach.* London: Routledge and Kegan Paul, 1983.

Nietzsche, Friedrich. *Twilight of the Idols.* Trans. R. J. Hollingdale. Harmondsworth, England: Penguin, 1990.

Nolan, Peter. "The Causation and Prevention of Famines: A Critique of A. K. Sen." *Journal of Peasant Studies* 21, no. 1 (1993): 1–28.

O'Ciosáin, Niall. "Hungry Grass." *Circa* (1995): 24–27.

Ó Gráda, Cormac. "Why Ireland Starved." *Times Literary Supplement,* 10 March 1995, 8.

Omaar, Rakiya, and Alex de Waal. "Humanitarianism Unbound? Current Dilemmas Facing Multi-Mandate Relief Operations in Political Emergencies." Discussion Paper no. 5. African Rights, 1994.

O'Neill, Onora. *Faces of Hunger: An Essay on Poverty, Justice, and Development.* Studies in Applied Philosophy, vol. 3. London: Allen & Unwin, 1986.

O'Neill, Thomas P. "The Organisation and Administration of Relief, 1845–1852." In *The Great Famine: Studies in Irish History 1845–1852,* ed. R. Dudley Edwards and T. Desmond Williams. Dublin: Browne and Nolan for the Irish Committee of Historical Sciences, 1956.

⚹ Osmani, S. R. "Comments on Alex de Waal's 'Reassessment of Entitlement Theory in the Light of Recent Famines in Africa.'" *Development and Change* 22 (1991): 587–96.

O'Sullivan, Patrick, ed. *The Meaning of the Famine.* New York: Leicester University Press, 1996.

O'Toole, Fintan. "Hungry Eyes." Prod. Mary Price, research Ellis Hill. BBC Radio 4, 1 November 1995.

Percival, John. *The Great Famine: Ireland's Potato Famine 1845–51.* London: BBC Books, 1995.

Philo, Greg. "From Buerk to Band Aid: The Media and the 1984 Ethiopian Famine." In *Getting the Message: News, Truth, and Power,* ed. Glasgow University Media Group. London: Routledge, 1993.

Ploughman, Penelope. "The American Print News Media 'Construction' of Five Natural Disasters." *Disasters* 19, no. 4 (1995): 308–26.

Póirtéir, Cathal. *The Great Irish Famine.* Thomas Davis Lecture Series. Cork: Mercier Press in association with RTE, 1995.

Póirtéir, Cathal, ed. *Famine Echoes*. Dublin: Gill and Macmillan, 1995.

Polanyi, Karl. *The Great Transformation: The Political and Economic Origins of Our Time*. Boston: Beacon Press, 1944.

Potts, Ian, and Michael Keating. *Humanitas II: Humanitarian Intervention*. Zeist, Netherlands: Television Trust for the Environment, 1992, video.

Propp, Vladimir. *Morphology of the Folktale*. Trans. Laurence Scott. 2d ed. Austin: University of Texas Press, 1968.

Ramsbotham, Oliver, and Tom Woodhouse. *Humanitarian Intervention in Contemporary Conflict: A Reconceptualisation*. Cambridge: Polity, 1996.

Rangasami, Amrita. "Failure of Exchange Entitlements Theory of Famine." *Economic and Political Weekly* 20, no. 41 (1985): 1747–52; no. 42 (1985): 1797–801.

Reed, Laura W., and Carl Kayson, eds. *Emerging Norms of Justified Intervention: A Collection of Essays from a Project of the American Academy of Arts and Sciences*. Cambridge: American Academy of Arts and Sciences, Committee on International Security Studies, 1993.

Reeves, Michelle. "The Politics of Charity." In *Looking beyond the Frame: Racism, Representation, and Resistance,* ed. Michelle Reeves and Jenny Hammond, 7–11. Oxford: Third World First, 1989.

Richards, Audrey I. *Land, Labour, and Diet in Northern Rhodesia: An Economic Study of the Bemba Tribe*. London: Oxford University Press for the International Institute of African Languages and Cultures, 1939.

Rijven, Stan, Greil Marcus, and Will Straw. *Rock for Ethiopia*. Papers from the Third International Conference on Popular Music Studies. IASPM Working Paper 7, IASPM, Montreal, July 1985.

Rindos, David. "Darwinism and Its Role in the Explanation of Domestication." In *Foraging and Farming: The Evolution of Plant Exploitation,* ed. David R. Harris and Gordon C. Hillman, 27–41. London: Unwin Hyman, 1989.

———. *The Origins of Agriculture: An Evolutionary Perspective*. New York: Academic Press, 1984.

Ruttan, Vernon W. *Why Food Aid?* Baltimore: Johns Hopkins University Press, 1993.

Sahlins, Marshall. *Stone Age Economics*. London: Tavistock, 1974.

Sahnoun, Mohamed. *Somalia: The Missed Opportunities*. Washington, D.C.: U.S. Institute for Peace, 1994.

Schaffer, Bernard, and H. Wen-hsien. "Distribution and the Theory of Access." *Development and Change* 6, no. 2 (1975): 13–36.

Scheper-Hughes, Nancy. *Death without Weeping: The Violence of Everyday Life in Brazil*. Berkeley: University of California Press, 1992.

———. "The Madness of Hunger: Sickness, Delirium, and Human Needs." *Culture, Medicine, and Psychiatry* 12, no. 4 (1988): 429–58.

Schram, Sanford F. *Words of Welfare: The Poverty of Social Science and the Social Science of Poverty.* Minneapolis: University of Minnesota Press, 1995.

Schultz, Theodore W. "Value of U.S. Farm Surpluses to Underdeveloped Countries." *Journal of Farm Economics* 42, no. 5 (1960): 1019–30.

Scott, J. C. *Weapons of the Weak: Everyday Forms of Peasant Resistance.* New Haven: Yale University Press, 1985.

Sen, Amartya. "The Causation and Prevention of Famines—A Reply." *Journal of Peasant Studies* 21, no. 1 (1993): 29–40.

———. "The Causes of Famine—A Reply." *Food Policy* 11, no. 2 (1986): 125–32.

———. "The Food Problem: Theory and Policy." *Third World Quarterly* 4, no. 3 (1982): 447–59.

———. "Population: Delusion and Reality." *New York Review of Books* 15, no. 15 (1994): 62–71.

———. *Poverty and Famines: An Essay on Entitlements and Deprivation.* Oxford: Clarendon Press, 1981.

———. "Rejoinder: An Untenable Hypothesis on the Causes of Famine—Reply." *Food Policy* 12, no. 1 (1987): 10–14.

Shaw, Martin. *Civil Society and Media in Global Crises: Representing Distant Violence.* London: Pinter, 1996.

Silkin, Trish, and Barbara Hendrie. "Research in the War Zones of Eritrea and Tigray." *Disasters* 21, no. 2 (1997): 166–76.

Simpson, Anne. "Charity Begins at Home." *Ten-8* 19 (1985): 21–26.

Singer, H. W. "Book Review: *Poverty and Famines* by Amartya Sen." *International Affairs* 58, no. 2 (1982): 335–36.

Singer, Peter. "Famine, Affluence, and Morality." *Philosophy and Public Affairs* 1, no. 3 (1972): 229–43.

Slim, Hugo. "Doing the Right Thing: Relief Agencies, Moral Dilemmas, and Moral Responsibility in Political Emergencies and War." *Disasters* 21, no. 3 (1997): 244–57.

Smith, Gayle E. "Emerging from Crisis: From Relief to Development." *Humanitarian Monitor*, February 1995, 28–29.

Sorenson, John. "Discourses on Eritrean Nationalism and Identity." *Journal of Modern African Studies* 29, no. 2 (1991): 301–17.

———. *Imagining Ethiopia: Struggles for History and Identity in the Horn of Africa.* New Brunswick, N.J.: Rutgers University Press, 1993.

Staten, Henry. *Wittgenstein and Derrida.* Oxford: Basil Blackwell, 1984.

Stockton, Nicholas. "In Defence of Humanitarianism." *Disasters* 22, no. 4 (1998): 352–60.

Swift, Jeremy. "Understanding and Preventing Famine and Famine Mortality." *IDS Bulletin* 24, no. 4 (1993): 1–15.

————. "Why Are Rural People Vulnerable to Famine?" *IDS Bulletin* 20, no. 2 (1989): 8–15.

Tal, Kalí. *Worlds of Hurt: Reading the Literature of Trauma*. Cambridge: Cambridge University Press, 1996.

Tester, Keith. *Media, Culture, and Morality*. London: Routledge, 1994.

Thompson, E. P. "The Moral Economy Reviewed." In *Customs in Common*, ed. E. P. Thompson, chapter 5. London: Merlin Press, 1991.

Tijmes, Pieter, and Reginald Luijf. "The Sustainability of Our Common Future: An Inquiry into the Foundations of an Ideology." *Technology in Society* 17, no. 3 (1995): 327–36.

Tilly, L. A. "Food Entitlement, Famine, and Conflict." In *Hunger and History: The Impact of Changing Food Productionand Consumption Patterns on Society*, ed. R. I. Rotberg and T. K. Rabb. Cambridge: Cambridge University Press, 1985.

Uvin, Peter. *The International Organisation of Hunger*. London: Kegan Paul, 1994.

van der Gaag, Nikki, and Cathy Nash. "Images of Africa: The UK Report (Sponsored by Oxfam and the EEC)." FAO/FFHC Rome, 1987.

Vaughan, Megan. *The Story of an African Famine: Gender and Famine in Twentieth-Century Malawi*. Cambridge: Cambridge University Press, 1987.

Walker, Martin. "Overcrowding Points to Global Famine." *The Guardian* (London), 15 August 1994, 18.

Watts, Michael. *Silent Violence: Food Famine and Peasantry in Northern Nigeria*. Berkeley: University of California Press, 1983.

Watts, Michael J., and Hans G. Bohle. "The Space of Vulnerability: The Causal Structure of Hunger and Famine." *Progress in Human Geography* 17, no. 1 (1993): 43–67.

Webb, Patrick, and Joachim von Braun. *Famine and Food Security in Ethiopia: Lessons for Africa*. Chichester, England: John Wiley for the International Food Policy Research Institute, 1994.

Weber, Cynthia. *Simulating Sovereignty: Intervention, the State, and Symbolic Exchange*. Cambridge Studies in International Relations, vol. 37. Cambridge: Cambridge University Press, 1995.

Wheeler, Nicholas J. "Making Sense of Humanitarian Outrage." *Irish Studies in International Affairs* 7 (1996): 31–40.

Wilson, Amrit. *The Challenge Road: Women and the Eritrean Revolution*. London: Earthscan, 1991.

Woodham-Smith, Cecil. *The Great Hunger*. London: Hamish Hamilton, 1962.

Xenos, Nicholas. *Scarcity and Modernity*. London: Routledge, 1989.

Yates, Robin D. S. "War, Food Shortages, and Relief Measures in Early

China." In *Hunger in History: Food Shortage, Poverty, and Deprivation,* ed. Lucile F. Newman. Oxford: Blackwell, 1990.

Zalewski, Marysia. "'All These Theories and Yet the Bodies Keep Piling up': Theories, Theorists, Theorising." In *International Theory: Positivism and Beyond,* ed. Steve Smith, Ken Booth, and Marysia Zalewski. Cambridge: Cambridge University Press, 1996.

Ziv, Ilan. *Consuming Hunger (1) Getting the Story (2) Shaping the Image.* BBC Channel 4 Broadcast, 18 and 19 February 1987. Tamouz Productions.

Žižek, Slavoj. "Beyond Discourse Analysis." In *New Reflections on the Revolutions of Our Time,* ed. Ernesto Laclau. London: Verso, 1990.

———. *Enjoy Your Symptom: Jacques Lacan in Hollywood and Out.* New York: Routledge, 1992.

———. *For They Know Not What They Do: Enjoyment as a Political Factor.* London: Verso, 1991.

———. *The Indivisible Remainder: An Essay on Schelling and Related Matters.* London: Verso, 1996.

———. *Looking Awry: An Introduction to Jacques Lacan through Popular Culture.* Cambridge: MIT Press, 1991.

———. *The Metastases of Enjoyment.* London: Verso, 1994.

———. *The Sublime Object of Ideology.* London: Verso, 1989.

———. *Tarrying with the Negative: Kant, Hegel, and the Critique of Ideology.* Post-Contemporary Interventions. Durham, N.C.: Duke University Press, 1993.

Žižek, Slavoj, ed. *Mapping Ideology.* London: Verso, 1994.

Index

JENNY EDKINS is lecturer in the Department of International Politics at the University of Wales, Aberystwyth, where she convenes a research seminar series on the politics of emergency. She is the author of *Poststructuralism and International Relations: Bringing the Political Back In* and coeditor (with Nalini Persram and Véronique Pin-Fat) of *Sovereignty and Subjectivity*.